The *Handbook of the International Phonetic Association* is a comprehensive guide to the Association's 'International Phonetic Alphabet'. The aim of the International Phonetic Alphabet is to provide a universally agreed system of notation for the sounds of languages, and for over a century the Alphabet has been widely used by phoneticians and others concerned with language. The *Handbook* presents the basics of phonetic analysis so that the principles underlying the Alphabet can be readily understood, and exemplifies the use of each of the phonetic symbols comprising the Alphabet. The application of the Alphabet is then extensively demonstrated by the inclusion of over two dozen 'Illustrations' – concise analyses of the sound systems of languages accompanied by a phonetic transcription of a passage of speech. These Illustrations cover languages from all over the world. The *Handbook* also includes a range of other useful information. The 'Extensions' to the International Phonetic Alphabet cover speech sounds beyond the sound systems of languages, such as those with paralinguistic functions and those encountered in pathological speech. A full listing is given of internationally agreed computer codings for phonetic symbols, including not only those of the International Phonetic Alphabet but also those of other traditions. And there is extensive information on the history of the International Phonetic Association and its current activities. The *Handbook* is an essential reference work for all those involved in the analysis of speech.

The International Phonetic Association exists to promote the study of the science of phonetics and the applications of that science. The Association can trace its history back to 1886, and since that time the most widely known aspect of its work has been the International Phonetic Alphabet. The *Handbook* has been produced collaboratively by leading phoneticians who have been on the Executive of the Association, and it incorporates (for instance in the case of the Illustrations) material provided by numerous members of the Association world wide.

Handbook of the International Phonetic Association

A guide to the use of the International Phonetic Alphabet

CAMBRIDGE
UNIVERSITY PRESS

PUBLISHED BY THE PRESS SYNDICATE OF THE UNIVERSITY OF CAMBRIDGE
The Pitt Building, Trumpington Street, Cambridge CB2 1RP, United Kingdom

CAMBRIDGE UNIVERSITY PRESS
The Edinburgh Building, Cambridge CB2 2RU, UK http: www.cup.cam.ac.uk
40 West 20th Street, New York, NY 10011–4211, USA http: www.cup.org
10 Stamford Road, Oakleigh, Melbourne 3166, Australia

© The International Phonetic Association 1999

First published 1999

Printed in United Kingdom at the University Press, Cambridge

A catalogue record for this book is available from the British Library

ISBN 0 521 65236 7 hardback
ISBN 0 521 63751 1 paperback

CONTENTS

PART 2: Illustrations of the IPA

PART 3: Appendices

Foreword

The *Handbook of the International Phonetic Association* is a resource containing concise information on the International Phonetic Alphabet and guidance on how to use it – a kind of 'user's manual'. It replaces the *Principles of the International Phonetic Association*, which has been out of print for some time and which had not been revised since 1949. But although the *Handbook* replaces some of the functions of the old *Principles*, it is a completely new work with wider objectives.

The old *Principles* contained a short tutorial on phonetic description, examples of the use of phonetic symbols, and a large number of 'specimens' consisting of very brief comments on the phonetics of a language and a transcription of the 'North Wind and the Sun' text translated into the language. Additionally, there was some information about the Association, and, printed on the inside covers, a brief history of it.

The new *Handbook* broadly speaking retains these components. It is divided into three parts: part 1 contains an introduction to phonetic description and exemplification of the use of the symbols; part 2 consists of 'Illustrations' of the use of the International Phonetic Alphabet for different languages (these Illustrations are ones which have appeared in the *Journal of the International Phonetic Association* since 1989); and part 3 contains appendices with a variety of reference material.

Beyond the basic similarity of structure, the *Handbook* is very different from the old *Principles*. Most superficially, perhaps, it reflects the changes which have been made in that most tangible and widely known product of the Association's work, the IPA Chart. Discussion and exemplification is based on the most recent (1996) edition of the chart. More substantively, the *Handbook* acknowledges the fact that over the past half century the advance of techniques for acoustic analysis means that many readers will be familiar with, and quite possibly working with, speech as an acoustic signal. This means it now seems appropriate to use an acoustic display such as a spectrogram not only as a way of presenting one facet of speech, but also to discuss problems which arise in the relation between a segmentally based system of notation and the physical speech event. The *Handbook* will also contain practical information to do with the use of the IPA on computers, such as the computer codes for phonetic symbols.

The most fundamental differences between the old *Principles* and the new *Handbook* perhaps arise from the expectation that the readership of the new work will be much less homogeneous than that envisaged for the old one. The new *Handbook* is intended to be a reference work not only for language teachers and phoneticians interested in the sounds of different languages, but also for speech technologists, speech pathologists, theoretical phonologists, and others.

This breadth of readership is to be encouraged, given the goal that the International Phonetic Alphabet (hereafter 'the IPA') should be a standard for the representation of speech. But it poses particular challenges for the writing of the 'tutorial' sections of the *Handbook*. The challenges are further increased by the vertical spread of readers from those who are experienced phoneticians to those who know nothing about phonetics. The breadth of readership has led perhaps to a more equivocal tone in the presentation of the premises behind the IPA than in the *Principles*. For instance, the way in which the IPA developed historically was closely bound up with a 'strictly segmented' phonemic view, and in section 10 the fact that there are alternatives in phonological theory is acknowledged. The vertical spread of readers poses the recurring question of how much or how little to say. The lower bound is presumably what a novice needs to pick up in order to have some idea of the principles governing the organization of the chart. The upper bound is the practical goal of a compact booklet, readily affordable by students, and concise enough to be easily digested by non-specialist readers.

The resulting text in part 1 is more discursive than that of the old *Principles*. It should be borne in mind, however, that it does not attempt the job either of a phonetics textbook, or of a critique of the IPA. Nowadays there are many good phonetics textbooks available, and it would be expected that students of phonetics would read one or more of these in conjunction with the *Handbook*. The purpose of the *Handbook* is not to provide a comprehensive or balanced education in phonetics, but to provide a concise summary of information needed for getting to grips with the IPA. Likewise, whilst a full-scale critique of the assumptions on which the IPA is founded is perhaps due, the practically-oriented *Handbook* is not the place for it. The IPA is a working tool for many, and whilst it may be possible to improve that tool, the role of the *Handbook* is that of an instruction manual for the tool which is currently available.

The creation of the *Handbook* has been in every sense a collaborative effort. The text in part 1 is largely the responsibility of Francis Nolan, and the exemplification of the use of sounds was provided by Peter Ladefoged and Ian Maddieson. Ian Maddieson, and Martin Barry, as successive editors of the *Journal of the International Phonetic Association*, have been responsible for overseeing and collating the rich and ever growing stock of Illustrations. Martin Ball was instrumental in formulating the Extensions to the IPA (appendix 3), and Mike MacMahon wrote appendix 4 on the history of the Association. John Esling is responsible for appendix 2 on the computer coding of symbols, and for most of the work involved in the final stages of preparing the *Handbook* including the final editing of the Illustrations. And, of course, particular thanks are due to the authors of the Illustrations, and to the large number of members of the International Phonetic Association who responded with suggestions and corrections when a draft of parts of the *Handbook* was published in the *Journal of the International Phonetic Association*.

THE INTERNATIONAL PHONETIC ALPHABET (revised to 1993, updated 1996)

CONSONANTS (PULMONIC)

	Bilabial	Labiodental	Dental	Alveolar	Postalveolar	Retroflex	Palatal	Velar	Uvular	Pharyngeal	Glottal
Plosive	p b			t d		ʈ ɖ	c ɟ	k ɡ	q ɢ		ʔ
Nasal	m	ɱ		n		ɳ	ɲ	ŋ	N		
Trill	ʙ			r					ʀ		
Tap or Flap				ɾ		ɽ					
Fricative	ɸ β	f v	θ ð	s z	ʃ ʒ	ʂ ʐ	ç ʝ	x ɣ	χ ʁ	ħ ʕ	h ɦ
Lateral fricative				ɬ ɮ							
Approximant		ʋ		ɹ		ɻ	j	ɰ			
Lateral approximant				l		ɭ	ʎ	ʟ			

Where symbols appear in pairs, the one to the right represents a voiced consonant. Shaded areas denote articulations judged impossible.

CONSONANTS (NON-PULMONIC)

Clicks		Voiced implosives		Ejectives	
ʘ	Bilabial	ɓ	Bilabial	ʼ	Examples:
ǀ	Dental	ɗ	Dental/alveolar	pʼ	Bilabial
ǃ	(Post)alveolar	ʄ	Palatal	tʼ	Dental/alveolar
ǂ	Palatoalveolar	ɠ	Velar	kʼ	Velar
ǁ	Alveolar lateral	ʛ	Uvular	sʼ	Alveolar fricative

OTHER SYMBOLS

ʍ	Voiceless labial-velar fricative	ɕ ʑ	Alveolo-palatal fricatives
w	Voiced labial-velar approximant	ɺ	Alveolar lateral flap
ɥ	Voiced labial-palatal approximant	ɧ	Simultaneous ʃ and x
ʜ	Voiceless epiglottal fricative		
ʢ	Voiced epiglottal fricative	Affricates and double articulations can be represented by two symbols joined by a tie bar if necessary.	k͡p t͡s
ʡ	Epiglottal plosive		

VOWELS

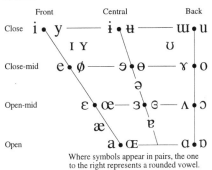

Where symbols appear in pairs, the one to the right represents a rounded vowel.

DIACRITICS Diacritics may be placed above a symbol with a descender, e.g. ŋ̊

◌̥	Voiceless	n̥ d̥	◌̈	Breathy voiced	b̤ a̤	◌̪	Dental	t̪ d̪
◌̬	Voiced	s̬ t̬	◌̰	Creaky voiced	b̰ a̰	◌̺	Apical	t̺ d̺
ʰ	Aspirated	tʰ dʰ	◌̼	Linguolabial	t̼ d̼	◌̻	Laminal	t̻ d̻
◌̹	More rounded	ɔ̹	ʷ	Labialized	tʷ dʷ	◌̃	Nasalized	ẽ
◌̜	Less rounded	ɔ̜	ʲ	Palatalized	tʲ dʲ	ⁿ	Nasal release	dⁿ
◌̟	Advanced	u̟	ˠ	Velarized	tˠ dˠ	ˡ	Lateral release	dˡ
◌̠	Retracted	e̠	ˤ	Pharyngealized	tˤ dˤ	◌̚	No audible release	d̚
◌̈	Centralized	ë	◌̴	Velarized or pharyngealized	ɫ			
◌̽	Mid-centralized	e̽	◌̝	Raised	e̝ (ɹ̝ = voiced alveolar fricative)			
◌̩	Syllabic	n̩	◌̞	Lowered	e̞ (β̞ = voiced bilabial approximant)			
◌̯	Non-syllabic	e̯	◌̘	Advanced Tongue Root	e̘			
◌˞	Rhoticity	ɚ a˞	◌̙	Retracted Tongue Root	e̙			

SUPRASEGMENTALS

ˈ	Primary stress
ˌ	Secondary stress ˌfoʊnəˈtɪʃən
ː	Long eː
ˑ	Half-long eˑ
◌̆	Extra-short ĕ
ǀ	Minor (foot) group
ǁ	Major (intonation) group
.	Syllable break ɹi.ækt
‿	Linking (absence of a break)

TONES AND WORD ACCENTS

LEVEL			CONTOUR		
e̋ or	˥	Extra high	ě or	˄	Rising
é	˦	High	ê	˅	Falling
ē	˧	Mid	e᷄	ˏ	High rising
è	˨	Low	e᷅	ˎ	Low rising
ȅ	˩	Extra low	e᷈	˟	Rising-falling
↓	Downstep		↗	Global rise	
↑	Upstep		↘	Global fall	

PART 1

Introduction to the IPA

1   What is the International Phonetic Alphabet?

The aim of the International Phonetic Association is to promote the study of the science of phonetics and the various practical applications of that science. For both these it is desirable to have a consistent way of representing the sounds of language in written form. From its foundation in 1886 the Association has been concerned to develop a set of symbols which would be convenient to use, but comprehensive enough to cope with the wide variety of sounds found in the languages of the world; and to encourage the use of this notation as widely as possible among those concerned with language. The system is generally known as the International Phonetic Alphabet. Both the Association and its Alphabet are widely referred to by the abbreviation IPA, and here the Alphabet will generally be abbreviated to 'the IPA'. The IPA is based on the Roman alphabet, which has the advantage of being widely familiar, but also includes letters and additional symbols from a variety of other sources. These additions are necessary because the variety of sounds in languages is much greater than the number of letters in the Roman alphabet. The use of sequences of phonetic symbols to represent speech is known as transcription.

The IPA can be used for many purposes. For instance, it can be used as a way to show pronunciation in a dictionary, to record a language in linguistic fieldwork, to form the basis of a writing system for a language, or to annotate acoustic and other displays in the analysis of speech. For all these tasks it is necessary to have a generally agreed set of symbols for designating sounds unambiguously, and the IPA aims to fulfil this role. The purpose of this *Handbook* is to provide a practical guide to the IPA and to the conventions associated with it.

Phonetics, like any science, develops over time. New facts emerge, new theories are created, and new solutions to old problems are invented. The notational system of any science reflects facts and theories, and so it is natural that from time to time the Alphabet should be modified to accommodate innovations. The Alphabet presented in this *Handbook* is the version revised by a Convention of the International Phonetic Association held in Kiel in 1989, subject to a subsequent set of minor modifications and corrections approved by the Council of the Association. Despite these and earlier changes, the Alphabet today shows striking continuity with the Association's Alphabet as it was at the end of the nineteenth century. The development of the IPA has, throughout the history of the Association, been guided by a set of 'Principles', and these are listed in appendix 1.

2   Phonetic description and the IPA Chart

Behind the system of notation known as the IPA lie a number of theoretical assumptions about speech and how it can best be analyzed. These include the following:
— Some aspects of speech are linguistically relevant, whilst others (such as personal voice quality) are not.
— Speech can be represented partly as a sequence of discrete sounds or 'segments'.
— Segments can usefully be divided into two major categories, consonants and vowels.
— The phonetic description of consonants and vowels can be made with reference to how

they are produced and to their auditory characteristics.

— In addition to the segments, a number of 'suprasegmental' aspects of speech, such as stress and tone, need to be represented independently of the segments.

The IPA is summarized in the 'IPA Chart', which is reproduced in its entirety after the foreword, and section by section in appendix 5; readers are encouraged to photocopy and enlarge the Chart for ease of reference. The structure of the Chart reflects the assumptions above. The following subsections provide a brief introduction to phonetic description in the context of these underlying assumptions, while referring to the relevant parts of the Chart. This introduction can only deal with a few important points, and readers who need a more thorough treatment of phonetic description should consult phonetics textbooks.

In introducing the IPA, it is necessary to refer to examples from languages. As far as possible, languages are used with which many readers may be acquainted, but of course this is not possible for many sounds. Variation also provides a problem: all languages have different accents and other varieties of pronunciation. When a sound is exemplified by a word in a particular language, this should be taken to mean that the sound can often be heard in that word, not that it will *always* occur in pronunciations of the word.

In the case of English, reference is made here mainly to two varieties, General American and Standard Southern British. These varieties are widely heard, in the United States and Britain respectively, in formal areas of broadcasting such as newscasts. General American is regarded as a variety which transcends regional divides. Standard Southern British (where 'Standard' should not be taken as implying a value judgment of 'correctness') is the modern equivalent of what has been called 'Received Pronunciation' ('RP'). It is an accent of the south east of England which operates as a prestige norm there and (to varying degrees) in other parts of the British Isles and beyond. Where necessary, reference will be made specifically to one of these varieties, but normally the term 'English' will be used, indicating that the sound occurs in both General American and Standard Southern British. In most cases, of course, the sound will also occur in many other varieties of English.

2.1   *Linguistically relevant information in speech*

Although phonetics as a science is interested in all aspects of speech, the focus of phonetic notation is on the linguistically relevant aspects. For instance, the IPA provides symbols to transcribe the distinct phonetic events corresponding to the English spelling *refuse* (['refjus] meaning 'rubbish' and [rɪˈfjuz] meaning 'to decline'), but the IPA does not provide symbols to indicate information such as 'spoken rapidly by a deep, hoarse, male voice'. Whilst in practice the distinction between what is linguistically relevant and what is not may not always be clear-cut, the principle of representing only what is linguistically relevant has guided the provision of symbols in the IPA. The need to go further, however, is now recognized by the 'Extensions to the IPA' presented in appendix 3.

2.2   *Segments*

Observation of the movements of the speech organs reveals that they are in almost continuous motion. Similarly the acoustic speech signal does not switch between successive steady states, but at many points changes gradually and at others consists of rapid transient events. Neither the movements of the speech organs nor the acoustic signal offers a clear division of speech into successive phonetic units. This may be surprising to those whose view of speech is influenced mainly by alphabetic writing, but it emerges clearly from (for instance) x-ray films and acoustic displays.

For example, the movements and the acoustic signal corresponding to the English word *worry* will show continuous change. Figure 1 presents a spectrogram of this word. Spectrograms are a way of making visible the patterns of energy in the acoustic signal. Time runs from left to right, and the dark bands reflect the changing resonances of the vocal tract as the word is pronounced. In the case of the word *worry*, the pattern ebbs and flows constantly, and there are no boundaries between successive sounds. Nonetheless the word can be segmented as [wɐɹi] – that is, as [w] + [ɐ] + [ɹ] + [i]. This segmentation is undoubtedly influenced by knowledge of where linguistically significant changes in sound can be made. A speaker could progress through the word making changes: in a British pronunciation, for instance, [wɐɹi] *worry,* [hɐɹi] *hurry,* [hæɹi] *Harry,* [hæti] *Hatty,* [hætə] *hatter.* There are thus four points at which the phonetic event can be changed significantly, and this is reflected in the analysis into four segments. Languages may vary in the points at which they allow changes to be made, and so segmentation may have to be tentative in a first transcription of an unknown language (see section 9). Nonetheless there is a great deal in common between languages in the way they organize sound, and so many initial guesses about the segmentation of an unfamiliar language are likely to be right.

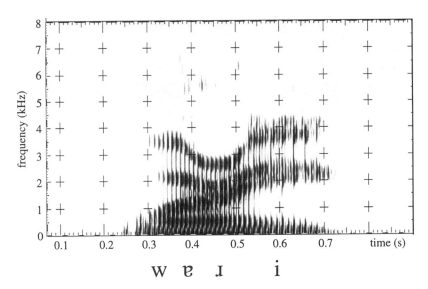

Figure 1 Spectrogram of the word *worry,* spoken in a Southern British accent.

Phonetic analysis is based on the crucial premise that it is possible to describe speech in terms of a sequence of segments, and on the further crucial assumption that each segment can be characterized by an articulatory target. 'Articulation' is the technical term for the activity of the vocal organs in making a speech sound. The description of the target is static, but this does not imply that the articulation itself is necessarily held static. So, for example, [ɹ] (as in the word *worry* above) is described as having a narrowing made by the tongue-tip near the back of the alveolar ridge (the flattish area behind the upper front teeth). The tongue-tip actually makes a continuous movement to and from that target, as reflected in the dipping pattern of higher resonances on the spectrogram in figure 1 between 0.4 and 0.5 s. In other sounds, a target will be held for a fixed amount of time. The important point is that the use of segments and associated 'target' descriptions allows for a very economical analysis of the complex and continuously varying events of speech.

2.3 The consonant-vowel distinction

Broadly, speech involves successive narrowing and opening of the vocal tract, the passage through which the air flows during speech. This can be seen clearly in an example such as *banana* ([bəˈnænə] or [bəˈnɑnə]), in which the vocal tract is closed three times (first by the lips and then twice by the tongue), each closure being followed by an opening of the vocal tract. The successive openings are the basis of syllables, and the word *banana* consists therefore of three syllables. The open part of the cycle is regarded as the centre, or nucleus, of the syllable.

Sounds like [b] and [n] which involve a closed, or nearly closed, vocal tract, are consonants. Sounds like [ə] and [ɑ] which involve an open vocal tract are vowels. More precisely, any sounds in which the flow of air out of the mouth is impeded at least enough to cause a disturbance of the airflow are consonants. So a sound such as [s], in which the 'hissing' that can be heard results from the airflow being made turbulent, is as much a consonant as [b]. Conversely any sounds in which the air flows out of the mouth unimpeded are vowels. The distinction between consonant and vowel is fundamental to the way segments are described in the framework underpinning the IPA.

It follows from the definitions of 'consonant' and 'vowel', and from the origin of the syllable in the repeated opening and narrowing of the vocal tract, that vowels are well suited to playing the role of syllable nuclei, and consonants are well suited to defining the margins of syllables. The relationship between syllables and type of sound is not, however, totally straightforward. For one thing, a sound which is a consonant may nonetheless act as a syllable centre. So in a common pronunciation of the English word *button* as [bʌtn̩] there are two syllables, but the nucleus of the second is a consonant, as judged from the way it is produced. Conversely in the word [jɛt] *yet*, the first sound, if prolonged, is very similar to the vowel of [hid] *heed,* and does not involve a narrowing extreme enough to produce friction. However because [j] plays the same role in the syllable as sounds which are by definition consonants (e.g. [b] in [bɛt] *bet*), it is often included in the class of consonants and described accordingly.

On the IPA Chart, there are separate sections for vowels and for consonants, reflecting different techniques for describing them. The different techniques arise from the more closed articulation of consonants and the more open articulation of vowels.

2.4 Consonants

Because consonants involve a narrowing or 'stricture' at an identifiable place in the vocal tract, phoneticians have traditionally classified a consonant in terms of its 'place of articulation'. The [t] of *ten*, for instance, requires an airtight seal between the upper rim of the tongue and the upper gum or teeth. Phonetic description of place of articulation, however, concentrates on a section or 'slice' through the mid-line of the vocal tract, the mid-sagittal plane as it is known, and in this plane the seal is made between the tip or blade of the tongue and the bony ridge behind the upper front teeth, the alveolar ridge. The sound is therefore described as alveolar. Figure 2 shows a mid-sagittal section of the vocal tract, with the different places of articulation labelled. As further examples, the [p] of *pen* is bilabial (the closure is made by the upper and lower lips), and the [k] of *Ken* velar (made by the back of the tongue against the soft palate or velum). Other places of articulation are exemplified in section 3.

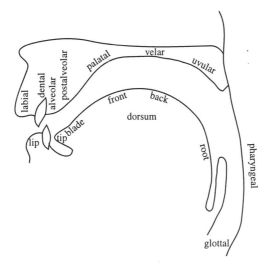

Figure 2 Mid-sagittal section of the vocal tract with labels for place of articulation

On the IPA Chart, symbols for the majority of consonants are to be found in the large table at the top. Place of articulation is reflected in the organization of this consonant table. Each column represents a place of articulation, reflected in the labels across the top of the table from bilabial at the left to glottal (consonants made by the vocal cords or vocal folds) at the right. The terms 'bilabial' and 'labiodental' indicate that the consonant is made by the lower lip against the upper lip and the upper front teeth respectively;

otherwise it is normally assumed that the sound at a named place of articulation is made by the articulator lying opposite the place of articulation (so alveolars are made with the tip of the tongue or the blade (which lies just behind the tip)). The exception to this is the term 'retroflex'. In retroflex sounds, the tip of the tongue is curled back from its normal position to a point behind the alveolar ridge. Usually alveolar [ɹ] shares some degree of this curling back of the tongue tip, which distinguishes it from other alveolars. Note that except in the case of fricatives only one symbol is provided for dental / alveolar / postalveolar; if necessary, these three places can be distinguished by the use of extra marks or 'diacritics' to form composite symbols, as discussed in section 2.8. For example, the dental / alveolar / postalveolar nasals can be represented as [n̪ n n̠] respectively.

The rows of the consonant table, labelled at the left side by terms such as plosive, nasal, trill, and so on, reflect another major descriptive dimension for consonants, namely 'manner of articulation'. Manner of articulation covers a number of distinct factors to do with the articulation of a sound. One is the degree of stricture (narrowing) of the vocal tract involved. If the articulation of the plosive [t] is modified so that the tongue tip or blade forms a narrow groove running from front to back along the alveolar ridge, instead of an airtight closure, air can escape. The airflow is turbulent, and this creates sound of a hissing kind known in phonetics as frication. Such a sound is called a fricative. In this case the resultant sound would be [s] as in *sin*. Other fricatives include [f] (as in *fin*) and [ʃ] (as in *shin*). If even less narrowing is made in the vocal tract, an approximant will result, in which the airflow is not turbulent and no frication is audible. Approximants are exemplified by the sound [j] at the start of *yet*, and the first sound in *red* in most varieties of English ([ɹ], [ɻ], or [ʋ] according to the variety).

'Manner of articulation' also includes important factors such as whether the velum (the soft part of the palate at the back of the mouth) is raised or lowered. If it is lowered, as for the sounds [m] and [n] in *man*, the resonances of the nasal cavity will contribute to the sounds. Consonants where this happens are called nasals. Laterals (lateral approximants such as English [l] in *let* and lateral fricatives such as Welsh [ɬ] in *llan* 'church (place-name element)' are sounds where air escapes not in the mid-line of the vocal tract but at the side. Trills are sounds like [r] in Spanish *perro* 'dog' in which the air is repeatedly interrupted by an articulator (in this case the tongue tip) vibrating in an airstream. A very short contact, similar in duration to one cycle of the vibration of a trill, is called a tap, such as the [ɾ] in Spanish *pero* 'but'.

A further important factor in the description of consonants is not shown in the column or row labels. This is whether the consonant is voiced or voiceless. In voiced consonants the vocal cords are producing acoustic energy by vibrating as air passes between them, and in voiceless ones they are not. A symbol on the left of a cell in the table is for a voiceless consonant, e.g. [p] and [ʔ], and one on the right is for a voiced consonant, e.g. [b] (the voiced counterpart of [p]) and [m]. Voicing distinctions are actually more fine-grained than implied by this two-way distinction, so it may be necessary to add to the notation allowed by the two basic symbols. For instance, the symbolization [ba pa pʰa] implies consonants in which the vocal cords are, respectively, vibrating during the plosive closure, vibrating only from the release of the closure, and vibrating only from a time well after the release (giving what is often known as an 'aspirated' plosive). Where a cell contains only one symbol, it indicates (with one exception) a voiced consonant and is placed on the right. The exception is the glottal plosive [ʔ] (as the vocal cords are closed, they are unable simultaneously to vibrate).

It should be clear that the consonant table is more than a list of symbols; it embodies a classificatory system for consonants. It allows the user to ask a question such as 'how should I symbolize a voiced sound involving complete closure at the uvula?' (The answer is [ɢ].) Or conversely, 'what sort of a sound is [ʝ]?' (The answer is one which is voiced, and in which frication can be heard resulting from a narrowing between the tongue front and the hard palate.)

Not all cells or halves of cells in the consonant table contain symbols. The gaps are of three kinds. Shaded cells occur where the intersection of a manner and a place of articulation define a sound which is thought not to be possible, either by definition (a nasal requires an oral occlusion combined with lowering of the velum, and so a pharyngeal or glottal nasal is ruled out), or because the sound is impossible or too difficult to produce, such as a velar trill or a bilabial lateral fricative. Unless phoneticians are mistaken in their view of the latter category of sound, no symbols will be needed for any of the shaded cells. An unshaded gap, such as the velar lateral fricative, may indicate that the sound in question can be produced, but has not been found in languages. It is always possible that a language will be discovered which requires the gap to be filled in. A case of this kind is the velar lateral approximant [ʟ], which only became generally known among phoneticians in the 1970s when it was reported in Kanite, a language of Papua New Guinea. An unshaded gap may also occur where a sound can be represented by using an existing symbol but giving it a slightly different value, with or without an added mark separate from the symbol. A symbol such as [β], shown on the chart in the position for a voiced bilabial fricative, can also be used to represent a voiced bilabial approximant if needed. In a similar way, no symbols are provided for voiceless nasals. A voiceless alveolar nasal can be written by adding the voiceless mark [̥] below the symbol [n] to form an appropriate composite symbol [n̥]. Many of the gaps on the chart could be filled in this way by the use of diacritics (sections 2.8 and 3). The formation of this kind of composite symbol is discussed further in the section on diacritics below.

2.5 Non-pulmonic consonants

All the symbols in the main consonant table imply consonants produced using air from the lungs ('pulmonic' consonants). Whilst some languages rely exclusively on air from the lungs for sound production, many languages additionally use one or both of two other 'airstream mechanisms' to produce some of their consonants. Symbols for these sounds are given in a separate box below and to the left of the main consonant table. These sounds are exemplified in section 3.

The more common of the two non-pulmonic airstream mechanisms used in languages, the 'glottalic', involves closing the glottis, and squeezing or expanding the air trapped between the glottis and a consonant stricture further forward in the vocal tract. If the air is squeezed, and therefore flows outwards – abruptly when a closure further forward is released, or briefly but continuously through a fricative stricture – the sound is known as an 'ejective'. Ejectives are symbolized by the appropriate voiceless consonant symbol with the addition of an apostrophe, e.g. [p'], [s']. If instead the air between the glottis and a closure further forward is expanded, reducing its pressure, air will flow into the mouth abruptly at the release of the forward closure. Usually the closure phase of such sounds is accompanied by vocal cord vibration, giving '(voiced) implosives' such as [ɓ]. If it is necessary to symbolize a voiceless version of such a sound, this can be done by adding a diacritic: [ɓ̥].

'Velaric' airstream sounds, usually known as 'clicks', again involve creating an enclosed cavity in which the pressure of the air can be changed, but this time the back closure is made not with the glottis but with the back of the tongue against the soft palate, such that air is sucked into the mouth when the closure further forward is released. The 'tut-tut' or 'tsk-tsk' sound, used by many English speakers as an indication of disapproval, is produced in this way, but only in isolation and not as part of ordinary words. Some other languages use clicks as consonants. A separate set of symbols such as [ǂ] is provided for clicks. Since any click involves a velar or uvular closure, it is possible to symbolize factors such as voicelessness, voicing, or nasality of the click by combining the click symbol with the appropriate velar or uvular symbol: [k͡ǂ ɡ͡ǂ ŋ͡ǂ], [q͡ǃ].

2.6 Vowels

Vowels are sounds which occur at syllable centres, and which, because they involve a less extreme narrowing of the vocal tract than consonants, cannot easily be described in terms of a 'place of articulation' as consonants can. Instead, they are classified in terms of an abstract 'vowel space', which is represented by the four-sided figure known as the 'Vowel Quadrilateral' (see the Chart, middle right). This space bears a relation, though not an exact one, to the position of the tongue in vowel production, as explained below.

Figure 3 shows a mid-sagittal section of the vocal tract with four superimposed outlines of the tongue's shape. For the vowel labelled [i], which is rather like the vowel of *heed* or French *si* 'if', the body of the tongue is displaced forwards and upwards in the mouth, towards the hard palate. The diagram shows a more extreme version of this vowel than normally found in English at least, made so that any further narrowing in the palatal region would cause the airflow to become turbulent, resulting in a fricative. This extreme vowel is taken as a fixed reference point for vowel description. Since the tongue is near the roof of the mouth this vowel is described as 'close', and since the highest point of the tongue is at the front of the area where vowel articulations are possible, it is described as 'front'.

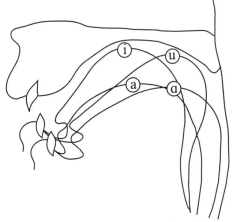

Figure 3 Mid-sagittal section of the vocal tract with the outline of the tongue shape for each of four extreme vowels superimposed.

Conversely, for the vowel labelled [ɑ], which is rather like the vowel of Standard Southern British or General American English *palm,* the tongue body is displaced downwards and backwards, narrowing the pharynx. The most extreme version of this vowel, made so that any further narrowing in the pharynx would result in a fricative, is taken as a second fixed reference point. The space between the tongue and the roof of the mouth is as large as possible, so this vowel is described as 'open', and the tongue is near the back of the mouth, so it is described as 'back'.

If the tongue body is raised as close as possible at the back of the mouth, just short of producing a velar consonant, and (as is common in languages) the lips are simultaneously rounded and protruded, the close back vowel [u] results (see figure 3), which is similar to the vowel of French *vous* 'you' or German *du* 'you'. And if a vowel is produced in which the highest point of the tongue is at the front of the mouth and the mouth is as open as possible, the result is [a]. This is rather like the quality of the vowel in *cat* in contemporary Standard Southern British English (other dialects may have less open qualities or less front qualities). These two extreme vowels may also be regarded as fixed references.

The first part of figure 4 shows that joining the circles representing the highest point of the tongue in these four extreme vowels gives the boundary of the space within which vowels can be produced. For the purposes of vowel description this space can be stylized as the quadrilateral shown in the second part of figure 4. Further reference vowels can now be defined as shown in the third part of figure 4. Specifically, two fully front vowels [e] and [ɛ] are defined between [i] and [a] so that the differences between each vowel and the next in the series are auditorily equal; and similarly, two fully back vowels [ɔ] and [o] are defined to give equidistant steps between [ɑ] and [u]. The use of auditory spacing in the definition of these vowels means vowel description is not based purely on articulation, and is one reason why the vowel quadrilateral must be regarded as an abstraction and not a direct mapping of tongue position. These vowels and those defined below are exemplified in section 3.

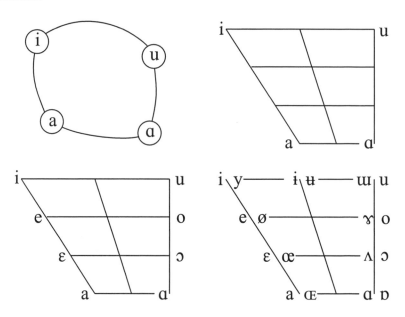

Figure 4 The vowel quadrilateral and cardinal vowels. Above, the relation between the vowel quadrilateral and the vowels shown in figure 3; below, the primary cardinal vowels and all cardinal vowels.

There are now four defined vowel heights: [i] and [u] are close vowels, [e] and [o] are close-mid vowels, [ɛ] and [ɔ] are open-mid vowels, and [a] and [ɑ] are open vowels (note that in this last pair the difference in letter shape is important, signifying a front vowel and a back vowel respectively). The vowel space can be seen to be taking on the form of a grid. The eight reference vowels are known as the 'primary cardinal vowels'. 'Cardinal' in this sense refers to points on which the system of description hinges. The description of the primary cardinal vowels outlined above differs slightly from that of the English phonetician Daniel Jones who first defined them, but is in accord with a widespread conception of them today. The primary cardinal vowels are often referred to by numbers ordered anticlockwise round the quadrilateral: 1 [i], 2 [e], 3 [ɛ], 4 [a], 5 [ɑ], 6 [ɔ], 7 [o], 8 [u].

So far, lip activity has been largely ignored. In the back series of cardinal vowels ([ɑ ɔ o u]) lip-rounding progressively increases, from none on [ɑ] to close rounding on

[u]. By convention unrounded vowels are placed to the left of the front or back line of the quadrilateral, and rounded vowels to the right. Conversely in the front series [a ɛ e i] the lips are neutral for [a], and become progressively more spread through the series to [i]. The fact that [i e ɛ a ɑ] are unrounded, and [ɔ o u] have increasing rounding, reflects a relationship commonly found in languages between vowel height, backness, and rounding. Lip activity is, however, independent of tongue position, and many languages exploit this in their vowel systems.

To reflect this, eight 'secondary cardinal vowels' are therefore defined which differ only in lip position from their primary counterparts. These are shown paired with their primary counterparts in the fourth part of figure 4. So, for example, of the close vowels [i y ɯ u], [i ɯ] have spread lips and [y u] have closely rounded lips; and of the open-mid vowels [ɛ œ ʌ ɔ], [ɛ ʌ] have slightly spread lips and [œ ɔ] have open rounding. A further two secondary cardinal vowels are defined; these are the close central vowels [ɨ] (spread) and [ʉ] (close rounded). The secondary cardinal vowels are sometimes referred to by the number of the corresponding primary cardinal vowel, for example [ø] is 'secondary cardinal 2', or they are numbered anticlockwise round the quadrilateral from 9 [y] to 16 [ɯ]. [ɨ] and [ʉ] are then numbered 17 and 18 respectively.

The complete set of IPA vowel symbols is shown in the quadrilateral on the Chart. In addition to the cardinal vowels already discussed, which lie on the outside edge of the quadrilateral, there are symbols for mid central vowels, and for vowels at a number of intermediate locations. There is a pair of symbols for unrounded and rounded close-mid central vowels, [ɘ ɵ], and a corresponding open-mid pair [ɜ ɞ]. The vowel [ə], often referred to as schwa, lies at the middle of the vowel quadrilateral, and [ɐ] lies between open-mid and open. The vowels [ɪ ʏ ʊ] are mid-centralized from [i y u] respectively.

Since the vowel space is continuous, it is a matter of chance whether a vowel in a language exactly coincides with one of the reference points symbolized on the quadrilateral. In particular, languages may use vowels which are similar to, but not as peripheral as, the reference points indicated by the cardinal vowels. If detailed phonetic description is required, most vowels in a language have to be placed in relation to a reference vowel, for instance 'a vowel centralized and lowered from cardinal [e]'. This description can be symbolized by adding diacritics (see section 2.8) to the cardinal vowel symbol: [ë̞].

2.7 Suprasegmentals

A number of properties of speech tend to form patterns which extend over more than one segment, and/or to vary independently of the segmental targets. This is particularly true of pitch, loudness, and perceived timing. These properties are often referred to as 'suprasegmentals', and part of the process of phonetic analysis is the separation of these properties from the rest of the speech event. The IPA provides a separate set of symbols for suprasegmentals, to be found on the Chart at the bottom right corner.

Pitch variation, for instance, can operate over complete utterances to convey meaning additional to that of the words in what is generally termed 'intonation'. This is true in all languages, though the complexity of the intonational system varies across languages. The symbol [‖] can be used to mark the end of the domain of an intonation pattern, and [|] to demarcate a smaller unit. The symbols [↗ ↘] for 'global rise' and 'global fall' respectively may also be useful for intonation, although a complete intonational transcription will require symbols not provided on the IPA Chart.

Another domain of pitch variation is the word or syllable, and such pitch variation serves to distinguish words in much the same way as their segmental make-up does. Languages in which pitch has this function are called tone languages, and are thought to form a majority of the languages of the world. In Thai, for example, [khaːˑ˥˩] with a falling pitch (indicated by the diagonal part of the symbol following the segments) means 'servant' and [khaːˑ˩] with rising pitch means 'leg'.

The IPA has two alternative sets of symbols for indicating tones. In languages in which lexical contrasts are predominantly dependent on the pitch movement on each syllable, such as Thai and the various forms of Chinese, so-called tone letters are often used. These letters, as in the Thai examples, indicate the tone of the preceding syllable by a vertical stroke with a line preceding it. The vertical stroke is assumed to represent five possible pitch heights within the speaker's range, and the position of the line shows the height and movement (if any) of the pitch on the preceding syllable. The tone letters are often used to indicate general tone movements. For example, if there is only one falling tone in a language, and no strong reason to draw attention to the particular level of its endpoints, it can be noted as going from the highest to the lowest level. Thus a transcription of the Standard Chinese word for 'scold' is [maˑ˩], although most Chinese speakers will not produce this syllable with a fall extending through their whole pitch range. It is also possible to use the tone letters to show more detailed transcriptions for certain purposes. Thus, the Thai high tone can be transcribed with the symbol [˥]; but measurements of the fundamental frequency in high tone syllables show that there is actually a rise and a fall in syllables of this sort, so the tone could be represented as [˦˥˦].

The other IPA system for transcribing tone has often been used for languages in which tonal contrasts depend predominantly on the pitch height in each syllable. There are three diacritics, corresponding to high [é], mid [ē] and low [è] tones, which can be placed above the segment bearing the tone (here exemplified by [e]). Thus the three tones in the West African language Yoruba can be transcribed as exemplified in the phrases [óbá] 'he/she met', [óbā] 'he/she hid', [óbà] 'it perched'. Notice that these tone symbols must not be interpreted as iconic; that is, although the 'acute accent' [´] looks rising, it in fact means 'high'. To represent a rising tone it is necessary to combine a 'low' and a 'high', and similarly for other contour tones. So a syllable such as [e] occurring on a rising tone is [ě], and on a falling tone is [ê]. On the other hand the 'tone letters' such as [e˥] (meaning 'high') and [e˩] (meaning 'rising') are directly iconic.

The chart shows the tone letter [˥]·as if it were equivalent to [˝], the extra-high tone symbol in the other set of symbols, and so on down the scale. But this is done only to simplify the layout of the chart. The two sets of symbols are not comparable in this way. The four tones of Standard Chinese are often symbolized as [ma˥] 'mother', [ma˥˩]

'scold', [maˀ˩] 'hemp', [maˀ˧] 'horse'. If they were transcribed in the other system they would be [má mâ má mà].

The symbols [ꜛ] for upstep and [ꜜ] for downstep are used to show modifications (raising or lowering) of the pitch indicated by ordinary tone symbols. Upstep occurs, for example, in Hausa in that the last of a series of high toned syllables before a low tone is pronounced with a higher pitch than the others. Thus the Hausa word [túrántʃí] 'English' has three high tones with the same pitch when said by itself. In the phrase [túránꜛtʃí nè] 'it is English', the raising of the high tone can be indicated by the modifier [ꜛ] as shown. Downstep occurs in the Ghanaian language Akan, as in the word [ɔkɔ́ꜜtɔ́] 'crab' which has a downstepped high tone on the last syllable. This tone is demonstrably a high in that it has the same pitch level as an initial high tone in a following word.

Symbols are also provided for indicating the relative prominence or stress of syllables, differing segmental length, and syllable divisions. The exact nature of syllable prominence or stress varies from language to language, but the IPA provides for up to three degrees of prominence to be indicated; in [ˌpærəsaɪˈkɒlədʒi] *parapsychology* the highest level occurs on the fourth syllable, and the second highest on the first syllable, while the remaining unmarked syllables are less prominent (a further division among these may be inferred from vowel quality, those syllables with [ə] being least prominent in English). Extra strong stress can be indicated by doubling the stress mark: [əˈˈmeɪzɪŋ] *amazing!* Segmental length can be marked on a continuum from short to long as [ĕ e eˑ eː], though the possibility exists to show even greater length as [eːː]. Syllable divisions, which it may be useful to indicate for phonological reasons or where the syllable division determines phonetic difference as in [naɪ.tr̥eɪt] *nitrate* versus [naɪt.ɹeɪt] *night-rate,* can be symbolized as shown. The use of suprasegmental symbols is further demonstrated in section 3.

2.8 Diacritics

Diacritics are small letter-shaped symbols or other marks which can be added to a vowel or consonant symbol to modify or refine its meaning in various ways. A symbol and any diacritic or diacritics attached to it are regarded as a single (complex) symbol. The set of diacritics approved by the International Phonetic Association is given in the table at the bottom left of the Chart.

A number of diacritics deal with different aspects of phonation. Two are available to reverse the voicing value otherwise implied by any symbol. Voiceless trills or nasals, for instance, for which there are otherwise no symbols, can be notated as [r̥], [n̥] etc. (some diacritics may be placed above a symbol when a descender on the symbol would interfere with legibility). Vowels which occur without voicing can also be indicated, e.g. [e̥]. More rarely employed is [̬] which indicates voicing in a symbol otherwise implying voicelessness. It sometimes indicates the spreading of voicing from an adjacent segment ('assimilation' of voicing), as in French [ʃak̬ʒuʁ] *chaque jour* 'each day'. It is a moot point whether [k̬] and [g] refer to phonetically identical sounds, and likewise [s] and [z̥]. It is possible that the distinction between [k] and [g] or between [s] and [z] can involve dimensions independent of vocal cord vibration, such as tenseness versus laxness of articulation, so that the possibility of notating voicing separately becomes important; but in any case, it can be convenient to be able to preserve the lexical shape of a word (e.g. French [ʃak] *chaque* 'each') while noting assimilation. The diacritic [ʰ] is used to indicate a release of air after a consonant, most commonly between a voiceless plosive and a vowel as in [tʰaɪ] *tie*. Two different phonation types which are used contrastively by some languages, creaky voice and breathy voice, can be indicated on vowels or consonants (see examples at the top of the second column of the diacritic table).

The diacritics shown in rows four to nine of the first column of the diacritic table, together with the diacritics for 'raised' and 'lowered' shown to the right in rows nine and ten, can be used to modify the lip or tongue position implied by a vowel symbol. Thus [ɥ] indicates a vowel like cardinal [u] but with a lip position further from the 'rounded' end of the 'spread-rounded' continuum than implied by the cardinal symbol, and (as seen in section 2.6 above) [ë̞] indicates a vowel centralized and lowered from cardinal [e]. Vowel qualities between [u] and [ʉ] might be symbolized [ʉ̠], indicating retraction relative to the central vowel, or (if nearer back than central) [u̟] or [ü] indicating fronting relative to the back vowel. The diacritic for 'mid-centralized' indicates a quality displaced in the direction of the mid central vowel [ə]; thus [ĕ] is equivalent to [ë̞], and [ŏ] to [ö̞].

The diacritics for 'raised' and 'lowered', when applied to a consonant symbol, change its manner category, so that [t̞] could be used to indicate an articulation like that of an alveolar plosive but one in which complete closure is not achieved, yielding a fricative-like sound (but lacking the grooved tongue shape of [s]) as in some Irish English pronunciations of the sound at the end of *right*. The diacritics for 'advanced' and 'retracted' are also commonly used to modify consonant place of articulation. So, for instance, a voiceless fricative at the front of the velar region could be symbolized [x̟], and a specifically postalveolar nasal [n̠].

The 'rhoticity' diacritic [˞] indicates a vowel with a specific auditory effect like that of the vowel in General American [fɑ˞] *far* and [fə˞] *fur* (the combination of the 'rhoticity' diacritic with [ə] is often written and printed [ɚ]). The auditory effect is probably caused by a constriction in the pharynx combined with an expansion of the space in the mouth in front of the tongue, either by curling the tongue tip up and back, or by retracting it into the tongue body while 'bunching' the tongue body up towards the pre-velar region. In some languages the tongue root functions independently of other determinants of vowel quality, adjusting the width of the pharynx, and at the bottom right of the table there are two diacritics to indicate advancement and retraction of the tongue root. The 'syllabic' diacritic is used to mark consonants which are acting as syllable nuclei, and the non-syllabic diacritic to mark vowels which are not fulfilling their customary syllabic role.

The 'dental' diacritic (third column) modifies those consonant symbols found under 'alveolar' to indicate unambiguously a dental articulation. As noted in section 2, although only one symbol is provided in the consonant table (except in the fricative row), dental / alveolar / postalveolar can be distinguished as [n̪ n n̠] (postalveolar being marked by the 'retracted' diacritic). The 'linguolabial' diacritic, which is used to symbolize an otherwise omitted (and very rare) consonantal type, indicates a sound made with the tip or blade of the tongue against the upper lip. The diacritic is used to modify the relevant alveolar consonant symbol. The diacritics for 'apical' and 'laminal' make specific which part of the frontmost area of the tongue is making an articulation: the tip (apical), or the blade (laminal).

Secondary articulations are narrowings of the vocal tract which are less narrow than the main one producing a consonant. The names palatalization, velarization, and pharyngealization, make explicit where the narrowing is. In one sense a secondary articulation is the superimposition of a close-vowel-like articulation on a consonant – [i] for palatalization, symbolized for instance [tʲ], [ɯ] for velarization ([tˠ]), and [ɑ] for pharyngealization ([tˤ]). Labialization strictly means reduction of the opening of the lips. However it has tended to be used for the commonly found combination of rounding (protrusion) of the lips accompanied by velar constriction. It is for such labially rounded velarization that the superscript [ʷ] is most appropriate. If it is necessary to distinguish a secondary reduction of the lip opening accompanied by neither protrusion nor velar constriction, a superscript [ʋ] (the symbol for a labiodental approximant) might be used. These superscript diacritics which are placed after the symbol look rather as if they imply a sequence of events; but strictly the notation means that the secondary articulation is simultaneous with the consonant. This is unlike the case of the aspiration diacritic (e.g. [tʰ]) where the plosive and the aspiration are sequential. The simultaneity of the secondary articulation is clearer from the alternative diacritic for symbolizing velarization or pharyngealization, [~], which is placed through the consonant symbol in question (often to the detriment of legibility). Nasalization, despite the similarity of name, is not a secondary articulation in the same sense, but the addition of the resonances of the nasal cavities to a sound. Vowels (e.g. [ẽ]) and consonants (e.g. [ɹ̃]) can be nasalized.

Finally, there are three diacritics in the third column dealing with release ('nasal release', 'lateral release', and 'no audible release'). All three show that a stop consonant has not been released into a vowel. Instead, the air escape is through the nose (e.g. [bʌtⁿn] *button*), round the side of the tongue (e.g. [bɒtˡɬ] *bottle*), or the air is not released until a later sound [ɹæg̚bæg] *ragbag*. The use of diacritics is further exemplified in section 3.

2.9 *Other symbols*
These symbols are included in their own section of the Chart for presentational convenience. The section contains several consonant symbols which would not fit easily into the 'place and manner' grid of the main consonant table. In some cases, such as the epiglottals and the alveolo-palatals, no column is provided for the place of articulation because of its rarity and the small number of types of sounds which are found there. In other cases, such as [w], the sound involves two places of articulation simultaneously, which makes it inconvenient to display in the table. If separate columns for all consonants with two places of articulation were provided, the size of the grid would become unmanageable. Most consonants that involve two simultaneous places of articulation are written by combining two symbols with the 'tie bar' [‿], for example [k͡p] which represents a voiceless labial-velar plosive.

3   Guide to IPA notation

3.1   Exemplification of the symbols

The general value of the symbols in the chart is listed below. In each case a symbol can be regarded as a shorthand equivalent to a phonetic description, and a way of representing the contrasting sounds that occur in a language. Thus [m] is equivalent to 'voiced bilabial nasal', and is also a way of representing one of the contrasting nasal sounds that occur in English and other languages.

When a symbol is said to be suitable for the representation of sounds in two languages, it does not necessarily mean that the sounds in the two languages are identical. Thus [p] is shown as being suitable for the transcription of *pea* in English, and also for *pis* in French; similarly [b] is shown as being suitable for the transcription of *bee* in English, and also for *bis* in French; but the corresponding sounds are not the same in the two languages. The IPA has resources for denoting the differences, if it is necessary to do so, as illustrated below in section 4; but at a more general level of description the symbols can be used to represent the sounds in either language.

All languages exhibit variation in their pronunciation. Sometimes an example below will only be valid for some varieties of a language. For instance the exemplification of [θ] by the English word *thief* is not valid for dialects which pronounce the ‹th› as a labiodental fricative [f] or a dental stop [t̪]. An example means that the symbol exemplified is, at least, appropriate for one or more widely spoken varieties of the language. In the case of English examples, where the variety is not further specified, it should be assumed that the exemplification is appropriate, at least, in General American English and Standard Southern British English (see section 2).

The symbols are exemplified in the order in which they appear on the chart; and they are discussed using the terms given as headings for the rows and columns. English (Eng.) and French (Fr.) examples are given when unambiguous. Where practical, an ortho-graphic version of the exemplifying word is provided, in italics. English glosses of words in other languages are given in quotation marks. The languages used for exemplification are identified at the end of the list at the end of this section.

PLOSIVES

p	Eng. *pea* [pi]; Fr. *pis* [pi] 'worst'	b	Eng. *bee* [bi]; Fr. *bis* [bis] 'encore'
t	Eng. *tea* [ti]; Fr. *thé* [te] 'tea'	d	Eng. *deep* [dip]; Fr. *dix* [dis] 'ten'
ʈ	Hindi [ʈal] 'postpone'	ɖ	Hindi [ɖal] 'branch'
c	Hungarian *tyúk* [cuːk] 'hen'	ɟ	Hungarian *gyúr* [ɟuːr] 'to knead'
k	Eng. *cap* [kæp]; Fr. *quand* [kɑ̃] 'when'; K'ekchi [kaʔa] 'grindstone'	g	Eng. *gap* [gæp]; Fr. *gant* [gɑ̃] 'glove'
q	K'ekchi [qa] 'our'	ɢ	Farsi [ɢar] 'cave'
ʔ	Hawaiian *Hawai'i* [hawaiʔi] '(place name)', *ha'a* [haʔa] 'dance'		

The plosives in the left-hand column above are said to be voiceless, and those on the right are said to be voiced. The extent of voicing may vary considerably. The voiceless consonants may be not only voiceless, but also aspirated; and the voiced consonants may be voiced throughout their duration, or may have voicing during only part of that time. Usually the use of a pair of symbols such as [p] and [b] in a given language signifies only that there is a contrast in the degree of voicing within that pair of sounds. Either of the variant letter shapes [g] and [ɡ] may be used to represent the voiced velar plosive.

NASALS

m Eng. *me* [mi]; Fr. *mis* [mi] 'put'
ɱ Eng. *emphasis* [ɛɱfəsɪs]
n Eng. *knee* [ni]; Fr. *nid* [ni] 'nest'
ɳ Malayalam [keɳɳi] 'link in a chain'
ɲ Fr. *agneau* [aɲo] 'lamb'; Malayalam [keɲɲi] 'boiled rice and water'
ŋ Eng. *hang* [hæŋ]
N Inuit [saaNNi] 'his bones'

Note that the symbols [t, d, n] listed above, and the symbols [r, ɾ, ɬ, ɭ, ɻ, l] which will be exemplified below, all represent sounds that can be either dental, or alveolar, or postalveolar. If there is a need to represent specifically one of these places of articulation, there are IPA resources for doing so, which will be exemplified later.

TRILLS

ʙ Kele [mbʙuen] 'fruit'
r Spanish *perro* [pero] 'dog'; Finnish *ranta* [rɑntɑ] 'shore'
ʀ Fr. *rat* [ʀa] 'rat'; Southern Swedish *ras* [ʀas] 'breed'

Note: most forms of English, French, German, Swedish do not have trills except in over-articulated speech, for instance when trying to be clear over a poor telephone line.

TAPS OR FLAPS

ɾ Spanish *pero* [peɾo] 'but'; Am. Eng. *atom* ['æɾəm]
ɽ Hausa *shaara* [ʃàːɽa] or [ʃàːɽa] 'sweeping'
(Some speakers of Hausa have [ɽ] and others have [ɺ].)

FRICATIVES

The fricatives in the left-hand column below are voiceless, and those on the right are voiced. To a somewhat lesser degree than in the case of the plosives, the extent of voicing may vary.

ɸ Ewe *e fa* [é ɸá] 'he polished'   β Ewe *eβe* [èβè] 'Ewe'

f   Eng. *fee* [fi]; Fr. *fixe* [fiks];
Ewe *e fa* [é fá] 'he was cold'

θ   Eng. *thief* [θif]

s   Eng. *see* [si]; Fr. *si* [si] 'if'

ʃ   Eng. *she* [ʃi]; Fr. *chic* [ʃik] 'chic'

ʂ   Standard Chinese *sha* [ʂa] 'to kill'

ç   German *ich* [ɪç] 'I'

x   German *hoch* [hox] 'high'

χ   Hebrew [maχar] 'he sold'

ħ   Hebrew [ħor] 'hole'

v   Eng. *vat* [væt]; Fr. *vie* [vi] 'life';
Ewe *eve* [èvè] 'two'

ð   Eng. *thee* [ði]

z   Eng. *zeal* [zil]; Fr. *zéro* [zeʁo] 'zero'

ʒ   Eng. *vision* [vɪʒn]; Fr. *joue* [ʒu] 'cheek'

ʐ   Standard Chinese *ráng* [ʐaŋ] 'to assist'

ʝ   Eng. variant of [j] in *yeast* [ʝist]

ɣ   Greek *γαλα* ['ɣala] 'milk'

ʁ   Fr. *riz* [ʁi] 'rice'

ʕ   Hebrew [ʕor] 'skin'

Although it is traditional to pair Hebrew and Arabic [ħ], [ʕ] as fricatives, the voiced sound [ʕ] is usually perceived as an approximant.

h   Eng. *he* [hi]

ɦ   Eng. *ahead* [əɦɛd]

[ɦ] represents a breathy voiced sound, rather than an ordinary voiced sound.

LATERAL FRICATIVES

ɬ   Zulu *hlanza* [ɬânzà] 'vomit';
Welsh *llan* [ɬan] 'church'

ɮ   Zulu *dlala* [ɮálà] 'play'

APPROXIMANTS

ʋ   Hindi [nɔʋẽ] 'ninth'

ɹ   Eng. *read* [ɹid]

ɻ   Hausa *shaara* [ʃàːɽa] or [ʃàːɻa] 'sweeping'
(Some speakers of Hausa have [ɽ] and others have [ɻ].)

j   Eng. *yes* [jɛs]; Fr. *yeux* [jø] 'eyes'

ɰ   Turkish *ağa* [aɰa] '(a title)'; Korean [ɰisa] 'doctor'

LATERAL APPROXIMANTS

l   Eng. *leaf* [lif]; Fr. *lit* [li] 'bed'

ɭ   Tamil [vaɭ] 'sword'; Swedish *pärla* [pæːɭa] 'pearl'

ʎ   Italian *figlio* [fiʎʎɔ] 'son'; Spanish *llegar* [ʎeˈɣaɾ] 'to arrive'

ʟ   Mid-Waghi *aglagle* [aʟaʟe] 'dizzy'

NON-PULMONIC CONSONANTS

CLICKS

ʘ   !Xóõ [k͡ʘôõ] 'dream'

ǀ   Xhosa *ukucola* [ukúk͡ǀola] 'to grind finely'

ǃ   Xhosa *ukuqoba* [ukúk͡ǃoɓa] 'to break stones'

ǂ !Xóõ [k͡ǂàã] 'bone'
‖ Xhosa *ukuxhoba* [ukúkǁʰoɓa] 'to arm oneself'

VOICED IMPLOSIVES

ɓ Sindhi [ɓəⁿi] 'field'
ɗ Sindhi [ɗɪnu] 'festival'
ʄ Sindhi [ʄətu] 'illiterate'
ɠ Sindhi [ɠənu] 'handle'
ʛ Mam [ʛa] 'fire'

EJECTIVES

p' Amharic [p'ap'as] 'bishop (loan word)'
t' Amharic [t'il] 'fight'
k' Amharic [k'alat] 'word'
s' Amharic [s'ahaɪ] 'sun'

VOWELS

The symbols on the vowel chart can be regarded as providing reference points in the vowel space. They can also be used to represent vowel qualities generally in the area of the corresponding reference points. With the vowel symbols it is especially important to note that they may represent slightly different sounds in different languages. For example, [i] may be used for the vowel in the English word *heed* or in the French word *lit* (bed), despite the fact that the English vowel may be slightly diphthongal and less close than the French vowel.

Because of their status as reference points, it is difficult to illustrate some of the vowel symbols appropriately in terms of particular languages; this is particularly true of the mid central vowels [ə, ɵ, ɜ, ɞ]. The symbols [ə] and [ɐ] are available for representing vowels in the mid central and lower central regions. [a] is often used for an open central vowel. The open front rounded reference quality [œ] is rarely found in languages, though reported for Austrian German.

The symbols in the right-hand column below specify vowels with more rounded lips than the corresponding symbols in the left-hand column.

i	Eng. *heed* [hid]; Fr. *lit* [li] 'bed'	y	Fr. *lu* [ly] 'read'; German *Füße* [fysə] 'feet'
ɪ	Eng. *hid* [hɪd]	ʏ	German *Flüsse* [flʏsə] 'rivers'; Swedish *nytta* [nʏtta] 'use (noun)'
e	Scottish Eng. *hay* [he]; Fr. *les* [le] 'the (pl.)'	ø	Fr. *peu* [pø] 'few'
ɛ	Eng. *head* [hɛd]; Fr. *lait* [lɛ] 'milk'	œ	Fr. *peur* [pœʁ] 'fear'
æ	Eng. *had* [hæd]		
a	Fr. *patte* [pat] 'paw'	Œ	Austrian German *Seil* [sŒ:] 'rope'

ɑ Eng. *father* [fɑðə(ɹ)]

ʌ Vietnamese [ʌŋ] 'favour' (This symbol is sometimes used for a different vowel, the central vowel in Eng. *hut* [hɐt].)

ɤ Vietnamese [tɤ] 'silk'

ɯ Vietnamese [tɯ̇] 'fourth'

ɨ Korean [g̊ɨm] 'gold'

ɒ British Eng. *bother* [bɒðə]

ɔ British Eng. *caught* [kɔt]; Ger. *Gott* [gɔt] 'god'; Vietnamese [tɔ] 'large'

o Fr. *lot* [lo] 'share'; Vietnamese [to] 'soup bowl'

ʊ Eng. *book* [bʊk]

u Eng. *school* [skuɫ]; Fr. *loup* [lu] 'wolf'; Vietnamese [tu] 'to drink'

ʉ Norwegian *butt* [bʉt] 'blunt'

OTHER SYMBOLS

ʍ Scottish Eng. *whether* [ʍɛðəɹ]

w Eng. *weather* [wɛðə(ɹ)]; Fr. *oui* [wi] 'yes'

ɥ Fr. *huit* [ɥit] 'eight'

ʜ Avar [maʜ] 'odour'

ʕ Avar [maʕ] 'nail'

ʡ Agul [jaʡar] 'centres'

ɕ Polish *Basia* [baɕa] 'Barbara (dim.)'

ɭ KiChaka [iɭaa] 'to dress oneself'

ɧ Some dialects of Swedish *schal* [ɧal] 'scarf' (Note: for some speakers there is little or no [ʃ] friction in this sound.)

Affricates and double articulations

k͡p, t͡ʃ etc. Eng. *chief* [t͡ʃif]; Yoruba *apa* [ak͡pá] 'arm'; Tswana *tsetse* [t͡sét͡sé] 'tsetse fly'
Note: the tie bar can be placed above or below the symbols to be linked.

SUPRASEGMENTALS

In general, only one or two degrees of stress are marked:

" may be used to indicate extra strong stress.

ˈ Eng. *phonetics* [fəˈnɛtɪks]

ˌ Eng. *phonetician* [ˌfoʊnəˈtɪʃən]

Length may be contrastive for vowels and/or consonants:

ː Finnish *matto* [matːɔ] 'carpet'; *maaton* [mɑːtɔn] 'landless'; *maatto* [mɑːtːɔ] 'electrical earth/ground'
Finnish *mato* [matɔ] 'worm'

Note: as in Finnish orthography, length can also be indicated in phonetic transcription by double letters: e.g. Finnish *maatto* [mɑɑttɔ] 'electrical earth/ground'.

Estonian has a three-way length or quantity contrast:

ː   Estonian *saada* [saːda] 'to get'
ˑ   Estonian *saada* [saˑda] 'send (imperative)'
    Estonian *sada* [sada] 'hundred'

Length is not contrastive (at least, without concomitant changes in quality) in English, but allophonic differences exemplify the use of the length diacritics:

ː   Eng. *bead* [biːd]
ˑ   Eng. *beat* [biˑt]
˘   Eng. *police* [pə̆liˑs]

White spaces can be used to indicate word boundaries. Syllable breaks can be marked when required. The other two boundary symbols are used to mark the domain of larger prosodic units. There is also a linking symbol that can be used for explicitly indicating the lack of a boundary.

.   Eng. *lamb prepared* [ˈlæm.pɹə.ˈpɛəd], *lamp repaired* [ˈlæmp.ɹə.ˈpɛəd]
| Eng. *Jack, preparing the way, went on* [ˈdʒæk | pɹəˈpeəɹɪŋ ðə ˈweɪ | wɛnt ˈɒn ‖]
‖   Fr. *Jacques, préparant le sol, tomba* [ʒak | pʁepaʁɑ̃ lə sɔl | tɔ̃ba ‖]
      'Jack, preparing the soil, fell down'
‿   Fr. *petit ami* [pətit‿ami] 'boyfriend'

As explained in the previous section, there are two alternative systems of tone transcription. The chart shows these two systems as if there were direct equivalencies between them. However, they are usually used in different ways.

˝   Bariba [ně ná nā kɔ̀] 'I am the one who came'
́   Yoruba *o bá* [ó bá] 'he/she met'
¯   Yoruba *o ba* [ó bā] 'he/she hid'
`   Yoruba *o bà* [ó bà] 'it perched'
˷   Trique [ě̀ʔ] 'bitter'

It is also possible to combine these symbols so that, for example, [ê] represents a high tone followed by a low tone on the vowel [e], i.e. a falling tone. Similarly [ě] represents a rising tone, and [ē̆] and [ê̆] represent high-rising and low-rising tones.

There are two symbols for showing that subsequent tones may be a step lower or higher. The introduction of a downstep is phonologically contrastive in the Igbo example below, but the Hausa upstep indicates only a predictable allophone.

ꜜ   Igbo *ụlọ anyị* [úꜜlɔ́ ꜜáɲí] 'our house'
ꜛ   Hausa [túránꜛtʃí nè] 'it is English'

The use of the other set of symbols is illustrated below.

	CHINESE (STANDARD)	CANTONESE	THAI
˥	[ma˥] 'mother'	[ʂik˥] 'to know'	
˦			
˧		[ʂi˧] 'to try'; [ʂit˧] 'to reveal'	
˨		[ʂi˨] 'matter'; [ʂik˨] 'to eat'	
˩		[ʂi˩] 'time'	
˥˩	[ma˥˩] 'scold'		[naː˥˩] 'face'
˦˥		[ʂi˦˥] 'poem'	
˧˨		[ʂi˧˨] 'city'	
˧˥	[ma˧˥] 'hemp'	[ʂi˧˥] 'to cause'	[naː˧˥] 'aunt/uncle'
˨˩	[ma˨˩] 'horse'		[naː˨˩] 'thick'
˦˥			[naː˦˥] 'paddy field'
˨˩			[naː˨˩] '(nickname)'

The symbols for global rise and global fall are appropriate for use in many languages to mark intonation.

↗   Eng. *No?* [↗ noʊ]

↘   Eng. *No.* [↘ noʊ], *How did you ever escape?* [↗haʊ dɪd ju ɛvər ɪ↘skeɪp]

DIACRITICS

The diacritics allow symbols to be created to represent many additional types of sounds. In the representation of many languages (including English) diacritics are necessary only when making detailed transcriptions.

◌̥   Burmese [n̥á] 'nose'

The voiceless diacritic can also be used to show that a symbol that usually represents a voiced sound in a particular language on some occasions represents a voiceless sound, as in a detailed transcription of conversational English *Please say* ... as [pl̥iz̥ se ...].

◌̬   The voiced diacritic can be used to show that a symbol that usually represents a voiceless sound in a particular language on some occasions represents a voiced sound, as in a detailed transcription of conversational English *back of* as [bæk̬ əv].

ʰ   Hindi [kʰan] 'mine'

Detailed transcription of English *pea, tea, key* [pʰi, tʰi, kʰi]

◌̗   Assamese [pɔt] 'to bury'

In some forms of English, e.g. Standard Southern British, over-rounded [ɔ] is found, e.g. *caught* [kɔ̹t].

◌̜   In many forms of English, e.g. Californian, under-rounded [ʊ] is found, e.g. *good* [gʊ̜d].

◌̟   Eng. [k̟] in *key* [k̟i]

◌̠   Eng. [t̠] in *tree* [t̠ɹi]

◌̈ Eng. [ɛ̈] in *well* [wɛ̈ɫ]
◌̽ Eng. [ŏ̽] in *November* [nŏ̽vɛmbə(ɹ)]
◌̩ Eng. [l̩] in *fiddle* [fɪdl̩]
◌̯ Spanish *poeta* [po̯'eta] 'poet'
◌˞ Am. Eng. [ə˞] in *bird* [bə˞d] This sound can also be written [ɹ̩].
◌̤ Hindi [kʊm̤ar] 'potter'
◌̰ Mazatec *nda'* [ndǽ̰] 'buttocks'
◌̼ Tangoa [t̼et̼e] 'butterfly'
◌ʷ Eng. [t] in *twin* [tʷɪn]; Cantonese [kʷɔk] '(family name)'
◌ʲ Russian [matʲ] 'mother'
◌ˠ Russian [lˠɨsɨj] 'bald'
◌ˤ Arabic [sˤad] (letter name)
◌̴ Eng. [l] in *hill* [hɪɫ]
◌̝ Some forms of South African Eng. [ɹ] in *dry* [dɹ̝aɪ]
◌̞ Danish [ð̞] in *lade* [læð̞ə] 'barn'
◌̘ Igbo *óbì* [ó̘bì̘] 'heart'
◌̙ Igbo *ụ̀bị̀* [ù̙bì̙] 'poverty of ability'
◌̪ Eng. [t̪] in *width* [wɪt̪θ]
◌̺ Ewe *e da* [é d̺à] 'he throws'
◌̻ Ewe *e ḍa* [é d̻à] 'he cooks'
◌̃ Fr. *fin* [fɛ̃] 'end'
◌ⁿ Russian [dⁿno] 'bottom'
◌ˡ Navajo [dˡőőʔ] 'prairie dog'
◌̚ Eng. [k̚] in *act* [æk̚t]

3.2 *Languages used for exemplification*

The principal country in which a language is spoken is given only when it is not apparent from the name.

Agul, Caucasian, spoken in the N.E. Caucasus.
Amharic, Afro-Asiatic, spoken in Ethiopia.
Arabic, Afro-Asiatic, spoken in many North African and Middle Eastern countries.
Assamese, Indo-European, spoken in India.
Avar, Caucasian, spoken in the N.E. Caucasus.
Bariba, Niger-Congo, spoken in Nigeria.
Burmese, Sino-Tibetan, spoken in Myanmar.
Cantonese, Sino-Tibetan, spoken in China.
Chinese (Standard), Sino-Tibetan.
Danish, Indo-European.
English, Indo-European.
Ewe, Niger-Congo, spoken in Ghana and Togo.
Farsi, Indo-European, spoken in Iran.

Finnish, Finno-Ugric.
French, Indo-European.
German, Indo-European.
Greek, Indo-European.
Hausa, Afro-Asiatic, spoken in Nigeria.
Hawaiian, Austronesian.
Hebrew, Afro-Asiatic, spoken in Israel.
Hindi, Indo-European, spoken in India.
Hungarian, Finno-Ugric.
Igbo, Niger-Congo, spoken in Nigeria.
Inuit, Eskimo-Aleut.
Italian, Indo-European.
K'ekchi, Mayan, spoken in Guatemala.
Kele, Austronesian, spoken in Papua New Guinea.
KiChaka, Niger-Congo, spoken in Tanzania.
Korean, Altaic.
Malayalam, Dravidian, spoken in India.
Mam, Mayan, spoken in Guatemala.
Mazatec, Oto-Manguean, spoken in Mexico.
Mid-Waghi, Papuan, spoken in Papua New Guinea.
Navajo, Na-Dene, spoken in United States.
Norwegian, Indo-European.
Polish, Indo-European.
Russian, Indo-European.
Sindhi, Indo-European, spoken in Pakistan.
Spanish, Indo-European.
Swedish, Indo-European.
Tamil, Dravidian, spoken in India.
Tangoa, Austronesian, spoken in Vanuatu.
Thai, Tai-Kadai.
Trique, Oto-Manguean, spoken in Mexico.
Tswana, Niger-Congo, spoken in Botswana.
Vietnamese, Austro-Asiatic.
Welsh, Indo-European.
Xhosa, Niger-Congo, spoken in South Africa.
!Xóõ, Khoisan, spoken in Botswana.
Yoruba, Niger-Congo, spoken in Nigeria.
Zulu, Niger-Congo, spoken in South Africa.

4 The phonemic principle

From its earliest days (see appendix 4) the International Phonetic Association has aimed to provide 'a separate sign for each distinctive sound; that is, for each sound which, being used instead of another, in the same language, can change the meaning of a word'. This notion of a 'distinctive sound' is what became widely known in the twentieth century as the phoneme. Its history is far longer, though. For instance, the phonemic principle is implicit in the invention of alphabetic writing. However a lot of languages, such as English, have spelling systems in which the relation between phonemes and letters of the alphabet has become obscured. This very fact was a motivation for the creation of a universally agreed system of phonetic notation. So, in English, the IPA provides a symbol /k/ which stands unambiguously for the phoneme which is variously written as ‹c› (*car*), ‹k› (*kettle*), ‹ck› (*back*), ‹ch› (*monarch*), ‹q› (*quick*), and in other ways.

Each language can be analyzed as having an inventory of phonemes. This inventory may range in size from around a dozen phonemes to nearer a hundred depending on the language. Conventionally, as in the English example above, symbols for the phonemes of a language are placed within oblique lines: / /.

In general, the symbol for a phoneme will be an unmodified letter of the IPA, but letters may also be combined to make a phoneme symbol (for instance /tʃ/, as at the beginning and end of English *church*; if necessary the phonological unity of the two segments can be shown by a tie bar: /t͡ʃ/). Diacritics may also be employed to create symbols for phonemes, thus reducing the need to create new letter shapes. This may be convenient in particular when a subset of the phonemic system of a language shares a phonetic property, as in the case of the nasalized vowel phonemes of French /ɛ̃ œ̃ ɑ̃ ɔ̃/, which when they stand alone represent French *hein* 'huh', *un* 'a, one', *an* 'year', and *on* 'one (impersonal pronoun)'.

The use of the phrase 'distinctive sound' above implies that there are other sounds which do not change the identity of a word, sounds which are not 'distinctive' in this technical sense. Central to the notion of the phoneme is the recognition that many finely distinct sounds can be phonetically identified which do not have the word-distinguishing role of, say, English /k/ and /t/ (as in /ki/ *key* vs. /ti/ *tea*). For instance, the English /k/ phoneme is made with a tongue closure further forward in the mouth before a front vowel (such as the /i/ of *key*) than before a back vowel (such as the /ɔ/ of *caw*). But crucially it is not possible, in English, to exchange these two varieties of /k/ to make two new words, so the two varieties of /k/ are not 'distinctive' in English.

A phoneme can be regarded as an element in an abstract linguistic system, an element which has to be realized in the physical world by an acoustic signal produced by vocal activity. Variation arises in the process of realization. Some of this variation can be attributed to the influence of adjacent sounds affecting the articulation, so for instance the /k/ of *key* may be thought of as being further forward to facilitate integration with the following /i/, while in other cases the variation seems to be merely a language-specific but phonetically unmotivated habit. Variant realizations of a phoneme are known as its allophones.

The IPA aims not only to provide symbols which can unambiguously represent phonemic inventories, but also to be able to represent details of phonetic realization. The above example could be represented as [k̟ʰiː] *key* and [k̠ʰɔː] *caw*, where the 'Subscript plus' and 'Under-bar' indicate advanced and retracted articulation respectively (see appendix 2 for diacritic names). A further detail of realization is also indicated here – the 'Superscript H' indicates aspiration, a delay in the onset of voicing after the voiceless plosive, characteristic of such plosives at the beginning of stressed syllables in many varieties of English. Square brackets are used conventionally to make clear that a symbol or sequence of symbols represents phonetic realizations rather than phonemes.

In providing the means to show the detail of phonetic realization in a given language, the IPA also achieves the delicacy of notation needed to compare the phonetic detail of different languages. For instance, although a phonemic representation /tru/ might be suitable for the English word *true* or the French word *trou*, the difference in pronunciation of the two words is reflected in phonetically more detailed representations such as [t̠ɹ̥ʉ] (*true*) and [t̪ʀ̥u] (*trou*). These show the dental realization of /t/ in French compared to the alveolar realization in English, here retracted under the influence of the following postalveolar; the uvular realization of /r/ in French compared to the postalveolar realization in English, both realizations devoiced after the voiceless plosive; and the fully back realization of /u/ in French compared to the central realization in (many varieties of) English.

5 Broad and narrow transcriptions

A connected text represented in terms of phonemes is known as a 'phonemic transcription', or, almost equivalently, a 'broad transcription'. The term 'broad' sometimes carries the extra implication that, as far as possible, unmodified letters of the roman alphabet have been used. This restriction may facilitate printing, and might be considered particularly if a phonemic transcription is to form the basis of a writing system. Under this definition a transcription of English *hideout* as /haidaut/ would be broad, while /haɪdaʊt/ would not be because it introduces letter shapes to the symbol for the phoneme /aɪ/ and the phoneme /aʊ/ which are not absolutely necessary for the unambiguous representation of the phonemes of English, but which may be desirable to remind the reader of the phonetic realization of these phonemes. Frequently, though, 'broad' is used merely as a way of referring to transcriptions which are phonemic, regardless of the letter shapes used to represent the phonemes. Phonemic transcriptions are one type of 'systematic' transcription, meaning they require the phonological patterns or 'system' of a language to be known before they can be made.

The term narrow transcription most commonly implies a transcription which contains details of the realization of phonemes. There are two ways in which such a transcription may come about. If a transcription is made in circumstances where nothing can be assumed about the phonological system, it is necessary to include all phonetic details because it is not clear which phonetic properties will turn out to be important. The transcription would be made taking into account only the phonetic properties of the speech. This type of narrow transcription, as might be made in the first stages of fieldwork, or when transcribing disordered speech, is sometimes called an impressionistic transcription or a general phonetic transcription. If an impressionistic transcription were made of an utterance of the English phrase *check the lens well* it might be [tʃe̞ʔk̚ǫ̈lēnzwæ̈ɫ]. This includes a glottalized velar stop, a dental approximant (the lowering diacritic indicating that the stricture was not close enough to cause frication), a velarized or pharyngealized lateral (probably involving, for many English speakers, a secondary articulation of 'uvularization' intermediate between velarized [lˠ] and pharyngealized [lˤ]), and three different vowel qualities in the stressed syllables, even though these vowels are the same in phonemic terms.

The other kind of narrow transcription containing realizational information is termed allophonic. If the relevant phonological system is known, a transcription can be devised which includes any number of additional symbols to indicate the phonetic realizations of the phonemes, i.e. their allophones. An allophonic transcription is also known as a systematic narrow transcription. In the knowledge that a possible phonemic analysis of *check the lens well* is /tʃekðəlɛnzwɛl/, one allophonic or systematic narrow transcription would, perhaps surprisingly, be [tʃe̞ʔk̚ǫ̈lēnzwæ̈ɫ], that is, one which is identical to the impressionistic transcription in the previous paragraph, incorporating all the phonetic detail which can be heard. The difference is that now it would be possible to express, in conventions, the relation between the allophones transcribed and the phonemes which they realize. Alternatively, it is possible (and customary) to be selective about the information which is explicitly incorporated into the allophonic transcription. The choice might be made, for instance, to leave out the information about vowel height (the closer vowel in *check* is triggered by the high tongue body position of the following velar, and the more open and retracted quality in *well* caused mainly by the secondary articulation of the following lateral), and about vowel nasalization (which is very general before a following nasal), giving a transcription which focuses on consonant realization: [tʃeʔk̚ǫlɛnzwɛɫ]. Minimally, if the focus of interest were glottalization of plosives, the allophonic transcription could be [tʃeʔk̚ðəlɛnzwɛl], or if the focus were the 'dark' lateral, [tʃekðəlɛnzwɛɫ]. These last two transcriptions look superficially very like a phonemic transcription, but they are in principle different because information has been included (albeit sparingly) which is not required for the unambiguous representation of the words. Narrowness is regarded as a continuum, so that [tʃekðəlɛnzwɛɫ] might be regarded as a slightly narrow (or 'narrowed') transcription, and [tʃe̞ʔk̚ǫ̈lēnzwæ̈ɫ] as very narrow. (In all these transcriptions, no spaces between words have been included. This is inevitable in an impressionistic transcription where it is not yet known how the utterance divides into words. In phonemic and allophonic transcriptions it is common to include spaces to aid legibility, but their theoretical validity is problematic.)

Any transcription is connected to a speech event by a set of conventions. In the case of an impressionistic ('general phonetic') transcription, the conventions are precisely those lying behind the IPA Chart, indicating for instance that the phonetic value of [ʔk̚] is a simultaneous velar and glottal closure. In the case of a phonemic transcription, the conventions also include the 'phonological rules' of the particular language which determine the realization of its phonemes, such as the fact that for some varieties of English the lateral phoneme /l/ is realized with an accompanying secondary articulation ([ɫ]) when not followed directly by a vowel or /j/ in the same word. Likewise, the realizational information which is not explicit in a particular allophonic transcription is, in principle, provided by conventions.

6   IPA transcriptions for a language

There can be many systems of phonemic transcription for the same variety of a language, all of which conform fully to the principles of the IPA. Sometimes the differences between the systems result from the fact that more than one phonetic symbol may be appropriate for a phoneme. For instance, the vowel phoneme of *get* in Standard Southern British English has allophones, according to phonetic environment, which mostly lie between the cardinal vowels [e] and [ɛ], some realizations being closer to one and some to the other. It is therefore permissible to choose either symbol as the one to represent the phoneme.

In other cases the differences between competing transcriptions result from alternative ways of representing the phonological contrast between sounds. In English, for example, the contrast between the words *bead* and *bid* has phonetic correlates in both vowel quality and vowel duration. A phonemic representation which explicitly notes this might use the symbols /iː/ and /ɪ/, where the difference in letter shape reflects the difference in vowel quality, and the length mark on the first letter reflects the difference in duration. But it is equally possible unambiguously to represent these phonemes as /iː/ and /i/ (where the phonemic symbol only explicitly shows the length difference), or as /i/ and /ɪ/ (where only quality is shown explicitly). All three pairs of symbols are in accord with the principles of the IPA (as long as the principle chosen for this pair of vowels is applied consistently throughout the vowels of the language).

Other differences may stem not from alternative representations of what is essentially the same phonemic analysis, as above, but from alternative phonemic analyses. For instance, English long vowels and diphthongs are often analyzed as unitary phonemes such as /iː/ (as in *heed*) and /aʊ/ (as in *how*). In this view, the fact that the phoneme symbol is made up of two phonetic symbols or a symbol and diacritic does not affect the status of a sound as a single phoneme in the analysis. Alternatively it is possible to analyze them as combinations of a short vowel and an approximant: /i/ + /j/ and /a/ + /w/, or even (in the case of long vowels) as combinations of short vowel phonemes (represented /i/, /u/ etc.) and a 'chroneme' /ː/: /i/ + /ː/ and /u/ + /ː/. It may not be possible to infer the particular analysis being used from the phonemic transcription. However the point here is that the representation resulting from any of these analyses is in keeping with the principles behind the IPA. The IPA does not provide a phonological analysis for a particular language, let alone a single 'correct' transcription, but rather the resources to express any analysis so that it is widely understood.

7 Working with the IPA

There are a number of practical issues that may arise when using the IPA. Some of these involve problems of how to refer to symbols. In what follows, reference will be made to appendix 2. This contains a comprehensive listing of symbols used in phonetics, including those of the IPA, but also many which are not recommended by the International Phonetic Association but which may be encountered. The listing indicates which symbols are not IPA usage, or which were once recommended but are no longer recommended. The listing was produced by the IPA Workgroup on Computer Coding, set up at the 1989 International Phonetic Association Convention in Kiel.

7.1 Symbol names

It is often useful to be able to refer to symbols by an agreed name. If it is a question of replacing [ɐ] by [ɒ], it is easier to say 'not "Turned A" but "Turned script A"' than to attempt a verbal description of the relevant symbols. Although the International Phonetic Association has never officially approved a set of names, many symbols have informally one or more names, and a greater degree of consensus has arisen as the result of the use of names in Pullum and Ladusaw's *Phonetic Symbol Guide* (2nd edition, 1996. University of Chicago Press). Appendix 2 therefore includes with each symbol a convenient and systematic name, most of which are those used by Pullum and Ladusaw.

7.2 Using the IPA in handwriting

There are cursive forms of IPA symbols, but it is doubtful if these are much in use today. They may have been of greater use when transcription by hand was the only way of recording speech, and so speed was essential. The cursive forms are harder for most people to decipher, and it is preferable to use handwritten versions which closely copy the printed form of the symbols.

7.3 Using the IPA in print

Printers should normally have a font including IPA symbols. Even if they do, however, there will be a danger of superficially similar symbols being mixed up (for instance [ɘ] with [θ] or [ɣ] with [ɤ]). Some publishers have tables in which unusual symbols can be identified by index numbers and letters, but practice is variable. It should therefore be noted that the Chart in appendix 2 provides for each symbol a unique identifying number, its 'IPA Number'. It may therefore be helpful to identify symbols which might prove difficult by that number, and to supply to printers and publishers a copy of the table.

7.4 Using the IPA on computers

Character sets including most or all of the IPA are available for several computing environments. Most straightforwardly a number of commercial and free fonts are available for Macintosh and Microsoft Windows. The situation in other computing environments may be less straightforward. One problem for those devising IPA character sets which has hindered the interchangeability of data containing phonetic symbols was the lack of an agreed standard coding for the symbols. The International Phonetic Association, through its Workgroup on Computer Coding, has worked with the International Standards Organization in its project to set up a universal character set (UCS) for all alphabets. An agreed set of UCS 16-bit codes is included in the list in appendix 2.

7.5 The IPA and braille

Over the years, a braille version of the International Phonetic Alphabet has evolved. A book by W. Percy Merrick and W. Potthoff, *A Braille Notation of the International Phonetic Alphabet with Keywords and Specimen Texts*, published in London by the Royal National Institute for the Blind in 1932 was reviewed in the Association's journal, *Le Maître Phonétique*, in 1936 by E. E. Quick (p. 51). This book is archived in the Library of Congress in the US and elsewhere, and has served as the basis for the development of a braille standard for the rendering of phonetics. The code book used for many years by the Canadian National Institute for the Blind and by many other institutions was a 1977 volume entitled the *Code of Braille Textbook Formats and Techniques*, published by the American Printing House for the Blind (1839 Frankfort Avenue, P.O. Box 6085, Louisville, Kentucky 40206-0085, USA. Tel. 1-800-223-1839). Rule XIX, section 45, of this book refers to phonetic notation, principles, and the phonetic alphabet, with indications of braille equivalents and illustrations of braille usage in print (dot) form. The book of codings was available at US$50 in print and US$235 in braille in 1996. A new edition of the book, *Braille Formats: Principles of Print to Braille Transcription 1997*, was released by the American Printing House for the Blind in September 1998. It is a 300-page volume with print and braille editions, each costing US$30. The phonetic symbols represented in *Braille Formats: Principles of Print to Braille Transcription 1997* are for the most part still valid and in use in the IPA. Some may no longer be in use; and some newer symbols added to the IPA more recently may not appear.

8 Going beyond the IPA

As noted in section 2, the descriptive resources of the IPA were developed principally for the linguistically relevant aspects of speech. This was because the whole tradition of phonetic description was concerned with the properties which realize the phonological systems of languages. A phonological system can be seen as the conventions which speakers of a language share about its sounds. Many aspects of individual utterances such as personal voice quality, emotive modifications of speech, accidental mis-articulations, dysfluencies, and speech pathologies are not relevant to the phonological system, and so phoneticians have tended to ignore such aspects when working on the phonology of a language. The IPA reflects this orientation, being, in essence, a system for describing the linguistic-phonetic properties of error-free utterances not specific to a particular individual. There are, however, many circumstances in which it is essential to be able to transcribe other properties of speech.

One important set of such properties constitutes a conventionalized system of communication beyond the verbal component of speech, and which is often referred to as paralanguage. This includes the use of phenomena such as voice quality, pitch range, and rate of utterance variously to convey aspects of the speaker's emotional state and attitude to other conversational participants, to indicate the status (e.g. confidentiality) of the information being conveyed, and to regulate the course of a conversation by encouraging or discouraging others from speaking. Researchers involved in the analysis of spoken interaction, for instance, clearly need resources for the description of such speech phenomena.

In other situations the phonetic properties of interest may be ones which realize the phonological system, but specifically in speakers who for one reason or another do not achieve normal realizations of the system. Most obviously, clinical practice and research in the field of speech pathology require a system of phonetic notation which will cope with sounds and combinations of sounds which lie outside the usual range. Research, too, on children's utterances during language acquisition, which contain many sounds that do not occur systematically in the languages of the world, also requires notational devices outside those provided by the IPA.

Researchers in these fields have, of course, developed their own notational devices as required. But clearly it would be preferable to have a widely agreed standard set of conventions for these additional applications, comparable to the standard provided by the IPA. With this aim the International Phonetic Association's Clinical Phonetics and Linguistics Group has proposed a set of 'Extensions to the IPA' for transcribing non-linguistic speech events, and other aspects of speech such as deviant or pathological speech. These are listed and explained in appendix 3.

9 Some problematic issues

9.1 Segmentation

In making an impressionistic transcription of a language whose phonological system is not known, uncertainties over the division of an utterance into segments may arise. Some articulatory sequences produce a speech signal which different languages may interpret as made up of a different number of segments. This is sometimes the case, for instance, when secondary articulations are added to primary articulations. An articulatory sequence such as would be represented by [lɔ] is relatively unproblematic. Here the syllable begins with a lateral, which involves a closure by the tongue tip or blade against the alveolar ridge, with the tongue body left free to anticipate the position required for the following vowel. The acoustic signal, as shown in the left half of the spectrogram in figure 5, clearly falls into two distinct parts corresponding to the lateral and the vowel. But if the tongue body is high during the lateral, there will be an [i]-like transition or palatal approximant between the consonant and the vowel – see the right half of figure 5. Given only the phonetic event, it is not clear whether to transcribe this sequence as three segments ([ljɔ]) or two segments ([lʲɔ], where the superscript 'j' indicates a modification of the lateral by palatalization, and not an additional segment).

There may be some evidence in the phonetic signal to help resolve the issue. For instance, if there is a noticeable [i]-like transition into the lateral from a preceding vowel as well as into the following vowel, it is more likely that the high tongue position is associated with the lateral. But ultimately the answer will lie in the phonological patterns of the language. If the language has sequences like [jɔ], where the palatal approximant appears independently of another consonant articulation, this points in the direction of treating it as a separate segment elsewhere (e.g. [ljɔ]). Pointing in the other direction would be the discovery that the language contrasted consonants extensively in terms of secondary articulation, even where an approximant would be unlikely to occur, for instance after a word-final voiceless fricative. Sequences such as [asj] and [asw] are not likely, since approximants normally occur adjacent to vowel nuclei, and such a contrast would normally be attributed to the consonant and phonemicized as /asʲ/ and /asʷ/, indicating contrastive secondary articulations of palatalization and labial-velarization. With this knowledge, then, [lʲɔ] would be seen as the segmentation more appropriate to the phonological patterning of the language.

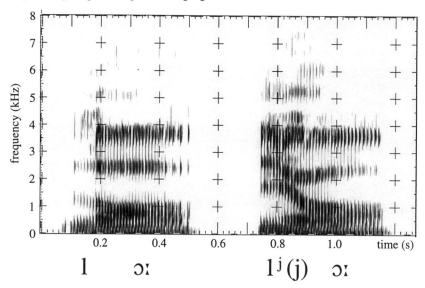

Figure 5 Spectrogram of [lɔ] and an utterance whose segmentation is ambiguously [lʲ]+[ɔ] or [l]+[j]+[ɔ].

The point of considering such examples is to underline the fact that the segmentation which phonetic description requires is not always transparently available in the phonetic event, and impressionistic transcriptions may have to contain unresolved ambiguities until sufficient is known about the structure of the particular language. Moreover, such uncertainties of segmentation will often form the basis of alternative proposals for phonemic interpretation.

9.2 Aligning transcriptions and speech

Even where the structure of the language is known, the alignment of a phonetic transcription with records of the physical speech event will sometimes be problematic. This is because the effects of a particular segment overlap with those of others, or, to put it another way, because the changes in the various parameters which make up speech (voicing, nasality, and so on) are neither instantaneous nor aligned simultaneously. The more closely the physical speech event is observed, the greater the tension between the segmentation derivable from the phonological structure of a language and that suggested by the structure of the physical signal.

The English word *sleeting*, for instance, is phonemically /sliːtɪŋ/, a sequence of six phonemes. The acoustic signal of this word as spoken by a speaker of a variety of English without voicing of word-medial /t/ is represented by the spectrogram in figure 6.

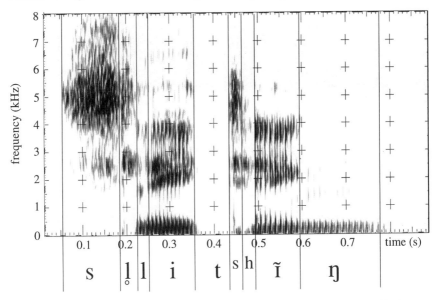

Figure 6 Spectrogram of the word *sleeting*, illustrating the complex relationship between acoustic patterns and phonemic segmentation.

This shows considerably more than six identifiably different successive aspects. A possible acoustic segmentation is indicated by the vertical lines drawn below the spectrogram. A narrow transcription can to an extent capture this acoustic segmentation, and might be suitable for some applications, for instance in speech technology research, where a close annotation of the acoustic signal is required. The representation [s̺l̥itˢʰĩŋ] given below the spectrogram reflects the fact that the voicelessness of the [s] persists into the first part of the lateral articulation, so there is no single acoustic phase corresponding to the 'voiced lateral approximant' phoneme; that the [t] is released first with a phase of affrication ([s]-like friction locatable to the alveolar region) and then aspiration (non-localizable [h]-like friction); and that the nasality of the final nasal stop is anticipated in the preceding vowel. In the case of the nasality, the narrow transcription captures the way in which cues to a particular phoneme are distributed beyond what would normally be considered the boundaries of the sound; the nasality on the vowel is an early indication that a nasal consonant is imminent. But other instances of this distribution of cues to a sound cannot be captured in an IPA transcription; for example, the changing acoustic pattern corresponding to [ɪ̃] is caused by the movement of the tongue body, during the vowel, from the alveolar [t] towards the velar closure of [ŋ]. This changing pattern is an important cue to the place of articulation of both consonants.

Problems of segmentation and alignment provide a challenge to one of the theoretical assumptions behind the IPA mentioned at the start of section 2, namely that 'speech can be represented partly as a sequence of discrete sounds or "segments"'. The word 'partly' acknowledges the fact that (section 2) 'in addition to the segments, a number of "suprasegmental" aspects of speech, such as stress and tone, need to be represented independently of the segments'. But it turns out that even the 'segmental' aspects of speech can prove harder to allocate unambiguously to a sequence of discrete segments than might be anticipated. This does not mean that the segmental assumption should be rejected. It is the foundation of phonetic description, and hence of the IPA. What it does mean is that users of the IPA should be aware that the analysis of speech in terms of segments does involve an analytic assumption, and that tensions between the analysis and the data will arise from time to time.

9.3 Transcribing the speaker or the hearer

The relation between a sequence of words and its phonetic realization, far from being unique, is highly variable. A speaker may choose to pronounce carefully, that is with a high degree of 'phonetic explicitness', or to take short cuts. Articulatory short cuts are sometimes known as phonetic reduction. There are tendencies, by no means absolute, for more phonetic reduction to happen the faster someone speaks and the more predictable the content of the speech is.

Many of the differences between explicit and reduced forms can be captured in IPA transcription. For instance, a careful utterance of the word *educated* in Standard Southern British English might be transcribed narrowly as [ɛdjʊkʰeɪtɪd], and a phonetically reduced utterance as [ɛ̈d͡ʑəχet̞əd̞], where unstressed vowels are mid-centralized, the first [d] and the following palatal are assimilated to the alveolo-palatal place of articulation, and the velar and alveolar voiceless plosives of the careful form are instead fricatives.

In other cases the transcriber is faced with theoretically problematic forms as a result of reduction. For instance in the phrase *mad cow*, a careful utterance of which would be [mæd̚kʰaʊ], the alveolar at the end of *mad* is susceptible in less careful pronunciation to assimilation to the place of articulation of the following velar. Traditionally, this might be transcribed as [mæg̚kʰaʊ], indicating complete loss of the alveolar. Instrumental records of articulation, however, show that sometimes in forms where the alveolar sound cannot be heard the speaker is nonetheless making a reduced tongue movement towards the alveolar ridge. There is then a discrepancy for such an utterance between the transcription which is 'right' for the hearer ([mæg˺kʰaʊ] as above) and one which would better reflect the speaker's behaviour – perhaps [mæɗ˺kʰaʊ], showing an incomplete articulation of the alveolar stop at the end of *mad*. Such a discrepancy violates an assumption implicit in phonetic description, namely that the form to be transcribed is common to speaker and hearer.

10   The IPA and phonological theory

The IPA is intended as a commonly agreed tool for analyzing and representing the phonetic properties of any language. Often, such phonetic analysis will be done in tandem with phonological analysis, that is, the discovery of ways in which sounds pattern in a language and interact with other levels of linguistic structure, particularly morphology (word-building). Views on how best to carry out phonological analysis are constantly evolving as new theories and their associated representational devices are developed.

Although it might be thought ideal if the IPA provided a means of representing phonetic facts independent of theoretical premises, it is inevitable that any means of representation which goes beyond simple replication (as by a tape recorder) must be shaped by hypotheses about the object being analyzed. Historically, the IPA has its roots in a tradition of phonology in which the notions of the phoneme, as a contrastive sound unit, and of allophones, as its variant phonetic realizations, are primary; and in which utterances are seen as the concatenation of the realizations of phonemes. The use of an alphabetic notation underlines the conceptualization of speech as a sequence of sounds.

That conceptualization was shown in the previous section to be sometimes at odds with the physical speech event. It has also been departed from several times in the phonological theories of the last hundred years. Distinctive Feature Theory stressed the importance not of the 'sound' or 'segment', but of the phonetic properties which co-occur in different combinations in sounds. Autosegmental Phonology, and before it Firthian Prosodic Analysis, broke free from the 'slicing' of speech into a single linear sequence of phoneme-sized slots, and allowed some phonetic properties to have larger domains (such as the syllable or word) where this seems in accord with the patterns of a language. Other developments have emphasized the importance of structures such as the mora, the syllable, the foot, and the phonological word in the organization of the phonetic properties of utterances.

These developments in theoretical phonology have had relatively little effect on the IPA. Distinctive Feature Theory has been indirectly acknowledged in the 1989 reformulation of the Principles of the IPA (see appendix 1); Principle 2 now includes the following:

The representation of [...] sounds uses a set of phonetic categories which describe how each sound is made. These categories define a number of natural classes of sounds that operate in phonological rules and historical sound changes. The symbols of the IPA are shorthand ways of indicating certain intersections of these categories. Thus [p] is a shorthand way of designating the intersection of the categories voiceless, bilabial, and plosive; [m] is the intersection of the categories voiced, bilabial, and nasal; and so on.

But there has been no loosening of the segmental 'slicing' of a traditional phonemic view. The IPA Chart, in its fundamental conception, remains much as it has been for over a century. Only in the case of those properties explicitly recognized as suprasegmental and in the 'Extensions to the IPA' (appendix 3) are devices provided for properties extending over domains larger than a segment.

The conservatism inherent in the IPA tradition has advantages. Phonemic analysis is still the most widely understood and practised form of phonological analysis, at least outside the ranks of theoretical phonologists, and its principles are fairly accessible to all those familiar with alphabetic writing systems. This favours a system of general phonetic description such as the IPA which is closely compatible with a phonemic view. Secondly, the inertia of the IPA protects it from the shorter-lived of the winds of phonological change, and provides an element of continuity which is particularly important to those who use the IPA as a tool for practical purposes. Nonetheless, the IPA should not be regarded as immutable, even in its fundamental assumptions, and there needs to be a continuing reappraisal of their appropriateness.

PART 2

Illustrations of the IPA

Part 2 of the *Handbook* contains the twenty-nine 'Illustrations' which have appeared in the *Journal of the International Phonetic Association* from 1989 to 1997. These are phonetic analyses of a language, showing how the IPA can be used in the description of its phonological inventory, and in the transcription of a continuous text.

The Illustrations include a transcription of a spoken text, traditionally a translation of the fable 'The North Wind and the Sun'. Of the Illustrations presented here, only that of Taba uses a different text. The British English text of the fable is given here for reference:

The North Wind and the Sun were disputing which was the stronger, when a traveller came along wrapped in a warm cloak. They agreed that the one who first succeeded in making the traveller take his cloak off should be considered stronger than the other. Then the North Wind blew as hard as he could, but the more he blew the more closely did the traveller fold his cloak around him; and at last the North Wind gave up the attempt. Then the Sun shone out warmly, and immediately the traveller took off his cloak. And so the North Wind was obliged to confess that the Sun was the stronger of the two.

Recordings of the words and text contained in most of the Illustrations are available to accompany the *Handbook.*

American English

PETER LADEFOGED

Department of Linguistics, UCLA, 405 Hilgard Avenue,
Los Angeles, CA 90095-1543, USA

There are many different dialects of English spoken in North America, so it is somewhat improper to refer to any one of them simply as 'American English'. The style of speech illustrated here is that of younger educated Americans in the Far-Western and some of the Mid-Western parts of the United States. The speech in the recording on which the transcription is based is that of a 21-year-old speaker who has lived all her life in Southern California. Speakers from other parts of the United States, such as the East coast and the Northern cities of the Mid-West have different dialects, nearly all of them being more conservative, with a greater number of vowels.

Consonants

	Bilabial	Labio-dental	Dental	Alveolar	Post-alveolar	Palatal	Velar	Glottal
Plosive	p　b			t　d			k　g	
Affricate					tʃ　dʒ			
Nasal	m			n			ŋ	
Fricative		f　v	θ　ð	s　z	ʃ　ʒ			h
Approximant				ɹ		j	w	
Lateral Approximant				l				

p	'pie'	t	'tie'	k	'kite'
b	'buy'	d	'die'	g	'guy'
m	'my'	n	'nigh'	ŋ	'hang'
f	'fie'	θ	'thigh'	h	'high'
v	'vie'	ð	'thy'	tʃ	'chin'
		s	'sigh'	dʒ	'gin'
		z	'zoo'	ʃ	'shy'
w	'why'	ɹ	'rye'	ʒ	'azure'
		l	'lie'	j	'you'

Vowels

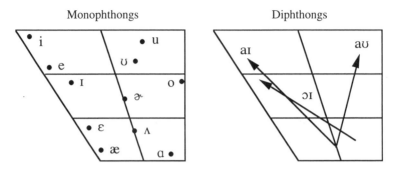

	Monophthongs		Diphthongs

The qualities of the vowels shown in the charts are based on observations of nine speakers of the dialect being described. The unstressed vowel [ə] is not shown on the chart as its quality varies considerably. Four different forms of transcription of the vowels are given in the list of key words. In (1), which is the style of transcription used in the first illustrative passage that follows, the differences in quality are explicit, the length and other differences among vowels being regarded as a matter of the conventions required for interpreting these particular symbols; in (2) the length differences are made explicit, with the quality differences being regarded as a matter of interpretation conventions; in (3) both length and quality differences are shown; and in (4) diphthongs are treated as consisting of a nucleus and an offglide. If only a single style of transcription had been given it would have been necessary to make all these aspects of vowel quality clear by means of additional conventions for interpreting the symbols. All of these (and several other) styles of transcription are properly regarded as IPA transcriptions of Californian English, provided that they are accompanied by suitable conventions. The vowel symbols in (1) are similar to those used in the 1949 *Principles*, the differences being that the 1949 version used [a] in words such as 'bad', [ə] in 'bud' and [ɪ] in 'bird'.

(1)	(2)	(3)	(4)	
i	iː	iː	iʲ	'bead'
ɪ	i	ɪ	ɪ	'bid'
e	eː	eː	eʲ	'bayed'
ɛ	e	ɛ	ɛ	'bed'
æ	æ	æ	æ	'bad'
ɑ	ɑ	ɑ	ɑ	'pod'
o	oː	oː	oʷ	'bode'
ʊ	u	ʊ	ʊə	'good'
u	uː	uː	uʷ	'booed'
ʌ	ʌ	ʌ	ʌ	'bud'
ɚ	ɚː	ɚː	ɚ	'bird'

	(1)	(2)	(3)	(4)	
	aɪ	aɪ	aɪ	aʲ	'buy'
	aʊ	aʊ	aʊ	aʷ	'bough'
	ɔɪ	ɔɪ	ɔɪ	ɔɪ	'boy'
	ə	ə	ə	ə	'a(bove)'

Stress

English has a very strong distinction between stressed and unstressed syllables, with stressed syllables being longer, louder, and often marked by a pitch excursion. Although stress placement is partially predictable, there are many instances where it is not, such as in noun/verb pairs like ['ɛksport/ɛk'sport] in contrast to [sə'port/sə'port]. Longer words frequently have one or more syllables with a secondary stress. Stress is transcribed using the marks ' (primary stress) and ˌ (secondary stress), as in [ˌfonə'tɪʃən] 'phonetician'.

Conventions

[p, t, k] are aspirated in word-initial position, and elsewhere when initial in a stressed syllable, but they are always unaspirated when following [s] in the same syllable, as in 'spy, sty, sky'. [b, d, g] have little or no voicing during the stop closure, except when between voiced sounds. When intervocalic and before an unstressed vowel, as in 'city, vicinity', [t] is a voiced flap, resembling [ɾ]. [d, n] are also flaps in similar circumstances. [l] is velarized except before [j].

The vowel symbols in column (1) have the qualities shown in the accompanying charts when pronounced in the key words. Vowels are raised before [ŋ] in the same syllable, so that the vowel in 'sing' is nearer that in 'seen' than that in 'sin', the vowel in 'sang' is close to that in 'sane', and the vowel in 'length' is intermediate between that in 'sing' and 'sang'. Vowels are lowered and centralized before [ɹ], and many contrasts are lost, so that 'merry, Mary, marry' and 'Murray' are often all pronounced ['mɚɹi]. [e] and [o] are usually slightly diphthongized. [u] and [ʊ] are unrounded, [ʊ] often being pronounced with spread lips. [u] is considerably fronted after [t, d, n, l], all of which are followed by a mid-high front glide when preceding [u], as in 'two, new', which are pronounced [tʲʉ, nʲʉ].

Transcription of recorded passage

Two transcriptions are given, the first being a broad phonemic transcription using the symbols in the charts above. This transcription should be interpreted with the aid of the conventions. The second transcription is a narrow phonetic transcription in which the conventions and other details have been incorporated. 'The' is often pronounced as [ðə] before words beginning with a vowel, but not on this recording. This speaker also has [h] in some words (e.g. 'he') where others might have omitted it.

Broad transcription

ðə 'nɔɹθ ˌwɪnd ən (ð)ə 'sʌn wɚ dɪs'pjutɪŋ 'wɪtʃ wəz ðə 'stɹɑŋgɚ, wɛn ə 'tɹævəlɚ ˌkem ə'lɑŋ 'ɹæpt ɪn ə 'wɔɹm 'klok. ðe ə'gɹid ðət ðə 'wʌn hu 'fɚst sək'sidəd ɪn 'mekɪŋ ðə 'tɹævəlɚ 'tek ɪz 'klok ˌɑf ʃʊd bi kən'sɪdɚd 'stɹɑŋgɚ ðən ðɪ 'əðɚ. ðɛn ðə 'nɔɹθ ˌwɪnd 'blu əz 'hɑɹd əz i 'kʊd, bət ðə 'mɔɹ hi 'blu ðə 'mɔɹ 'klosli dɪd ðə'tɹævlɚ 'fold hɪz 'klok ə'ɹaʊnd ɪm; ˌæn ət 'læst ðə 'nɔɹθ ˌwɪnd ˌgev 'ʌp ði ə'tɛmpt. 'ðɛn ðə 'sʌn 'ʃaɪnd ˌaʊt 'wɔɹmli, ənd ɹ'midiətli ðə 'tɹævlɚ 'tʊk ˌɑf ɪz 'klok. ən 'so ðə 'nɔɹθ ˌwɪnd wəz ə'blaɪʒ tɪ kən'fɛs ðət ðə 'sʌn wəz ðə 'stɹɑŋgɚ əv ðə 'tu.

Narrow transcription

ðə 'nɔɹθ ˌwɪnd ən ə 'sʌn wɚ dɪs'pjurɪŋ 'wɪtʃ wəz ðə 'stɹɑŋgɚ, wɛn ə 'tɹævlɚ ˌkem ə'lɑŋ 'ɹæpt ɪn ə 'wɔɹm 'klok. ðe ə'gɹid ðət ðə 'wʌn hu 'fɚst sək'sidəd ɪn 'mekɪŋ ðə 'tɹævlɚ 'tek ɪz 'klok ˌɑf ʃʊd bi kən'sɪdɚd 'stɹɑŋgɚ ðən ðɪ 'ʌðɚ. 'ðɛn ðə 'nɔɹθ ˌwɪnd 'blu əz 'hɑɹd əz hi 'kʊd, bət ðə 'mɔɹ hi 'blu ðə 'mɔɹ 'klosli dɪd ðə'tɹævlɚ 'fold hɪz 'klok ə'ɹaʊnd hɪm; ˌæn ət 'læst ðə 'nɔɹθ ˌwɪnd ˌgev 'ʌp ði ə'tɛmpt. 'ðɛn ðə 'sʌn 'ʃaɪnd ˌaʊt 'wɔɹmli, ən ɹ'midiətli ðə 'tɹævlɚ ˌtʊk 'ɑf ɪz 'klok. ən 'so ðə 'nɔɹθ ˌwɪnd wəz ə'blaɪʒ tɪ kən'fɛs ðət ðə 'sʌn wəz ðə 'stɹɑŋgɚ əv ðə 'tu.

Orthographic version

The North Wind and the Sun were disputing which was the stronger, when a traveler came along wrapped in a warm cloak. They agreed that the one who first succeeded in making the traveler take his cloak off should be considered stronger than the other. Then the North Wind blew as hard as he could, but the more he blew the more closely did the traveler fold his cloak around him; and at last the North Wind gave up the attempt. Then the Sun shined out warmly, and immediately the traveler took off his cloak. And so the North Wind was obliged to confess that the Sun was the stronger of the two.

Amharic

KATRINA HAYWARD* AND RICHARD J. HAYWARD**

*Department of South East Asia, **Department of Africa, School of Oriental and African Studies,
Thornhaugh Street, Russell Square, London WC1H 0XG, UK

Amharic, the national language of Ethiopia is the Semitic language with the greatest number of speakers after Arabic. However, while there are large numbers of people throughout Ethiopia who speak Amharic as a second language, mother-tongue speakers are concentrated in the highland plateau extending from somewhat south of Addis Ababa, the capital, northwards to a line running approximately WNW from Korem. This territory is bounded to the east and west by lowland areas where other languages are spoken.

Some good descriptions of Amharic phonetics and phonology are to be found in Armbruster (1908: 4–50), Cohen (1970: 29–68), Ullendorff (1955), and Podolsky (1991). As regards its dialect situation, Amharic is in great need of systematic research. The only published work on the subject (Habte Mariam Marcos 1973) is both useful and suggestive for future work, but it is a brief pioneering effort. The speech of Addis Ababa has emerged as the standard dialect and has wide currency across all Amharic-speaking communities. The most divergent dialect is that of Gojjam province, though the Mänz and Wällo varieties also show their own marked features, especially in phonology.

Consonants

	Bilabial	Labio-dental	Alveolar		Post-alveolar		Palatal	Velar		Glottal	Labialized Velar	
Plosive	(p) b		t	d				k	g		kʷ	gʷ
Affricate					tʃ	dʒ						
Nasal	m			n			ɲ					
Fricative		f	s	z	ʃ	ʒ				h		
Tap/Trill				r								
Approximant	w						j					
Lateral Approximant				l								
Ejective Stop	(p')		t'					k'			kʷ'	
Ejective Affricate					tʃ'							
Ejective Fricative			s'									

Additional labialized consonants: fʷ, bʷ, mʷ, pʷ', tʷ', hʷ

p	posta	'post (mail)'
b	bəkk'ələ	'it sprouted'
p'	p'app'as	'church patriarch'
m	məkkərə	'he advised'
f	fəllək'ə	'it gushed up'

t	təkkələ	'he planted'
d	dərrəsə	'he arrived'
t'	t'ərrəgə	'he swept'
n	nəddəfə	'it stung'
s	səbbərə	'he broke s.t.'
z	zəffənə	'he sang'
s'	s'afə	'he wrote'
tʃ	tʃəlləmə	'it got dark'
dʒ	dʒemmərə	'he began'
tʃ'	tʃ'ərrəsə	'he finished'
r	rəzzəmə	'it became long'
ʃ	ʃərrəbə	'he plaited'
ʒ	ʒembər	'sun'
l	ləmmənə	'he begged'
ɲ	təɲɲa	'he lay down'
j	jəlləm	'there is not'

k	kəbbəbə	'he encircled'
g	gərrəmən	'it surprised me'
k'	k'əddədə	'he tore s.t.'
h	hakim	'doctor'

w	wat'ə	'he swallowed s.t.'
pʷ'	pʷ'agʷʊme	'13th month'
bʷ	bʷambʷa	'pipe (conduit)'
mʷ	mʷammʷa	'it dissolved'
fʷ	fʷaffʷa	'falling water of waterfall'

tʷ'	tʷ'af	'wax taper'

kʷ	kʷas	'ball'
kʷ'	kʷ'akʷ'ate	'whooping cough'
gʷ	gʷaggʷa	'he became full of suspense'
hʷ	hʷala	'after'

Ato Yalew Kebede is a 29-year-old male Amhara whose speech was recorded and transcribed for this illustration. He was also responsible for the translation of 'The North Wind and the Sun'. He grew up in Gondar, an urban centre noted for its 'good' Amharic. Gondar Amharic is extremely close to the Addis Ababa standard dialect in all its features. However, one or two things emerge in the passage which identify the origin of the speaker; for example, [bəgənza fək'adu] instead of standard [bəgəzza fək'adu] 'by his own will'.

The voiceless bilabial stops /p, p', pʷ'/ are extremely rare, and are confined to words of foreign origin. Phonologically, the postalveolar affricates pattern with the stops. Because of its affinity with the labialized consonants, we have placed /w/ in the 'labial' column. All consonants with the exception of /p, pʷ', tʷ', h, hʷ/ have geminate counterparts. In the case of /ɲ/, single and geminate do not contrast phonologically, and it is usually claimed that the geminate variant occurs intervocalically, while the single variant occurs elsewhere. Consonants may be geminated (strengthened) following nasals; an interesting example in our text is /bət'inkare/ 'in strength' (see further below).

Vowels

<table>
<tr><td>i</td><td>kis</td><td>'pocket'</td></tr>
<tr><td>ɨ</td><td>mɨn</td><td>'what?'</td></tr>
<tr><td>ɪ</td><td>jɪh ~ jɨh</td><td>'this'</td></tr>
<tr><td>e</td><td>k'es</td><td>'priest'</td></tr>
<tr><td>ɛ</td><td>jɛmmil</td><td>'he who says'</td></tr>
<tr><td>a</td><td>bal</td><td>'husband'</td></tr>
<tr><td>ə</td><td>kəbt</td><td>'cattle'</td></tr>
<tr><td>ɔ</td><td>gʷɔrf</td><td>'flood'</td></tr>
<tr><td>o</td><td>s'om</td><td>'fast' (n)</td></tr>
<tr><td>ʊ</td><td>kʷ'ʊlf</td><td>'lock'</td></tr>
<tr><td>u</td><td>t'ut</td><td>'breast'</td></tr>
</table>

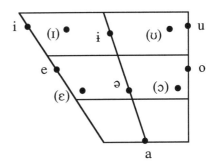

Phonetic diphthongs [aɪ], [aʊ], [əɪ], and [əʊ] occur, but phonotactic patterns suggest that these should be analysed as sequences of /a/ or /ə/ followed by /j/ or /w/. The latter interpretation is the one adopted in the transcription of the specimen passage below.

The vowels written /ɨ/ and /ə/ here are often represented by the symbols /ə/ and /ä/ respectively. It is possible to argue that /ɨ/ is not present in underlying representations, but is always epenthetic (see Hetzron 1964; Hayward 1986). In general in the Ethiopic script, each symbol represents a consonant plus a vowel; for example መ = /mə/, ሜ = /me/ and ማ = /ma/. However, the symbol for a consonant plus /ɨ/ also does duty for a consonant standing on its own, i.e. ም = /mɨ/ or /m/.

The vowels represented by the symbols [ɪ, ʊ, ɛ, ɔ] are not independent phonemes, but allophones of the central vowels /ɨ/ and /ə/. Following postalveolar and palatal consonants, (which, from a phonological point of view, form a 'palatal' series), /ɨ/ and /ə/ are often fronted to /ɪ/ and /ɛ/. Following labialized consonants and /w/, /ɨ/ and /ə/ typically have retracted and rounded pronunciations ([ʊ] and [ɔ]). Spelling also needs to be taken into account here, since a literate speaker, whose spelling of a particular form indicates /ɨ/ or /ə/, may pronounce [ɨ] or [ə], especially in careful speech (thus, the variation jɪh ~ jɨh noted above). In the specimen passage below, we have written [ɪ, ʊ, ɛ, ɔ], rather than more strictly phonemic /ɨ/ and /ə/, in such cases.

The question also arises of whether [ɪ, ʊ, ɛ, ɔ] (as allophones of central vowels) are really distinct from the independent phonemes /i/, /u/, /e/, and /o/ respectively, as our chart indicates. With regard to the back rounded vowels, the issue is further complicated by the fact that consonants preceding them have anticipatory lip rounding. For example, the /k/ in /ku/ is phonetically [kʷ], and for this reason it is often difficult to choose between /kʷʊ/ (= /kʷɨ/ in a more strictly phonemic interpretation) and /ku/ on strictly phonetic grounds. In non-final closed syllables and final syllables closed by two consonants, the two series of vowels do not contrast. We have interpreted all vowels in these environments as phonemic central vowels. For example, we have written /gʷʊlbət/ rather than /gulbət/ 'strength', and /wʊdd/ rather than /wudd/ 'dear, expensive'. This contrasts with our informant's spellings of the same words, which indicate 'gu-' and 'wu-' respectively.

In non-final open syllables and final syllables closed by a single consonant, both series of vowels may occur. In such environments, there is potentially a length contrast, /i, u, e, o/ being susceptible to prolongation. Prototypically, these long vowels contrast with short /ɪ, ʊ, ɛ, ɔ/ in both duration and quality, but there is a less certain middle ground. In the case of verbs and their derivatives, morphological considerations will often lead to a decision in favour of phonemic central vowels. For example, in the case of /kʷʼʊtʼir/ 'number', the decision to write /kʷʼʊ-/ (/kʷʼɨ/ in a more strictly phonemic representation) was influenced by the cognate verb /kʷʼɔttʼərə/ 'he counted'. This belongs to the same verb class as /kʼəttʼərə/ 'he hired' and should, therefore, have the same underlying stem vowels; thus, a phonemicization /kʷʼəttʼərə/ is to be preferred to /kʼottʼərə/. Our /kʷʼʊtʼir/ agrees with our informant's spelling, which also indicates an initial labialized velar. However, we found it very difficult to decide between /bəkkʷʊl/ and /bəkkul/ 'side, direction', where no such cognate forms are available for comparison. Our final choice of /bəkkʷʊl/ contrasts with the '-kkul' of our informant's spelling. (The complexity of the situation is well-described in Ullendorff 1951; cf. especially pp. 82–3.)

Stress
Stress is weak, and its position is variable. Further investigation is needed concerning the relationship between stress and intonation on the one hand and between stress and gemination on the other.

Conventions
/p, t, tʃ, k, kʷ/ are all moderately aspirated. Voiced obstruents are devoiced pre-pausally and when a voiceless obstruent follows, for example in /libs/ 'clothes', [lib̥s]. /b/ is realized as an approximant [β] medially between sonorants (for example, in /gʷʊlbət/ [gʷʊlβət]). /l/ is always clear, never dark. Single /r/ is a tap, geminate /rr/ a trill. When they precede the vowels /i/ and /e/, but more especially the latter, consonants may be strongly palatalized, for example in /gize/ [gʲizʲe] 'time'.

In rural speech, /p/ may be replaced by /f/. In initial position, /ʒ/ is now found only in the speech of Mänz. In Addis Ababa, it has been replaced by the affricate /dʒ/. /ɲ/ occurs initially in only one or two rare words. /sʼ/ is most commonly pronounced as an affricate, [t͡sʼ]. It is tending to merge with /tʼ/, especially in initial position. However, complex regional and sociolinguistic factors affect the occurrence of initial /sʼ/, which may be retained in certain lexical items in educated speech. Our informant consistently pronounced initial [t͡sʼ] in the word /sʼəhaj/ 'sun'.

/h/ is voiced between vowels, and may be realized simply as breathy voice on a preceding and/or following vowel (for example, in /bəzzihɨm/ 'and on these terms', phonetically [bəzzɨ̤ːm]). Following /i/ or /ɨ/, /h/ is typically pronounced as a palatal fricative [ç]. Thus, the form [bəzzi] 'at this' (/bəzzih/) would be pronounced [bəzziç] in isolation or in slow speech.

A prothetic [ɨ] is often inserted before word-initial /r/, for example [ɨrəʒʒim] 'tall' (no examples occur in the text). [ɨ] may also be inserted after word-final consonants, when the following word begins with a consonant. In our speaker's rendering of the text below, there is variation, for example [lɨbsi ləbso] with epenthesis, but [lɨbs k'adimo] without it. Such cases of epenthetic [ɨ] are not noted in the transcription. Another case of epenthetic [ɨ] in our informant's rendering of the text which is not noted in the transcription, but which needs to be mentioned, occurs in the form /bət'inkare/ [bət'inɨkkare]. Here, the /k/ undergoes post-nasal strengthening and this conditions [ɨ] insertion. In other cases, [ɨ] may be devoiced and so short that it is barely audible. This occurs in two forms in our text, when it follows the feminine prefix /t-/ (in these morphological contexts geminated to tt-): [sɨttɨdʒemmɨr] 'when she was beginning' and [jemmɨttɨbalt'] 'she who is greatest'. In the second of these, the pronunciation of /b/ as [β] confirms the presence of the vowel.

Transcription of recorded passage

s'əhajɪnna kəsəmen jemminəfsəw nəfas

s'əhajɪnna kəsəmen bəkkʷʊl jemminəfsəw nəfas ine neɲ t'ənkarra ine neɲ t'ənkarra bəmmil jɪkkərakkəru nəbbər. bəzzi gize and məŋgədeɲɲa jebɨrd məkkələkəja lɨbs ləbso jɪggʷaz nəbbər. kəzjam məŋgədeɲɲəw ləbɨrd məkkələkəja ləbsot jemmihedəw lɨbs k'ədimo jaswɔllək'ə bət'inkare jɪbəlt'al bəmmil təsmammu. bəzzihɨm məsərət kəsəmen bəkkʷʊl jemminəfsəw nəfas ballə bəlelləw gʷʊlbət bəhajl nəffəsə. honom gɨn bəhajl bənəffəsə kʷ'ʊt'ir məŋgədeɲɲəw jebasəwnu bələbbəsəw lɨbs jɪddʒəbbɔn jemmər. bəmətʃ'ərrəʃam kəsəmen bəkkʷʊl jemminəfsəw nəfas bəgənza fək'adu akʷ'omə. s'ahajm bətərawa wətt'atʃɪnna muk'ətwan mawrəd sɨttɨdʒemmɨr məŋgədeɲɲəw mɨnimm saj kʷ'ɔj wɔdijawnu jeləbbəsəwl lɨbs awɔllək'ə. bəmətʃ'ərrəʃam kəsəmen bəkkʷʊl jemminəfsəw nəfas s'əhaj bət'inkare kəssu jemmɨttɨbəlt' məhonwan jaləwʊdd bəgɨdd ammənə.

Orthographic version

ፀሐይና ከሰማን ቡኩል የሚነፍሰው ነፋስ

ፀሐይና ከሰማን ቡኩል የሚነፍሰው ነፋስ እኔ ነኝ ጠንካራ እኔ ነኝ ጠንካራ በሚል ይከራከሩ ነበር። በዚህ ዚሊ አንድ መንገደኛ የጠርድ መከላከያ ልብስ ለብሶ ይዝዝ ነበር። ከዚያም መንገደኛው ለጠርድ መከላከያ ለብሶት የሚይደውን ልብስ ቀድሞ ያስወለቀ በጥ ንካሬ ይበልጣል በሚል ተስማሙ። በዚህም መሠረት ከሰማን ቡኩል የሚነፍሰው ነፋስ ባለበላቸው ጉልበት በሀይል ነፈሰ። ሆኖም ግን በሀይል በነፈሰ ቁጥር መንገደኛው የባሰውት በለበሰው ልብስ ይጀበን ጀመር። በመጨረሻም ከሰማን ቡኩል የሚነፍሰው ነፋስ በገንዛ ፈቃዱ አቆመ። ፀሐይም በተራፕ ወጣችና መቁጠን ማውረድ አትጀምር መንገደኛው ምንም ሳይቀይ ወዲያወት የለበሰውን ልብስ አወለቀ። በመጨረሻም ከሰማን ቡኩል የሚነፍሰው ነፋስ ፀሐይ በጥንካሬ ከሱ የምትበልጥ መሆኗን ያለውድ በገድ አመነ።

References

ARMBRUSTER, C. H. (1908). *Initia Amharica: An Introduction to Spoken Amharic.* Cambridge: The University Press.

COHEN, M. (1970). *Traité de langue amharique (Abyssinie).* Paris: Institut d'ethnologie.

HABTE MARIAM MARCOS (1973). Regional variations in Amharic. *Journal of Ethiopian Studies* 11, 113–29.

HAYWARD, R. J. (1986). The high central vowel in Amharic: New approaches to an old problem. In Fishman, J. A. et al. (editors), *The Fergusonian Impact, Vol. 1: From Phonology to Society.* Berlin, New York, Amsterdam: Mouton de Gruyter.

HETZRON, R. (1964). La voyelle du sixième ordre en amharique. *Journal of African Languages* 3, 179–90.

PODOLSKY, B. (1991). *Historical Phonetics of Amharic.* University of Tel-Aviv.

ULLENDORFF, E. (1951). The labiovelars in the Ethiopian languages. *Rassegna di Studi Etiopici* 10, 71–84.

ULLENDORFF, E. (1955). *The Semitic Languages of Ethiopia: A Comparative Phonology.* London: Taylor's (Foreign) Press.

Arabic

ROBIN THELWALL* AND M. AKRAM SA'ADEDDIN**

*2121 1st Avenue NW, Calgary, AB T2N 0B6, Canada
**University of Kuwait, Kuwait City

There are many tendentious issues in proposing a text in any form of Standard or Classical Arabic in spoken form. We will not justify the present text more than to say that the speaker was born in Safad, North Palestine, lived and was educated in Beirut from age 8 to 15, subsequently studied and taught in Damascus, studied phonetics in Scotland and since then has resided in Scotland and Kuwait.

It seems widely accepted that there are two dominant (prestigeful) dialect centres of gravity for Spoken Arabic: first, that of Al-Shaam (greater Syria, from the Mediterranean coast to the eastern edge of the Fertile Crescent) and, second, Egypt (focused on Al-Azhar Mosque and University in Cairo). This is not to disregard the status of the Arabian Peninsula, Iraq or other areas as the sources of models, but the matter remains to be adequately investigated.

Consonants

	Bilabial	Labio-dental	Dental	Alveolar	Post-alveolar	Palatal	Velar	Uvular	Pharyn-geal	Glottal
Plosive	b		t d				k	q		ʔ
Nasal	m		n							
Fricative		f	θ ð	s z	ʃ		x ɣ		ħ	h
Affricate					dʒ					
Trill				r						
Approximant						j	w			
Lateral Approximant				l						

Pharyngealized consonants: tˤ, dˤ, sˤ, ðˤ, lˤ, ʔˤ

Note: /ʔˤ/ is represented as /ʕ/ in the transcriptions below.

			t	tiːn	'figs'	k	kalb	'dog'
b	balla	'recovered'	d	diːn	'religion'	q	qalb	'heart'
m	malla	'got bored'	n	nadda	'released'	ʔ	saʔala	'asked'
f	dafara	'stank'	s	saːra	'walked'	x	xilaːf	'dispute'
θ	daθara	'covered'	z	zaːra	'visited'	ɣ	ɣilaːf	'cover' (n)

ð	haakaða	'thus'	ʃ	ʃadda	'doubling mark'	ʕ	saʕala	'coughed'
						ħ	ħuruwb	'wars'
			dʒ	dʒadda	'grandmother'			
			r	rawʔa	'splendour'	h	huruwb	'escape' (n)
			l	lawʔa	'sorrow'	j	jaraqaan	'jaundice'
						w	wasˤl	'receipt'
sˤ	sˤarf	'exchange'	tˤ	xitˤaab	'letter'			
ðˤ	ðˤarf	'envelope'	dˤ	xidˤaab	'henna'			
			lˤ	alˤʕˤaa	'god'			

Vowels

i	ʕidd	'promise!'				u	ʕudd	'come back!'
ij	ʕijd	'feast'	a	ʕadd	'counted'	uw	ʕuwd	'lute'
aj	ʕajn	'eye'	aa	ʕaadd	'came back'	aw	ʕawd	'return'

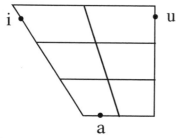

a

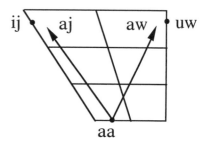

aa

Stress

Stress within Arabic words falls on the final heavy syllable of the morpheme, disregarding suffixes. A heavy syllable is defined as having either a long vowel or a (C)VCC structure. In words with no heavy syllable the matter is still to be investigated for spoken Modern Standard Arabic, and it is assumed that the stress patterns operating in the background Colloquial Arabic of the speaker will operate.

Syllabification and the determiner [al-]

The assimilation of the consonant of the definite article to following [+ coronal] segments is shown in the transcription. The vowel is assimilated to the final vowel of the preceding word, if any. Since word division is shown according to orthographic conventions, we have left out the vowel of the determiner in such cases. The actual realization is, of course, continuous.

Conventions

/t, k / are aspirated, /tˤ/ is unaspirated, /tˤ, dˤ, sˤ, ðˤ/ are Retracted Tongue Root, involving simultaneous pharyngealization and greater or lesser degrees of velarization. The convenient phonological term within Arabic phonetic studies is 'emphasis/emphatic'.

These consonants exert a strong co-articulatory effect on all sounds in preceding and following syllables in given lexemes. This is not blocked by labials, the labialized /ʃ/, and /r /. Only /j / blocks the process. / ʕ/ is a Retracted Tongue Root glottal stop. This realization is supported by Gairdner (1925), Al-Ani (1970) and Kästner (1981) as well as extensive observation of a range of speakers from different regional origins residing in Kuwait at present (1990). Nowhere have we observed a pharyngeal fricative. /x/ is accompanied by uvular trill. Geminate consonants in word-final position in pre-pausal realization have an incipient syllable onset with [ə], e.g. / ʕadd/ → [ʕad.də], where [.] represents a syllable boundary. In context they are realized without this feature.

The primary vowel allophones are conditioned by the presence or absence of neighbouring emphatics in the same word and by word-final position for non-emphatic contexts. /a/ has three main allophones: [ɑ] before Retracted Tongue Root consonants, [ɐ] before word boundary, and [a] elsewhere, taking phonological length into account. Length is neutralized in open syllables. /i/ and /ij/ become [ɨ] before Retracted Tongue Root and pharyngeal consonants. This may be more retracted than a high central unrounded vowel, reaching towards [ɣ]. In most contemporary colloquial dialects there is no phonological opposition between [i] and [u]. /u/ and /uw/ become [ʊ] and [ɣ] before Retracted Tongue Root and pharyngeal consonants. In word final position the length opposition is neutralized.

Points of particular interest in the sound system include:
1. The 'dʒim', which is here pronounced as a voiced lenis palato-alveolar affricate (Gairdner 1925: 23; see however Kästner 1981: 65, where it is described as a fricative).
2. The 'ðˤaaʔ', which is here pronounced /ðˤ/ 'a voiced dental fricative with tongue root retraction and concomitant pharyngealization and velarization'. See Kästner (1981: 62ff), and in contrast, Gairdner (1925: 21).
3. The 'ʕajn', which is realized as a pharyngealized glottal stop (see also Kästner 1981: 49; Al-Ani 1970: 62–71; and Gairdner 1925: 28–9).
There are various different reflexes of these sounds in the present day spoken dialects of Arabic, and in the phonetic descriptions of past dialects, which it is irrelevant to pursue here.

Transcription of recorded passage
kaanat rijhu ʃʃamaali tatadʒaadalu wa ʃʃamsa fij ʔajjin minhumaa kaanat ʔaqwaa min alʔuxraa, wa ʔið bi-musaafirin jatˤluʕu mutalaffiʕan biʕabaaʔatin samijka. fa tafaqataa ʕalaa ʕtibaari ssaabiqi fij ʔidʒbaari lmusaafiri ʕalaa xalʕi ʕabaaʔatihi lʔaqwaa. ʕasˤafati rijhu ʃʃamaali biʔaqsˤaa ma statˤaaʕat min quwwa. wa laakin kullumaa zdaada lʕasˤf izdaada lmusaafiru tadaqɖuran biʕabaaʔatih, ʔilaa ʔan ʔusqitˤa fij jadi rrijh fa taxallat ʕan muhaawalatihaa. baʕdaʔiðin satˤaʕati ʃʃamsu bidifʔihaa, fa maakaana min almusaafiri ʔillaa ʔan xalaʕa ʕabaaʔatahu ʕalaa ttauw. wa haakaða idˤtˤurat rijhu ʃʃamaali ʔilaa liʕtiraafi biʔanna ʃʃamsa kaanat hija lʔaqwaa.

Orthographic version

كانت ريح الشمال تتجادل والشمس في أي منهما كانت أقوى من الاخرى. وإذ بمسافر
يطلع متلفعا بعباءة سميكة . فاتفقتا على اعتبار السابق في اجبار المسافر على خلع عباءته
الاقوى . عصفت ريح الشمال بأقصى ما استطاعت من قوة . ولكن كلما ازداد العصف
ازداد المسافر تدثرا بعباءته الى ان أسقط في يد الريح فتخلت عن محاولتها . بعدئذ سطعت
الشمس بدفئها فما كان من المسافر الا ان خلع عباءته على التو . وهكذا اضطرت ريح
الشمال الى الاعتراف بان الشمس كانت هي الاقوى .

References

AL-ANI, S. H. (1970). *Arabic Phonology: An Acoustical and Physiological Investigation*. The Hague: Mouton.

GAIRDNER, W. H. T. (1925). *The Phonetics of Arabic*. London: Oxford University Press.

KÄSTNER, H. (1981). *Phonetik und Phonologie des modernen Hocharabisch*. Leipzig: Verlag Enzyklopädie.

Bulgarian

ELMAR TERNES* AND TATJANA VLADIMIROVA-BUHTZ**

*Institut für Phonetik, Allgemeine Sprachwissenschaft und Indogermanistik, Universität Hamburg,
Bogenallee 11, D-20144 Hamburg, Germany
**Aumattenweg 2, D-79117 Freiburg im Breisgau, Germany

The style of speech illustrated is Standard Bulgarian as used by people with an academic background. Historically, the Standard contains elements of western and eastern Bulgarian, but in its present form, it cannot be localized in any particular region.

The speech on the recording is that of a 33-year-old speaker holding a post at the University of Sofia. Bulgarian examples are given in a transliteration from Cyrillic script.

Consonants

	Bilabial	Labio-dental	Alveolar	Post-alveolar	Palatal	Velar
Plosive	p b		t d			k ɡ
Nasal	m		n			
Fricative		f v	s z	ʃ ʒ		x
Affricate			ts dz	tʃ dʒ		
Trill			r			
Approximant					j	
Lateral Approximant			l			

p	*pija*	'I drink'	t	*tom*	'volume'	k	*kol*	'pole'
b	*bija*	'I beat'	d	*dom*	'home'	ɡ	*gol*	'naked'
			ts	*tsar*	'tsar'	tʃ	*tšar*	'charm'
			dz	*dzift*	'tar'	dʒ	*džob*	'pocket'
m	*most*	'bridge'	n	*nos*	'nose'	x	*halka*	'ring'
f	*far*	'lighthouse'	s	*sărna*	'roe'	ʃ	*šal*	'scarf'
v	*var*	'limestone'	z	*zărna*	'corn' (pl)	ʒ	*žal*	'pity'
r	*roza*	'rose'	l	*lale*	'tulip'	j	*jak*	'strong'

The phonemic analysis underlying the present transcription does not assume the existence of palatalized consonants. An alternative analysis postulates the following palatalized consonants: / pʲ, bʲ, tʲ, dʲ, kʲ, ɡʲ, tsʲ, dzʲ, mʲ, nʲ, rʲ, fʲ, vʲ, sʲ, zʲ, xʲ, lʲ /.

The nature of palatalization in Bulgarian is different from that in Russian. Its occurrence is very restricted. Before front vowels and [j], palatalization does not go beyond the degree that is conditioned by the inevitable play of coarticulation. Before back vowels palatalization may unambiguously be interpreted as C plus [j]. In syllable and word final position it does not occur.

Vowels

i	*kit*	'whale'
ɛ	*pet*	'five'
a	*mlad*	'young'
ɔ	*rod*	'kin'
u	*lud*	'crazy'
ɤ	*păt*	'path'
[o] (unstressed only)		
[koˈga]	*koga*	'when'
[ɐ] (unstressed only)		
[ˈdumɐ]	*duma*	'word'

[o] is a neutralization of /u/ and /ɔ/, [ɐ] is a neutralization of /a/ and /ɤ/, both in unstressed syllables.

Stress

Stress is distinctive:

[ˈparɐ]	*para*	'steam'
[pɐˈra]	*para*	'coin'

Conventions

/p, t, k/ are unaspirated. /b, d, g/ are fully voiced. /t, d, ts, dz, n, r, s, z, l/ are prealveolar. /r/ is a trill. /x/ has only slight friction. /l/ is velarized [ɫ] before [a, ɔ, u, ɤ, o, ɐ] as well as in syllable and word final position.

[o, ɐ] may be somewhat more closed than shown in the figure in unstressed syllables after stress.

Transcription of recorded passage

ˈsɛvɛrnijɐt ˈvjatɐr i ˈslɤntsɛto sɛ prɛˈpirɛxɐ ˈkɔj ɛ ˈpɔsilɛn, koˈgato ɛdin ˈpɤtnik, zɐˈvit f ˈtɔplɐ ˈdrɛxɐ, ˈminɐ pokrɛj ˈtjax. tɛ rɛˈʃixɐ tʃɛ ˈtɔzi, ˈkɔjto ˈprɤf nɐˈkarɐ ˈpɤtnikɐ dɐ si svɐˈli ˈdrɛxɐtɐ, ʃtɛ sɛ ˈstʃitɐ ˈpɔsilɛn od ˈdrugijɐ. toˈgavɐ ˈsɛvɛrnijɐt ˈvjatɐr zɐˈpɔtʃnɐ dɐ ˈduxɐ s ˈfsitʃkɐ ˈsilɐ, no ˈkɔlkoto ˈpɔsilno ˈvjatɐrɐt ˈduxɐʃɛ, ˈtɔlkovɐ ˈpɔplɐtno ˈpɤtnikɐt oˈvivɐʃɛ ˈdrɛxɐtɐ okolo ˈsɛbɛ si. ˈnaj ˈpɔslɛ ˈsɛvɛrnijɐt ˈvjatɐr prɛˈkɤsnɐ oˈsilijɐtɐ si. toˈgavɐ ˈslɤntsɛto zɐˈpɔtʃnɐ dɐ ˈgrɛɐ ˈsilno, i ˈpɤtnikɐt vɛdˈnagɐ svɐˈli ˈdrɛxɐtɐ si. i tɐˈka, ˈsɛvɛrnijɐt ˈvjatɐr ˈbɛʃɛ priˈnudɛn dɐ priˈznaɛ, tʃɛ ˈslɤntsɛto ɛ ˈpɔsilno ot ˈnɛgo.

Orthographic Version

Северният вятър и слънцето се препираха, кой е по-силен, когато
един пътник, завит в топла дреха, мина покрай тях. Те решиха,
че този, който пръв накара пътника да си свали дрехата, ще се
счита по-силен от другия. Тогава северният вятър започна да
духа с всичка сила, но колкото по-силно вятърът духаше,
толкова по-плътно пътникът увиваше дрехата около себе си.
Най-после северният вятър прекъсна усилията си. Тогава
слънцето започна да грее силно, и пътникът веднага свали
дрехата си. И така, северният вятър беше принуден да признае, че
слънцето е по-силно от него.

Acknowledgement

We are grateful to Mohammad-Reza Majidi for help with the computer program used in preparing the
original manuscript of this paper.

Chinese (Hong Kong Cantonese)

ERIC ZEE

Phonetics Laboratory, Department of Chinese, Translation and Linguistics,
City University of Hong Kong, 83 Tat Chee Avenue, Kowloon, Hong Kong

The style of speech illustrated is that typical of the educated younger generation in Hong Kong. The recording is that of a 22-year-old male university student who has lived all his life in Hong Kong.

Consonants

	Bilabial	Labio-dental	Dental	Alveolar	Post-alveolar	Palatal	Velar	Labial-Velar	Glottal
Plosive	p pʰ			t tʰ			k kʰ	kʷ kʷʰ	
Affricate				ts tsʰ					
Nasal	m			n			ŋ		
Fricative		f		s					h
Approximant						j		w	
Lateral Approximant			l						

p	paˈ	'father'	t	taˈ	'dozen'	k	kaˈ	'to add'
pʰ	pʰaˈ	'to lie prone'	tʰ	tʰaˈ	'he/she'	kʰ	kʰaˈ	'truck'
m	maˈ	'mother'	n	pʰanˈ	'to climb'	ŋ	pʰaŋˈ	'to cook'
f	faˈ	'flower'	s	saˈ	'sand'			
			ts	tsaˈ	'to hold'			
			tsʰ	tsʰaˈ	'fork'			
w	waˈ	'frog'	j	jɐuˈ	'worry'			
			l	lɐuˈ	'angry'			
						kʷ	kʷaˈ	'melon'
						kʷʰ	kʷʰaˈ	'to boast'
						h	haˈ	'shrimp'

Vowels

Monophthongs

(1) or (2)

i	iː	si˥	'silk'	hip˧	'to assist'	him˥	'moderate'
y	yː	sy˥	'book'	hyt˧	'blood'	syn˥	'sour'
ɛ	ɛː	sɛ˥	'to lend'	hɛk˧	'to eat'	sɛŋ˥	'sound'
œ	œː	hœ˥	'boot'	sœk˥	'to whittle'	sœŋ˥	'hurt'
a	aː	sa˥	'sand'	hak˧	'guest'	sam˥	'three'
ɔ	ɔː	sɔ˥	'comb'	hɔk˧	'shell'	fɔŋ˥	'square'
u	uː	fu˥	'husband'	fut˧	'wide'	fun˥	'cheerful'
ɪ	ɪ			sɪk˥	'colour'	sɪŋ˥	'star'
ɵ	ɵ			sɵt˥	'shirt'	sɵn˥	'to inquire'
ɐ	ɐ			sɐp˥	'wet'	sɐm˥	'heart'
ʊ	ʊ			sʊk˥	'uncle'	sʊŋ˥	'loose'

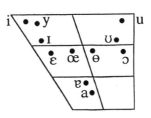

Diphthongs

(1) or (2)

ai	aːi	sai˥	'to waste'
ɐi	ɐi	sɐi˥	'west'
au	aːu	sau˥	'basket'
ɐu	ɐu	sɐu˥	'to receive'
ei	ei	hei˥	'rare'
ɛu	ɛːu	tɛu˧	'to throw'
ɵy	ɵy	sɵy˥	'bad'
ɔi	ɔːi	sɔi˥	'gill'
ui	uːi	fui˥	'ash'
iu	iːu	siu˥	'to burn'
ou	ou	sou˥	'beard'

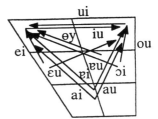

Tones

˥	(high, level)	si˥	'silk'	sɪk˥	'colour'
˧	(mid, level)	si˧	'to try'	sit˧	'to reveal'
˨	(low-mid, level)	si˨	'matter'	sɪk˨	'to eat'
˩	(low-mid to low, falling)	si˩	'time'		
˩˥	(low-mid to high, rising)	si˩˥	'history'		
˨˧	(low-mid to mid, rising)	si˨˧	'city'		

Conventions

(a) Consonants, vowels and diphthongs

Syllable-final plosives [p, t, k] are unreleased, i.e. [p˺, t˺, k˺]. Syllable-initial [t, tʰ, n] and final [t, n] are apico-laminal denti-alveolar; syllable-initial [s, ts, tsʰ] are laminal alveolar; and syllable-initial [l] is apical denti-alveolar or apical alveolar. [n] rarely occurs in syllable-initial position; syllable-initial [ŋ] is often deleted. [i, y, ɛ, œ, a, ɔ, u] occur in open syllables as well as syllables closed by a plosive or nasal. In open syllables, [i, y, u] are about cardinal; [ɛ] = [e̞]; [œ] = [ø̞]; [ɔ] = [o̞]; and [a] = [a̠]; [i, y, u, ɛ, œ̞, ɔ̞, a̠] are lowered in syllables closed by a plosive or nasal. [i, y, ɛ, œ, a, ɔ, u] are long in open syllables and short (a third shorter) in syllables closed by a plosive or nasal. [ɪ, ɵ, ɛ, ʊ] which occur only in syllables closed by a plosive or nasal are extra-short (two thirds shorter than [i, y, ɛ, œ, a, ɔ, u] in open syllables). All diphthongs are long; the first elements in [ai, au, ɔi, ui, iu, ɛu] are longer than the second elements; and the first elements in [ɐi, ɐu, ei, ɵy, ou] are similar to the second elements in length. [au] = [aʊ]; [ai] = [aɪ]; and [ɛu] = [ɛʊ]. The alternative transcriptions for vowels and diphthongs given above differ in whether these length distinctions are indicated.

(b) Tones

[˥, ˧, ˨, ˩, ˩˧, ˨˦] (= high; mid; low-mid; low-mid to low, falling; low-mid to high, rising; low-mid to mid, rising) are long tones; [˧] is relatively shorter. The short or extra-short variants of [˥, ˧, ˨] occur on syllables closed by a plosive. On a compound-final syllable, [˧, ˨] and their variants and [˧] are often replaced by [˩˥].

Transcription of recorded passage

jɐu˨ jɛt˥ tsʰi˨ ‖ pɛk˥ fuŋ˥ tʰuŋ˩ tʰai˨ jœŋ˩ hei˥ tou˨ au˨ kɛm˥ pin˥ kɔ˨ lɛk˥ ti˥ ‖ kʰɵy˨˦ tei˨ am˥ am˥ tʰɐi˥ tou˥ jɐu˨ kɔ˨ jɛn˥ haŋ˩ kʷɔ˨ ‖ li˥ kɔ˨ jɛn˥ tsœk˨ tsy˨ kin˨ tai˨ lɐu˥ ‖ kʰɵy˨ tei˨ tsɐu˨ wa˨ lak˨ ‖ pin˥ kɔ˨ hɔ˥ ji˨ tsɪŋ˥ tou˨ li˥ kɔ˨ jɛn˥ tsʰɵy˩ tsɔ˥ kin˨ lɐu˥ lɛ˥ ‖ tsɐu˨ syn˨ pin˥ kɔ˨ lɛk˥ ti˥ lak˨ ‖ jy˥ si˨ ‖ pɛk˥ fuŋ˥ tsɐu˨ pɔk˨ mɛŋ˨ kɛm˨ tsʰɵy˥ ‖ tim˥ tsi˥ ‖ kʰɵy˨˦ jyt˨ tsʰɵy˥ tɛk˥ sɐi˥ lei˨ ‖ kɔ˥ kɔ˨ jɛn˥ tsɐu˨ jyt˨ hei˨ la˥ sɛt˨ kin˨ lɐu˥ ‖ tsɵy˨ hɐu˨ ‖ pɛk˥ fuŋ˥ mou˨ sai˨ fu˥ ‖ wei˨ jɐu˨ fɔŋ˨ hei˨ ‖ kɛn˥ tsy˨ ‖ tʰai˨ jœŋ˩ tsʰɵt˥ lɛi˨ sai˨ tsɔ˥ jɛt˥ tsɛn˨ ‖ kɔ˥ kɔ˨ jɛn˥ tsɐu˨ tsɪk˥ hak˥ tsʰɵy˩ tsɔ˥ kin˨ lɐu˥ lak˨ ‖ jy˥ si˨ ‖ pɛk˥ fuŋ˥ wei˨ jɐu˨ jɪŋ˨ sy˥ la˥ ‖

Orthographic version (non-standard, vernacular)

　　有一次，北風同太陽喺度拗緊邊個叻啲。佢哋啱啱睇到有個人行過，哩個人着住件大褸。佢哋就話嘞，邊個可以整到哩個人除咗件褸呢，就算邊個叻啲嘞。於是，北風就搏命咁吹。點知，佢越吹得犀利，嗰個人就越係噚實件褸。最後，北風冇晒符，唯有放棄。跟住，太陽出嚟晒咗一陣，嗰個人就即刻除咗件褸嘞。於是，北風唯有認輸啦。

Catalan

JOAN F. CARBONELL* AND JOAQUIM LLISTERRI**

*Department of Phonetics and Linguistics, University College, London NW1 2HE, UK
**Departament de Filologia Espanyola, Facultat de Filosofia i Lletres, Universitat Autònoma de Barcelona, 08193 Bellaterra, Barcelona, Spain

The style of speech illustrated below is that of an educated speaker of Central Catalan as spoken in the area of Barcelona. The speech illustrated in the recording is that of a 26-year-old male speaker whose speech is representative of that variety.

Consonants

	Bilabial	Labio-dental	Dental	Alveolar	Post-alveolar	Palatal	Velar
Plosive	p b		t d				k ɡ
Affricate					tʃ dʒ		
Nasal	m			n		ɲ	ŋ
Trill				r			
Tap or Flap				ɾ			
Fricative		f		s z	ʃ ʒ		
Central Approximant						j	w
Lateral Approximant				l		ʎ	

/v/ does not occur in the Central Catalan system, but is present in some dialects (e.g. Majorcan Catalan, in the Camp de Tarragona).

p	*piga*	'speck'	t	*talla*	'size'	k	*casa*	'house'
b	*biga*	'beam'	d	*dalla*	'scythe'	ɡ	*gasa*	'lint'
						tʃ	*metxa*	'fuse' (n)
						dʒ	*metge*	'doctor'
m	*mama*	'mum'	n	*mana*	'he commands'	ɲ	*manya*	'skill'
						ŋ	*sang*	'blood'
			r	*serra*	'saw' (n)	ɾ	*cera*	'wax'
f	*fosc*	'dark'	s	*passar*	'to pass'	ʃ	*eixut*	'dry'
			z	*pesar*	'to weigh'	ʒ	*ajut*	'help'
			j	*iaia*	'grandma'	w	*veuen*	'they see'
			l	*pala*	'shovel'	ʎ	*palla*	'straw'

Vowels

The seven vowels /i/, /e/, /ɛ/, /a/, /o/, /ɔ/, /u/ occur in stressed syllables. If the syllables lose their stress /e/, /ɛ/, /a/ are reduced to schwa [ə] and /o/, /ɔ/ to [u]. The high vowels /i/, /u/ retain their quality in unstressed positions.

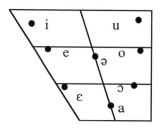

Stressed vowels

i	*ric*	'I laugh'
e	*cec*	'blind'
ɛ	*sec*	'dry'
a	*sac*	'sack' (n)
ɔ	*soc*	'log' (n)
o	*sóc*	'I am'
u	*suc*	'juice'

Unstressed vowels

i	*idea*	'idea'
u	*usar*	'to use'
ə	*amor*	'love' (n)

The phonetic diphthongs always begin or end with a high vocoid element. This may be interpreted as one of the independent phonemes /j/ or /w/, or may be regarded as an allophonic variant of a high vowel, /i/ or /u/. The first hypothesis seems more reasonable. On the one hand, both [uj] and [wi] can occur, so that the relative prominence of the components cannot be derived from their position in the syllable. On the other hand, the possibility of having both [wi] and [iw] shows that they are commutable. Therefore, it is best to consider /j/ and /w/ as underlying non-syllabic elements, rather than to derive them from /i/ and /u/.

Diphthongs are formed with a vowel and /j/ and /w/ either preceding (rising diphthong) or following (falling diphthong). Examples are given below.

ej	*rei*	'king'	ɛw	*peu*	'foot'
uj	*avui*	'today'	ow	*pou*	'well' (n)
ja	*iaia*	'grandma'	wa	*quatre*	'four'
je	*veiem*	'we see'	wə	*aigua*	'water'

Stress and accent

Stress may fall on the last syllable of a word, [kumbər'sa] 'to chat', on the penultimate syllable, [kum'pɛndrə] 'to understand', or on the antepenultimate, ['kapsulə] 'capsule'. All lexical words have one stressed syllable, though compound words regularly retain the stress associated with each element, e.g. *parallamps* ['parə'ʎams] 'lightning conductor'; similarly adverbs formed with *-ment* may be double-stressed, *bonament* ['bɔnə'men] 'willingly'. Most monosyllabic function words are always weak, even if stressed and accented.

Although the vowel reduction process suggests that stress is not distinctive, there are some minimal pairs where stress is contrastive, like *surti* ['surti], subjunctive form of 'to go out' and *sortir* [sur'ti], infinitive form of 'to go out'.

Differences between dialects
There are two main dialects of Catalan: Eastern Catalan and Western Catalan. Each dialect is further subdivided into different subdialects. The standard pronunciation of Catalan can be considered that of educated Central Catalan, a variety of Eastern Catalan.

The two main dialects differ noticeably in the treatment of unstressed vowels: while Western Catalan does not show vowel reduction processes in unstressed syllables, in Eastern Catalan dialects /e/, /ɛ/ and /a/ merge into schwa [ə] and /o/ and /ɔ/ merge into [u] in unstressed positions, while /i/ and /u/ retain their quality. In other words, in most Eastern dialects unstressed syllables will only contain one of the three vowel qualities [i], [u] or [ə]. In Western dialects [e], [o] and [a] also occur as unstressed vowels.

Conventions
The three voiced plosives have approximant variants [β], [ð], [ɣ] in onset positions (except after pause) after a vowel, or a liquid (except for /d/ after /l/). Elsewhere, these segments are realized as plosives. The voicing contrast of all the obstruents is neutralized word-finally due to the processes of word-final devoicing and voicing assimilation. All obstruents are devoiced word-finally before a pause. Moreover, the plosives have voiced allophones before a voiced consonant, but voiceless allophones before a vowel or a voiceless consonant. The fricatives behave similarly, but, unlike plosives, they also assimilate voicing before a vowel. This results in morphophonemic alternations, like *pes* [pɛs] 'weight' – *pesar* [pə'za] 'to weigh'.

Voiceless plosives are unaspirated; voiced allophones of the voiced plosives are voiced throughout. /b/ and /g/ are geminated before /l/ in the same syllable, if internally in a word after a stressed vowel: *poble* ['pɔbblə] 'village'. In Barcelona, the voiced geminates are currently devoiced, ['pɔpplə] or reduced to an unvoiced stop ['pɔplə], while in other dialects the stops are realized as approximants, i.e. ['pɔβlə]. The geminates [nn] and [mm] also occur in careful speech in words like *innecessari* [innəsə'sari] 'unnecessary' and *immens* [im'mɛns] 'huge'. There is also a geminate lateral [ll] as in *illusió* [illu'zio] 'illusion', but it is usually reduced to [l] in colloquial speech. The geminate [ʎʎ] appears in words like *espatlla* [əs'paʎʎə] 'shoulder'. /l/ has some degree of velarization in all positions, but is darker before a pause or consonant.

Final clusters of nasal or lateral stops are reduced by dropping the stop, which is usually restored if a morpheme starting with a vowel is added: *pont* [pɔn] 'bridge' – *pontet* [pun'tɛt] 'small bridge'. Final /r/ is lost before a word boundary or before the plural morpheme in most words, including infinitives, but is restored before a morpheme starting with a vowel:

color [ku'lo] 'colour' but *coloraina* [kulu'rajnə] 'bright colours'. There are however a number of exceptions, like *futur* [fu'tur] 'future'.

In emphatic speech and in certain dialects, initial postalveolar fricatives are affricated: *ximple* ['(t)ʃimplə] 'foolish', *germà* [(d)ʒər'ma] 'brother'. Underlying /v/ is realized as /b/ in Central Catalan; [b] or [β] occur before a vowel and [w] occurs finally; this results in alternations between [b] or [β] and [w]. Thus *blava* ['blaβə] 'blue' (fem) vs. *blau* [blaw] 'blue' (masc).

Transcription of recorded passage

lə trəmun'tanə j əl sɔl əz ðispu'taβən | sustə'niŋ 'kað u k eʎ 'erə l mes fɔr | kwan də 'soptə | 'bewən um biə'dʒe kə s ə'kɔstə mbuli'kat ən unə 'ɣraŋ 'kapə ‖ baŋ kumbə'ni kə l ki pri'me fə'riə kə l βiə'dʒe s trə'ɣes lə 'kapə | sə'riə tiŋ'gup pəl mes fɔr ‖ lə trəmun'tanə s 'pɔz ə βu'fa m 'totə lə 'seβə 'furiə | pə'rɔ kɔm mez βu'faβə | mez əl βiə'dʒe s əβri'ɣaβə m lə 'kapə ‖ ə lə fi | ba də'ʃa 'korə ferli 'trewrə ‖ ələ'zɔrəz əl sɔl kumən'sa ðə βri'ʎa | j əl kab d um mu'men | əl βiə'dʒe | ben əskəl'fat | əs trɛw lə 'kapə ‖ ə'ʃi | lə trəmun'tanə βa 'βɛ ðə kuɱfə'sa kə l sɔl 'erə l mes fɔr ‖

Orthographic version

This text was published in the *Principles of the International Phonetic Association* edited in 1912 but was omitted from the specimens in the subsequent versions of the *Principles*. It had appeared for the first time in *Le Maître Phonétique* vol. 26 ns. 7–8 (1911) p. 119 and was prepared by Josep M. Arteaga (Barcelona, 1846–1913), a Catalan phonetician who became a member of the Council of the IPA in 1907.

La tramuntana i el sol es disputaven, sostenint cada u que ell era el més fort, quan de sobte, veuen un viatger que s'acosta embolicat en una gran capa. Van convenir que el qui primer faria que el viatger es tragués la capa seria tingut pel més fort. La tramuntana es posa a bufar amb tota la seva fúria; però com més bufava, més el viatger s'abrigava amb la capa; a la fi, va deixar còrrer fer-li treure. Aleshores el sol començà de brillar, i al cap d'un moment, el viatger, ben escalfat, es treu la capa. Així, la tramuntana va haver de confessar que el sol era el més fort.

Acknowledgements

We would like to thank Carme de la Mota and Antonio Ríos for their useful comments and suggestions.

References

ALARCOS, E. (1983). *Estudis de lingüística catalana*. Barcelona: Ariel.
BADIA I MARGARIT, A. M. (1951). *Gramática histórica catalana*. Barcelona: Noguer. Catalan translation: València, Tres i Quatre, 1981.
BADIA I MARGARIT, A. M. (1988). *Sons i fonemes de la llengua catalana*. Barcelona: Publicacions de la Universitat de Barcelona.

BONET, E.-LLORET, M.-R. (1998). *Fonologia catalana*. Barcelona: Ariel.

GILI, J. (1974). *Introductory Catalan Grammar*. Oxford: Dolphin Books.

HUALDE, J. I. (1992). *Catalan*. London: Routledge.

INSTITUT D'ESTUDIS CATALANS. (1990). *Proposta per a un estàndard oral de la llengua catalana I: Fonètica*. Barcelona: Institut d'Estudis Catalans.

RECASENS, D. (1991). *Fonètica descriptiva del català*. Barcelona: Institut d'Estudis Catalans.

RECASENS, D. (1993). *Fonètica i fonologia*. Barcelona: Enciclopèdia Catalana.

VENY, J. (1985). *Introducció a la dialectologia catalana*. Barcelona: Enciclopèdia Catalana.

WHEELER, M. W. (1979). *Phonology of Catalan*. Oxford: Basil Blackwell.

YATES, A. (1975). *Catalan*. London: Hodder and Stoughton (Teach Yourself Books).

Croatian

ERNESTINA LANDAU

Vučetićev prilaz 5, 10020 Zagreb, Croatia

MIJO LONČARIĆ

Institute of Croatian Language, Strossmayerov trg 2, 10000 Zagreb, Croatia

DAMIR HORGA AND IVO ŠKARIĆ

Department of Phonetics, Faculty of Philosophy, University of Zagreb, 10000 Zagreb, Croatia

Croatian is one of the Slavic languages. As the national language of Croats, it consists of three main dialects, Štokavian, Kajkavian and Čakavian, named after the different forms of the interrogative pronoun meaning 'what' /ʃtô/, /kâj/ and /tʃâ/, orthographically *što, kaj, ča*. Standard Croatian was established in the eighteenth and nineteenth centuries. It is based on the New Štokavian Jekavian dialect.

The speech on the accompanying recording is that of a 57-year-old female announcer at the Croatian Television Network reading in a colloquial style. The style of speech illustrated is that of many educated speakers of Standard Croatian as spoken in the Republic of Croatia.

Consonants

	Bilabial	Labiodental	Dental	Alveolar	Postalveolar	Palatal	Velar
Plosive	p b		t d				k g
Affricate			ts		tʃ dʒ	tɕ dʑ	
Nasal	m			n		ɲ	
Fricative		f	s z		ʃ ʒ		x
Trill				r			
Approximant		ʋ				j	
Lateral Approximant				l		ʎ	

p   pǐːtɕe *píće* 'drink' (n)   t   tǔːga *túga* 'sorrow'   k   kôːst *kôst* 'bone'
b   bǐːtɕe *bíće* 'creature'   d   dǔːga *dúga* 'rainbow'   g   gôːst *gôst* 'guest'

				ts	tsâr	*cȁr*	'czar'					
				tʃ	tʃêp	*čȅp*	'cork'	tɕ	lě:tɕa	*léća*	'lentils'	
				dʒ	dʒêp	*džȅp*	'pocket'	dʑ	lě:dʑa	*léđa*	'back' (n)	
m	mô:j	*môj*	'my'	n	nô:s	*nôs*	'nose'	ɲ	ɲô:j	*njôj*	'to her'	
f	fǎ:za	*fáza*	'phase'	s	sělo	*sèlo*	'village'	x	xî:r	*hîr*	'caprice'	
ʋ	vǎ:za	*váza*	'vase'	z	zǎ:jam	*zájam*	'loan'					
				ʃ	ʃâ:l	*šâl*	'scarf'					
				ʒ	ʒâ:l	*žâl*	'beach'					
				r	râ:d	*râd*	'work' (n)	j	jûg	*jȕg*	'South'	
				l	lô:v	*lôv*	'chase'	ʎ	ʎêti	*ljȅti*	'in summer'	

Vowels

The system of Croatian vowels consists of five monophthongal vowels, /i, e, a, o, u/, which occur distinctively short and long, and a diphthong /ie/ occurring only in a long syllable. These vowels have more or less constant qualities in stressed and unstressed positions. There is also a syllabic trill /r̩/ which can either be long (4 to 5 contacts) or short (1 to 2 contacts). When occurring between two consonants, it is sometimes pronounced together with nonphonemic [ə], i.e. as [ər], e.g. [ʋə̂rt] *vȓt* 'garden'. A short [ə] also occurs in certain other contexts, as for example in pronouncing the names of some letters.

The diphthong /ie/ begins at the position of the /i/ monophthong and ends at the position of the monophthong /e/. It can also be pronounced [ije], but this still functions as a single syllable.

Short
i ʋîle *vȉle* 'hayfork'
e têk *tȅk* 'only'
a pâs *pȁs* 'dog'
o kôd *kȍd* 'by, at'
u dûga *dȕga* 'stave'

Long
i: ʋî:le *víle* 'fairies'
e: tê:k *têk* 'appetite'
a: pâ:s *pâs* 'belt'
o: kô:d *kôd* 'code'
u: dǔ:ga *dúga* 'rainbow'

[ə] [pâ̩rst] *pȓst* 'finger'
ie biělo *bijélo* 'white' (adj)

Conventions

When /f, ts, x/ precede a voiced obstruent they occur as [v, dz, ɣ]: [grôv‿bi] *grȍf bi* 'the earl would', [ŏtadz‿bi] *ȍtac bi* 'father would', [ŏʋiɣ‿bi] *ȍvih bi* 'of these...would'.

(There are similar alternations affecting other voiceless obstruents, but these may be regarded as the replacement of one phoneme with another; similarly, voiced obstruents alternate with their voiceless counterparts when followed by a voiceless obstruent.)

The post-alveolar affricates /ʃ, ʒ/ appear as the palatal sibilants [ɕ, ʑ] when they precede /tɕ, dʑ/: [mîɕ‿tɕe] *mȉš će* 'the mouse will', [pûːʑ‿tɕe] *pûž će* 'the snail will'. /ʋ/ occurs as [w] before the vowel /u/: [wûːk] *vûk* 'wolf'. /m/ occurs as [ɱ] before /f, ʋ/: [trǎɱʋaj] *trȁmvaj* 'tram'. /n/ occurs as [ŋ] before /k, g/: [stâːŋka] *stânka* 'pause'. /x/ occurs as [h] when it is initial in a consonant cluster: [hmêʎ] *hmȅlj* 'hops'.

A sequence of vowels across a word boundary may be separated by a glottal stop: [iː‿ʔônda] *i ȍnda* 'and then'.

Stress and accent

In addition to the contrast of length mentioned in connection with vowels, Croatian also has rising ([ˇ]) and falling ([ˆ]) pitch accents. It is traditional to regard these two distinctions as forming a four-way contrast of word accent, namely, long rising (´), short rising (`), long falling (ˆ) and short falling (ˇ); (ˉ) denotes length on an unstressed vowel. The parenthesized signs above are not part of the usual orthography, but are used to mark the accents in specialized linguistic works. The syllable on which the distinctive pitch movement begins and in which it may be completed is the stressed syllable. Monosyllabic (full) words always have a falling accent: /mêtʃ/ *mȇč* '(sporting) match', /mêːd/ *mȇd* 'honey'. Falling accents may also occur on the first syllable of a disyllabic or longer word, e.g. /mâma/ *mȁma* 'mama', /fôrma/ *fȍrma* 'form (n)', but they do not fall on later syllables apart from a few exclamations, e.g. /ahâ/ *ahȁ* 'aha!', and loan words, e.g. /ʒelêː/ *želê* 'jelly'. Rising accents may occur on any syllable but the last of a word, e.g. /zǐːma/ *zíma* 'winter', /terǎsa/ *teràsa* 'terrace', /ǐzʋiɲěːɲe/ *izvinjénje* 'excuse (n)' (with a secondary accent on the initial /i/).

There are two groups of words, proclitics and enclitics, which form a unit with the following or preceding stressed word respectively. Enclitics are always unstressed: /ôːn‿ti‿je tô: rêkao/ *ôn ti je tô rȅkao* 'he told you that'. Proclitics can be either unstressed or stressed. They are unstressed when the following word has a rising tone, e.g. /u‿ʋȍdi/ *u vòdi* 'in water', /pri‿rǎːdu/ *pri rádu* 'at work', but they can be stressed when the following word has a falling tone, e.g. /ôko/ *ȍko* 'eye' but /û‿oko/ *ȕ oko* 'in the eye'; /grâːd/ *grȃd* 'town' but /û‿graːd/ *ȕ grȃd* 'to town'; /ʃûma/ *šȕma* 'wood' but /ǔ‿ʃumi/ *ù šumi* 'in the wood'.

The stress position in Croatian is relatively free. Unstressed syllables preceding the stressed one are always short while the unstressed syllables following the stressed one can either be short or long, e.g. /kûtɕa/ *kȕća* 'a house' vs. /kûːtɕaː/ *kȕćā* 'houses (gen pl)'. The unstressed syllables are shorter than the corresponding stressed ones, by about 50 per cent in the case of long vowels and 30 per cent in the case of short ones.

Transcription of recorded passage

‖ sjêʋeːrniː lĕdeniː ʋjêtar i‿sûːntse‿su‿se prĕpirali o‿sʋõjoj snăːzi ‖ stôga ŏdlutʃeː da‿ŏnome ôd‿ɲiːx prîpadne pôbjeda kŏjiː sʋŭːtʃeː | tʃôʋjeka pûːtnika ‖ ʋjêtar zăpotʃe snâːʒno pŭːxati | a‿bŭduːtçi da‿je tʃôʋjek tʃʋfːsto dřʒao ôdjetçu | năʋali ôːn jôʃ jâtʃeː ‖ tʃôʋjek pâːk jôʃ jâtʃeː ot‿stûdeni přĭtisnuːt | naʋŭːtʃeː nă‿sebe jôʃ ʋîʃeː ôdjetçeː | dôk‿se ʋjêtar ne‿ŭmoriː i‿prĕpustiː‿ga tâda sûːntsu ‖ ŏnoː u‿potʃĕːtku zăsija ŭmjereno ‖ kâd‿je tʃôʋjek skîⁿnuo suʋĭːʃak ôdjetçeː | pŏʋiːsi ŏnoː jôʃ jâtʃeː ʒêgu | dôk‿se tʃôʋjek | u‿nemogŭːtçnosti da‿ŏdoli sŭntʃeʋoːj toplĭni ne‿sʋŭːtʃeː | i‿nĕ‿podzeː na‿kŭːpaɲe u‿rijĕːku tekŭtçitsu ‖ prîːtʃa pokăzujeː da‿je‿tʃêːsto uspjĕʃnijeː uʋjerăːʋaːɲe | nĕgoli năːsiːʎe ‖

Orthographic version with diacritics

Sjȅvērnī lèdenī vjȅtar i Sûnce su se prèpirali o svòjoj snázi. Stȍga òdlučē da ònome ȍd njîh prìpadne pȍbjeda kòjī svúčē čȍvjeka pûtnika. Vjȅtar zàpoče snâžno púhati, a bùdūći da je čȍvjek čvȑsto dȑžao ȍdjeću, nàvali ôn jȍš jȃčē. Čȍvjek pâk, jȍš jȁčē od stȕdeni prìtisnūt, navúčē nà sebe jȍš vȉšē ȍdjećē, dȍk se vjȅtar ne ùmorī i prȅpustī ga tâda Sûncu. Ònō u počétku zàsija ùmjereno. Kȁd je čȍvjek skȉnuo suvȉšak ȍdjećē, pòvīsi ònō jȍš jȁčē žȅgu dȍk se čȍvjek, u nemogúćnosti da òdoli sùnčevōj toplìni, ne svúčē i nè pođē na kúpanje u rijéku tekùćicu. Prîča pokàzujē da je čȅsto uspjèšnijē uvjerávānje nègoli násīlje.

Orthographic version

Sjeverni ledeni vjetar i Sunce su se prepirali o svojoj snazi. Stoga odluče da onome od njih pripadne pobjeda koji svuče čovjeka putnika. Vjetar započe snažno puhati, a budući da je čovjek čvrsto držao odjeću, navali on još jače. Čovjek pak, još jače od studeni pritisnut, navuče na sebe još više odjeće, dok se vjetar ne umori i prepusti ga tada Suncu. Ono u početku zasija umjereno. Kad je čovjek skinuo suvišak odjeće, povisi ono još jače žegu dok se čovjek, u nemogućnosti da odoli sunčevoj toplini, ne svu če i ne pođe na kupanje u rijeku tekućicu. Priča pokazuje da je često uspješnije uvjeravanje negoli nasilje.

Czech

JANA DANKOVIČOVÁ

Department of Phonetics and Linguistics, University College London,
4 Stephenson Way, London NW1 2HE, UK

Czech belongs to the western group of Slavic languages and is spoken as a mother tongue mainly in the Czech Republic. In its two provinces of Bohemia and Moravia it is spoken by about 10 million people. There are also some relatively large Czech-speaking communities in North America and smaller, isolated ones in neighbouring European countries. The closest related languages are Slovak and Polish.

A continuous tradition of Czech writing begins in the late thirteenth century. A recognisably near-modern spoken language and written standard had evolved by the sixteenth century. The spoken language continued to develop after the establishment of a relatively stable written standard. Thus when the written form underwent a modernizing revival from the late eighteenth century, the result was a noticeable divergence between written and spoken usage. This state has persisted to the present day.

The transcription of the sample text is based on the speech of a native speaker from Prague speaking standard Czech.

Consonants

	Bilabial	Labiodental	Alveolar	Postalveolar	Palatal	Velar	Glottal
Plosive	p b		t d		c ɟ	k ɡ	
Nasal	m		n		ɲ		
Fricative		f v	s z	ʃ ʒ		x	ɦ
Affricate			t͡s	t͡ʃ			
Trill			r ̺r				
Approximant					j		
Lateral Approximant			l				

All the plosives occur in voiced/voiceless pairs and are normally not aspirated. The glottal stop, while not phonemic, is typically used before vowels at the beginning of words or between vowels within the word after a prefix. Apart from the glottal and velar fricatives, all the fricatives occur in voiced/voiceless pairs. The glottal fricative is always voiced. The velar fricative is normally voiceless, although its voiced counterpart [ɣ] may occur allophonically. For more detail about the interaction between the glottal and velar fricatives with respect to assimilation, see the section on Assimilation below. Two affricate phonemes occur, a voiceless alveolar /t͡s/ and a voiceless post-alveolar /t͡ʃ/. They both have an allophonic voiced counterpart arising from voicing assimilation (see below).

There are two trills, /r/, as in *ruka* /ruka/ 'hand', and /ř/, as in *řeka* /řeka/ 'river'. The first one is an alveolar apical trill with 1–3 periods of vibration. It is immune from voicing assimilation and occurs voiced in all positions in the word. In the case of /ř/, the place of articulation is normally similar to that for /r/. Although it may be produced with the blade of the tongue, the main differentiating characteristic from /r/ is the number of vibrations, which may be 1–2 greater than in /r/, and their lesser amplitude than for the vibrations in /r/. Also, the constriction is narrower and the velocity of air greater. This sound often starts as a trill but continues as a fricative and thus probably the best term for it is 'alveolar trill fricative' with the symbol /ř/. (The laminal diacritic /ř̪/ used in Ladefoged and Maddieson (1996) does not capture the sound's defining property.) A voiceless allophone of /ř/ occurs in places where voicing assimilation applies.

There are three nasal phonemes, /m/, /n/ and /ɲ/. A labiodental nasal may occur allophonically, as the result of assimilation of the place of articulation with a following labiodental fricative. The velar nasal occurs allophonically before a velar stop, and in this position it is obligatory. The lateral /l/ is always voiced and, in standard Czech, it has a clear or neutral quality in all positions in the word. However, some Czech dialects have a phonemic contrast between /l/ (which is often palatalized) and dark /ɫ/. The bilabial nasal /m/, lateral /l/, and sonorant trill /r/ can be syllabic, e.g. *sedm* /sɛdm̩/ 'seven'; *vlk* /vl̩k/ 'wolf'; *vrba* /vr̩ba/ 'willow'.

p	pɛro	*pero*	'pen'	f	fakulta	*fakulta*	'faculty'
b	bota	*bota*	'shoe'	v	vaːza	*váza*	'vase'
t	tɛnto	*tento*	'this'	s	siːla	*síla*	'strength'
d	duːm	*dům*	'house'	z	zɪma	*zima*	'winter'
c	cɛlo	*tělo*	'body'	ʃ	ʃɛst	*šest*	'six'
ɟ	ɟɛlo	*dělo*	'gun'	ʒ	ʒɛna	*žena*	'woman'
k	kolo	*kolo*	'wheel'	x	xlɛba	*chleba*	'bread'
g	galɛrɪjɛ	*galerie*	'gallery'	ɦ	ɦora	*hora*	'mountain'
m	matka	*matka*	'mother'	r	ruka	*ruka*	'hand'
n	noɦa	*noha*	'leg'	ř	řɛka	*řeka*	'river'
ɲ	ɲɛt͡so	*něco*	'something'	j	jɛdɛn	*jeden*	'one'
t͡s	t͡sɛna	*cena*	'price'	l	lɛs	*les*	'forest'
t͡ʃ	t͡ʃɪstiː	*čistý*	'clean'				

Vowels

The vowel system consists of a set of five short vowels /ɪ ɛ a o u/, their long counterparts /iː ɛː aː oː uː/, and three diphthongs, all falling: /ou/, /au/ and /ɛu/ (the last two can be found only in loan words). The short and long vowels are in opposition in all positions.

The quality cf short non-low vowels and their corresponding long counterparts differs, in general, only to a small extent. However, in the pair /ɪ/ and /iː/, the short vowel is noticeably less close and more central than the long one. The greater difference in quality between these two vowels than in the case of the other vowel pairs is reflected by the usage here of a different vowel symbol for each of the two. The vowel /oː/ has a phonemic status only in loan words (and therefore in the table below it is shown in brackets). The short /a/ is pronounced usually as marginally fronter than the long /aː/. Vowel distinctions are preserved in unstressed positions.

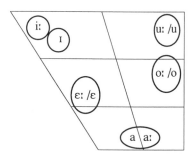

ɪ	mɪlɛ	*mile*	'nicely'	iː	miːlɛ	*míle*	'mile'
ɛ	lɛt	*let*	'flight'	ɛː	lɛːt	*lét*	'summer (gen pl)'
a	ɾat	*řad*	'row (gen pl)'	aː	ɾaːt	*řád*	'order'
o	voda	*voda*	'water'	(oː)	goːl	*gól*	'goal'
u	domu	*domu*	'house (gen sg)'	uː	domuː	*domů*	'home (adv)'
ou	mouxa	*moucha*	'fly (n)'				
(au)	auto	*auto*	'car'				
(ɛu)	nɛutraːlɲiː	*neutrální*	'neutral'				

Assimilation

Czech has assimilations of place and manner of articulation, and also voicing assimilation. Both assimilation of place of articulation and of voicing are normally anticipatory. Some examples of assimilation of place were mentioned in the discussion of consonants. Assimilation of manner of articulation is relatively rare; if it occurs, it usually concerns combinations of /t/ and /s/, /t/ and /ʃ/, /d/ and /z/, or /d/ and /ʒ/, which may become affricates /t͡s/, /t͡ʃ/, /d͡z/ and /d͡ʒ/ respectively (e.g. *dětský* can be pronounced either as [ɟɛtskiː] or

[jɛt͡ski:]).
Voicing assimilation affects most consonants. Apart from matching voicing to the following consonant, it also causes devoicing at the end of a word before a pause. When subject to voicing assimilation, the voiced glottal fricative /ɦ/ and voiceless velar fricative /x/ behave like a voiced/voiceless pair. For instance, in *běh Prahou* /ɦ/ in *běh* is realized as [x].

Suprasegmentals
Primary lexical stress falls on the first syllable of a word; thus it does not have a contrastive phonological role and functions rather as an indication of the word boundary. The stress marks in the transcription below indicate which syllables were accented by the speaker in the recorded passage. ‖ represents the major and | the minor intonation phrase boundary.

Transcription of recorded passage
ˈsɛvɛraːk a ˈslunt͡sɛ sɛ ˈɦaːdalɪ | ɡdo ˈz ɲɪx jɛ ˈsɪɲɛjʃiː ‖ f tom ˈspatr̝ɪlɪ ˈpot͡sɛstnɛːɦo | ˈktɛri: ˈkraːt͡ʃɛl ˈzaɦalɛn ˈplaːʃcɛm ‖ ˈujɛdnalɪ tɛdɪ | ʒɛ ˈtɛn sɛ maː ˈpovaʒovat ˈza sɪɲɛjʃiːɦo ‖ ɡdo ˈprvɲi: ˈdokaːʒɛ | ˈabɪsɪ ˈpot͡sɛstni: ˈsvlɛːkl ˈplaːʃc ‖ ˈtu zat͡ʃal ˈsɛvɛraːk ˈfoukat ˈzɛ fʃi: ˈsi:lɪ ‖ alɛ t͡ʃi:m vi:t͡s ˈfoukal ‖ ci:m ˈvi:t͡s sɛ ˈpot͡sɛstni: ˈzaɦaloval ˈdo svɛːɦo ˈplaːscɛ ‖ ˈkonɛt͡ʃɲɛ sɛ ˈsɛvɛraːk ˈvzdal ˈmarnɛːɦo ˈuːsɪli: ‖ ˈpak zat͡ʃalo ˈslunt͡sɛ ˈsvi:cɪt a ˈɦr̝aːt ‖ a ˈza ɲɛjaki: ˈokamʒɪk ˈpot͡sɛstni: | ˈktɛrɛːmu bɪlo ˈɦorko ‖ ˈsxoɟɪl ˈplaːʃc ‖ ˈtak musɛl ˈsɛvɛraːk ˈuznat | ʒɛ ˈslunt͡sɛ jɛ ˈsɪɲɛjʃi: ‖

Orthographic version
Severák a Slunce se hádali, kdo z nich je silnější. V tom spatřili pocestného, který kráčel zahalen pláštěm. Ujednali tedy, že ten se má považovat za silnějšího, kdo první dokáže, aby si pocestný svlékl plášť. Tu začal Severák foukat ze vší síly, ale čím víc foukal, tím víc se pocestný zahaloval do svého pláště. Konečně se Severák vzdal marného úsilí. Pak začalo Slunce svítit a hřát a za nějaký okamžik pocestný, kterému bylo horko, shodil plášť. Tak musel Severák uznat, že Slunce je silnější.

Acknowledgements
I would like to thank Martin Barry, Francis Nolan, Zdena Palková, Miroslav Ptáček, Přemysl Janota, Marie Svobodová and James Naughton for their comments and suggestions.

References
KUČERA, H. (1961). *The Phonology of Czech*. The Hague: Mouton & Co.
LADEFOGED, P. AND MADDIESON, I. (1996). *The Sounds of the World's Languages*.
　　Oxford: Blackwell.
PALKOVÁ, Z. (1994). *Fonetika a fonologie češtiny*. Prague: Karolinum.
ROMPORTL, M. (1973). *Základy fonetiky*. Prague: Státní Pedagogické Nakladatelství.

Dutch

CARLOS GUSSENHOVEN

Vakgroep Engels-Amerikaans, Katholieke Universiteit Nijmegen,
Erasmusplein 1, 6525 HT Nijmegen, The Netherlands

Apart from the Republic of Surinam and the Leeward islands of the Dutch Antilles, Aruba, Bonaire and Curaçao, where Dutch is an official language, Dutch is spoken in the Netherlands and the northwestern half of Belgium by about 20 million speakers. Variation in the pronunciation of educated European Dutch is substantial. For instance, the Belgian varieties (also collectively known as Flemish) tend to have monophthongal realizations of [eː, øː, oː] as opposed to realizations as closing diphthongs in the Netherlands. More generally, the southern varieties tend to have a full set of voiced fricatives /v, z, ɣ/ by the side of /f, s, x/ – which system of voiced fricatives is reduced to just /v, z/ or just /z/ as one gets closer to the prestigious western part of the Netherlands ('Randstad'). (There is great variability in the voicing of fricatives. Low-prestige urban varieties in the west may also lack /z/.) Roughly south of a line Rotterdam-Nijmegen, which is marked by the rivers Rhine, Meuse and Waal, /x, ɣ/ are velar, while to the north the corresponding voiceless fricative is post-velar or uvular. The phoneme /r/ tends to be alveolar in Belgium, in Amsterdam and in the north-east of the Netherlands, but uvular elsewhere. The variety illustrated represents Western, educated, middle-generation speech, and a careful colloquial style. More information is given by Collins and Mees (1982), Mees and Collins (1983), and Booij (1995).

Consonants

	Bilabial	Labio-dental	Alveolar	Post-alveolar	Palatal	Velar	Uvular	Glottal
Plosive	p b		t d	(c)		k		(ʔ)
Nasal	m		n	(ɲ)		ŋ		
Fricative		f v	s z	(ʃ) (ʒ)			χ	ɦ
Tap			ɾ					
Approximant		ʋ			j			
Lateral Approximant			l					

p	*pen*	'pen'	t	*tak*	'bough'	k	*kat*	'cat'
b	*ben*	'(I) am'	d	*dak*	'roof'	χ	*gat*	'hole'
			([c]	*ketjap*	'soy sauce')			

m	*mens*	'human being'	n	*nek*	'neck'	ŋ	*eng*	'narrow'
			([ɲ]	*oranje*	'orange' adj)			
f	*fiets*	'bicycle'	s	*sok*	'sock'	([ʃ]	*chef*	'section head')
v	*oven*	'oven'	z	*zeep*	'soap'	([ʒ]	*jury*	'jury')
ʋ	*wang*	'cheek'	j	*jas*	'coat'	([ʔ]	*beamen*	'confirm')
l	*lente*	'springtime'	ɾ	*rat*	'rat'	ɦ	*hoed*	'hat'

/p, t, k/ are voiceless unaspirated, /b, d/ are fully voiced. Alveolars (except /r/) are laminal and /s, z/ may have only mid-to-low pitched friction. [c, ɲ, ʃ] are the variants of /t, n, s/ that occur before /j/. In fact, all occurrences of these sounds can be analyzed as sequences of alveolar-plus-/j/; by analogy, [ʒ] could be seen as /zj/ and is therefore parenthesized in the chart above. [c, ɲ, ʃ, ʒ] are prepalatal, the tip of the tongue being held in the lower jaw. /ʋ/ tends to be only weakly voiced. /ʋ/ is [ʋ] in the onset, and [β̞] in the coda. /r/ is [ɾ] in the onset, and [ɹ] in the coda; in careful speech, a trill may occur word-initially. [ʔ] precedes vowel-initial syllables within words after /aː, ə/; because of its predictable distribution it is also shown in parentheses.

Voiced obstruents and /ɦ/ do not occur in the coda; /v/ is restricted to positions between voiced segments within the word. Marginal [g] (not listed) occurs in a small number of loans.

Sentence phonology is characterized by a number of consonantal adjustments. Sequences of identical consonants are reduced to single consonants by a process of degemination. Progressive devoicing will affect fricatives after obstruents, while obstruents may be voiced before /b, d/. Moreover, post-sonorant word-final fricatives, particularly /s/, may be voiced before vowels.

Vowels

Dutch has a set of lax vowels, a set of tense vowels, and a reduced vowel. The first column gives the lax vowels and the reduced vowel /ə/, the second column the tense vowels. Vowels in the third column are marginal in the language, and only appear in recent loans. The nasalized vowels [ɛ̃ː, ãː, ɔ̃ː] (not listed) also have this status. There are also three wide diphthongs.

ɪ	*bit*	'bit'	i	*biet*	'beetroot'	iː	*analyse*	'analysis'
ʏ	*hut*	'cabin'	y	*fuut*	'grebe'	yː	*centrifuge*	'spindryer'
ɛ	*bed*	'bed'	eː	*beet*	'bite'	ɛː	*serre*	'conservatory'
ə	*'t*	'the'	øː	*neus*	'nose'	œː	*oeuvre*	'works'

ɑ	*bad*	'bath'	aː	*zaad*	'seed'			
ɔ	*bot*	'bone'	oː	*boot*	'boat'	ɔː	*zone*	'zone'
			u	*hoed*	'hat'	uː	*cruise*	'cruise'

εi	*ei*	'egg'
œy	*ui*	'onion'
ʌu	*zout*	'salt'

/i, y, u/ are long before /r/ in the same stress foot. /eː, øː, oː/ are narrow closing diphthongs ([ei, øy, ou]), except before /r/ in the same word, when they are pronounced [eə, øə, oə].

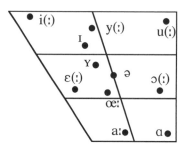 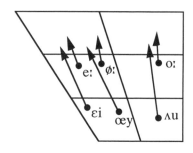

Stress and accentuation

Main stress falls on the antepenult, the penult, or the final syllable of the word if the penult· is open, and on the penult or the final syllable if the penult is closed. The long marginal vowels only occur in stressed syllables. In unstressed syllables, the otherwise long [eː, øː, oː, aː] are short. Minimal pairs are rare, examples being *canon* ['kaːnɔn] 'canon', *kanon* [ka'nɔn] 'cannon'; *Servisch* ['sɛrvis] 'Serbian', *servies* [sɛr'vis] 'dinner service'.

Largely depending on focus, intonational pitch accents will occur on the syllable with main stress of some words, marked with ['] in the transcription. The realization of these pitch accents will extend as far as the next pitch accent or the single bar |, which marks off a minor intonational phrase. Utterance-final boundary tones may be added before the double bar ‖.

Transcription of recorded passage

də 'noːrdəʋɪnt ɛn də 'zɔn | ɦadə ən dɪs'kʏsi oːvər də 'fraːχ | 'ʋi fan ɦʏn 'tʋeːə də 'stɛrəkstə ʋas | tun ər 'jœyst imant foːr'bɛi kʋam | di ən 'dɪkə 'ʋarmə 'jas aːnɦat ‖ zə spraːkə 'af | dat ʋi də foːrbɛiχaŋər dərtu zʌu 'krɛiχə zəɲ 'jas œy tə trɛkə | də 'stɛrəkstə zʌu zɛin ‖ də 'noːrdəʋɪnt bəχɔn œyt 'alə maχ tə 'blaːzə ‖ maːr u 'ɦardər i 'blis | dɛs tə 'dɪχtər də foːrbɛiχaŋər zəɲ jaz ɔm zɪχ 'ɦeːn trɔk ‖ tən'slɔtə χaf tə noːrdəʋɪnt ət maːr 'ɔp ‖ fər'fɔlχənz bəχɔn də 'zɔn | 'kraχtəχ tə 'straːlə | ɛn ɔ'mɪdələk daː'rɔp | trɔk tə foːrbɛiχaŋər zəɲ 'jaz œyt ‖ də 'noːrdəʋɪnt kɔn tun slɛχs bə'ʔaːmə | datə 'zɔn də 'stɛrəkstə ʋas.

Orthographic version

De noordenwind en de zon hadden een discussie over de vraag wie van hun tweeën de sterkste was, toen er juist iemand voorbij kwam die een dikke, warme jas aanhad. Ze spraken af dat wie de voorbijganger ertoe zou krijgen zijn jas uit te trekken de sterkste zou zijn. De noordenwind begon uit alle macht te blazen, maar hoe harder hij blies, des te dichter de voorbijganger zijn jas om zich heen trok. Tenslotte gaf de noordenwind het maar op. Vervolgens begon de zon krachtig te stralen, en onmiddellijk daarop trok de voorbijganger zijn jas uit. De noordenwind kon toen slechts beamen dat de zon de sterkste was.

References

BOOIJ, E. E. (1995). *The Phonology of Dutch.* Oxford University Press.

COLLINS, B. AND MEES, I. (1982). A phonetic description of the consonant system of Standard Dutch. *Journal of the International Phonetic Association* 12, 2–12.

MEES, I. AND COLLINS, B. (1983). A phonetic description of the vowel system of Standard Dutch. *Journal of the International Phonetic Association* 13, 64–75.

French

CÉCILE FOUGERON* AND CAROLINE L. SMITH**

Phonetics Laboratory, UCLA, 405 Hilgard Avenue, Los Angeles, CA 90095-1543, USA
and
Institut de Phonétique, CNRS URA1027, Université Paris III, France
**Eloquent Technology Inc, Ithaca, NY, USA*

The following description of French is based on the speech of a young Parisian female speaker. Varieties of French have almost identical inventories; the main differences are to be found in the maintenance or loss of certain contrasts.

Vowels

Oral vowels. French vowels, which are all monophthongs, are normally described using four values for height and two or possibly three (front, central, back) for backness. All back vowels are rounded; there are both rounded and unrounded sets of front vowels.

The mid-high and mid-low vowels have limited overlap in their distributions, but cannot be regarded as allophones. The contrast between [e] and [ɛ] is found in open syllables in final position (e.g. [se] *ses* (3rd person possessive, plural) vs. [sɛ] *sait* 'knows' and [pwaɲɛ] *poignet* 'wrist' vs. [pwaɲe] *poignée* 'handful'). Elsewhere, [e] occurs in open syllables and [ɛ] in closed syllables: compare [se.vir] *sévir* 'to rage' vs. [sɛʁ.viʁ] *servir* 'to serve'. For the other pairs of mid vowels, the contrast between mid-high and mid-low is limited for the most part to closed monosyllables. In other environments, the mid-low vowels [œ] and [ɔ] occur in closed syllables and the mid-high vowels [ø] and [o] in open syllables. However, in addition to this general rule, the nature of the syllable-final consonant also has an effect: the mid-high vowels [ø] and [o] are found in syllables ending

i	si	*si*	'if'		u	su	*sous*	'under'
e	se	*ses*	'his, hers' (pl)		o	so	*sot*	'silly'
ɛ	sɛ	*sait*	'knows'		ɔ	sɔʁ	*sort*	'fate'
	sɛʁ	*serre*	'greenhouse'					
y	sy	*su*	'known'					
ø	sø	*ceux*	'these'					
œ	sœʁ	*soeur*	'sister'					
ə	sə	*ce*	'this'					
a	sa	*sa*	'his, hers' (f)					

in [z], and [o] is not found even in monosyllables ending in [ʁ], [ɲ], and [g] (Delattre 1966; Léon 1992). It is noticeable that our speaker often produces a markedly centralized allophone of [ɔ], especially before [ʁ]. This is transcribed [ɔ̈] in the passage below. Some speakers have a contrast between two low vowels [a] and [ɑ]; our speaker has only one low vowel, [a], which is central. Schwa, [ə], is also a central vowel, with some rounding.

Some speakers retain a contrast between long and short vowels in a very few words, but most speakers no longer maintain any length contrast.

Nasalized vowels. Traditionally, French is described as having four distinctively nasalized vowels, [ɛ̃], [ɑ̃], [ɔ̃], and [œ̃]. However, our speaker, like many others, lacks [œ̃], which is replaced by [ɛ̃].

The vowel [ɛ̃] is produced with tongue and lip position very similar to its oral counterpart [ɛ]; however, several articulatory studies (e.g. Zerling 1984; Lonchamp 1988) have suggested that [ɑ̃] and [ɔ̃] differ substantially from their supposed oral counterparts [ɑ] and [ɔ]. The position of the tongue is similar in [ɑ̃] and [ɔ̃], and the main articulatory difference is that [ɔ̃] has a greater degree of lip rounding. These authors suggest that other symbols might be more appropriate for transcribing these two vowels, but we have retained the traditional usage as none of the alternative proposals has gained widespread acceptance.

ɑ̃	sɑ̃	*sans*	'without'
ɔ̃	sɔ̃	*son*	'his, hers' (m sg)
ɛ̃	sɛ̃	*saint*	'saint'

Consonants

	Bilabial	Labio-dental	Dental	Palato-alveolar	Palatal	Velar	Uvular
Plosive	p　b		t　d			k　g	
Nasal	m		n		ɲ	(ŋ)	
Fricative		f　v	s　z	ʃ　ʒ			ʁ
Lateral Approximant			l				

	Palatal	Labial-Palatal	Labial-Velar
Central Approximants	j	ɥ	w

p	pu	*pou*	'louse'		f	fu	*fou*	'crazy'
b	bu	*boue*	'mud'		v	vu	*vous*	'you' (pl)
t	tu	*tout*	'all'		s	su	*sous*	'under'
d	du	*doux*	'sweet'		z	zo	*zoo*	'zoo'

k	ku	*cou*	'neck'	ʃ	ʃu	*chou*	'cabbage'
g	gu	*goût*	'taste'	ʒ	ʒu	*joue*	'cheek'
				ʁ	ʁu	*roue*	'wheel'
m	mu	*mou*	'soft'	l	lu	*loup*	'wolf'
n	nu	*nous*	'we, us'				
ɲ	aɲo	*agneau*	'lamb'	w	swɛ̃	*soin*	'care'
ŋ	paʁkiŋ	*parking*	'parking lot'	j	sjɛ̃	*sien*	'his, hers'
				ɥ	sɥɛ̃	*suint*	'grease on sheep's wool'

French voiced stops are typically fully voiced throughout; voiceless ones are described as unaspirated. When preceding high vowels, they are often followed by a short period of aspiration and/or frication. The velar nasal occurs only in final position in borrowed (usually English) words.

French has one rhotic, whose production varies considerably among speakers and phonetic contexts. The speaker presented here uses a uvular fricative [ʁ] that is sometimes reduced to an approximant [ʁ], particularly in final position; it may also be devoiced (for examples see the transcribed text), and can be reduced to zero in some word-final positions. For other speakers, a uvular trill [ʀ] is also fairly common, and an apical trill [r] occurs in some dialects. Vowels are often lengthened before this segment.

The approximants [w], [ɥ], and [j] each correspond to a high vowel, [u], [y], and [i] respectively. There are a few minimal pairs where the approximant and corresponding vowel contrast, but there are also many cases where they are in free variation. Contrasts between [j] and [i] occur chiefly in final position, as in [abej] *abeille* 'bee' vs. [abei] *abbaye* 'monastery'.

Word-final consonants are always released, and in keeping with a general favouring of open syllables, they are usually resyllabified as onsets when followed by a vowel-initial word (*enchaînement*). Underlying word-final consonants that are not pronounced before a consonant, are pronounced only when preceding a vowel in the same rhythmic group. This process, known as *liaison*, also contributes to this canonical open-syllable pattern.

Prosody

Although French is often described as having stress on word-final syllables, in connected speech this is pre-empted by the accent on the final syllable of a group of words (sense group or accentual group, see Vaissière 1992 for discussion).

Transcription of recorded passage

The transcriptional style adopted in this illustration is a relatively narrow one, which reflects the particular pronunciation used in the recording of the passage made for the illustration.

la biz e lə sɔlɛʲ sə dispytɛ ‖ ʃakɛ̃ asyʁɑ̃ kilɛtɛ lə ply fɔʁ̥ ‖ kɑ̃t ilzɔ̃ vy ɛ̃ vwɑjaʒœ ki savɑ̃sɛ ‖ ɑ̃vlope dɑ̃ sɔ̃ mɑ̃to ‖ iː sɔ̃ tɔ̃be dakɔ̃ʁ̥ kə səlɥi ki aʁivʁe ləpʁ̥əmje a lə lɥi fɛʁote ‖ səʁə ʁəgaʁde kɔ̃m lə ply fɔʁ̥ ‖ alɔ̃ʁ̥ la biz sɛ̦ miz a sufle də tut se fɔʁ̥s ‖ mɛ ply ɛl suflɛ ply lə vwɑjaʒœʁ̥ sɛʁɛ sɔ̃ mɑ̃totuʁ̥ də lɥi ‖ finalmɑ̃ ɛl ʁənõsa lə lɥi fɛʁote ‖ alɔ̃ʁ̥ lə sɔlɛʲ kɔmɑ̃sa bʁ̥ije ‖ e o bu dɛ̦̃ mɔmɑ̃ lə vwɑjaʒœ ʁeʃofe ota sɔ̃ mɑ̃to ‖ ɛ̃si la biz dy ʁəkɔnɛt kə lə sɔlɛʲ ɛtɛ lə ply fɔʁ̥.

Orthographic version

La bise et le soleil se disputaient, chacun assurant qu'il était le plus fort. Quand ils ont vu un voyageur qui s'avançait, enveloppé dans son manteau, ils sont tombés d'accord que celui qui arriverait le premier à le lui faire ôter serait regardé comme le plus fort. Alors, la bise s'est mise à souffler de toutes ses forces, mais plus elle soufflait, plus le voyageur serrait son manteau autour de lui. Finalement, elle renonça à le lui faire ôter. Alors, le soleil commença à briller et au bout d'un moment le voyageur, réchauffé, ôta son manteau. Ainsi, la bise dut reconnaître que le soleil était le plus fort.

Acknowledgement
The first author was supported by an *Allocation de recherche M.R.T.* awarded to the *D.E.A. de phonétique de Paris.*

References
DELATTRE, P. (1966). *Studies in French and Comparative Phonetics.* The Hague: Mouton.

LÉON, P. (1992). *Phonétisme et prononciations du français.* Paris: Nathan.

LONCHAMP, F. (1988). *Étude sur la production et la perception de la parole, les indices acoustiques de la nasalité vocalique, la modification du timbre par la fréquence fondamentale.* Thèse de Doctorat d'État, Université de Nancy II.

VAISSIÈRE, J. (1992). Rhythm, accentuation and final lengthening in French. In Sundberg, J., Nord, L. and Carlson, R. (editors), *Music, Language, Speech and Brain* (Stockholm: Wenner-Gren International Symposium Series 59), 108–20.

ZERLING, J-P. (1984). Phénomènes de nasalité et de nasalisation vocaliques: étude cinéradiographique pour deux locuteurs. *Travaux de l'Institut de Phonétique de Strasbourg* 16, 241–66.

Galician

XOSÉ L. REGUEIRA

Instituto da Lingua Galega and Dept. de Filoloxía Galega
University of Santiago de Compostela, 15703 Santiago, Spain

Galician is a Romance language closely related to Portuguese. It is spoken in the far northwestern part of the Iberian Peninsula. As a result of historical circumstances, Spanish has exerted a strong political and cultural influence over this region since the end of the Middle Ages, and there is in consequence in Galicia today a socially ascendant Spanish-speaking urban minority, while the rest of the population maintains Galician as its mother tongue. As a result, Galician is in a situation of language shift and the spoken language now includes numerous loan-words from Spanish. However, in recent decades Galician has been recognized as an official language in Galicia along with Spanish, and the language has gone through a process of standardization and social recovery.

The language variety described here is that of colloquial Galician as spoken by a middle-aged male speaker whose speech may be considered representative of an informal variety used by educated urban speakers.

Consonants

	Bilabial	Labio-dental	Dental	Alveolar	Post-alveolar	Palatal	Velar
Plosive	p b		t d			ɟ	k ɡ
Affricate					t͡ʃ		
Nasal	m			n		ɲ	ŋ
Trill				r			
Tap				ɾ			
Fricative		f	θ	s̺	ʃ		
Approximant						j	w
Lateral Approximant				l			

Some varieties of the language, particularly among elderly speakers, display two contrasting lateral consonants, one alveolar [l] and the other palatal [ʎ]. However, in the language of most speakers, especially in urban and younger speakers, the palatal lateral consonant has been replaced by a voiced palatal plosive [ɟ], as can be seen in the table above.

In the dialects of western Galician, instead of /θ/ and /s̺/ there is only one fricative consonant, usually realized as a voiceless lamino-alveolar fricative [s]. This phenomenon is known as *seseo* (Fernández Rei 1991: 189–215). Another dialectal characteristic which is encountered chiefly in the western half of the Galician-speaking region is known as *gheada*; this dialectal feature consists of the absence of the voiceless velar plosive /g/, which is replaced by a voiceless fricative with several possible realizations, including pharyngeal [ħ], uvular [χ], velar [x] and glottal [h]. Standard Galician, including the variety of pronunciation described here, does not show these variants.

p	'papo	*papo*	'jowl'		ʃ	'ʃa	*xa*	'already'
b	'bimbjo	*vimbio*	'wicker'		m	'mĩmo	*mimo*	'cuddle' (n)
t	'tiṇta	*tinta*	'ink'		n	'nẽno	*neno*	'child'
d	'doṇdo	*dondo*	'soft'		ɲ	'aɲo	*año*	'lamb'
ɟ	'aɟo	*allo*	'garlic'		ŋ	'uŋɑ	*unha*	'a', 'one'
k	'kuko	*cuco*	'cuckoo'		r	ko'reɾ	*correr*	'to run'
g	'gɑŋgɑ	*ganga*	'bargain'		ɾ	'owɾo	*ouro*	'gold'
t͡ʃ	't͡ʃut͡ʃo	*chucho*	'kiss'		l	'liŋgwa	*lingua*	'language'
f	'fofo	*fofo*	'flabby'		j	'baja	*vaia*	'goes' (subj)
θ	'θiṇθa	*cinza*	'ash'		w	'bow	*vou*	'I go'
s̺	's̺is̺o	*siso*	'good sense'					

The approximants [j] and [w] may appear after a vowel, giving rise to sequences such as [ew], [ow], [ej], [oj], etc. While in most phonetic descriptions of Galician these are labelled diphthongs, in the present description they are viewed as sequences of vowel plus consonant, rather than as sequences of two vowels.

Vowels

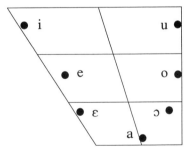

Nasalization is not distinctive for vowels, but any vowel can become fully or partially nasalized in contact with a nasal. The effect is strongest when a vowel occurs between two nasal consonants, and nasalization is systematically indicated for this sequence of sounds in the examples in this article. (In the recorded passage, nasalization is indicated *wherever* the speaker produced a nasalized vowel, i.e. in more than just the NVN context.)

i	'biɾ	*vir*	'to come'	ɔ	'nɔş	*nós*	'we'
e	'teɾ	*ter*	'to have'	o	'koro	*corro*	'I run'
ɛ	'bɛro	*berro*	'shout' (n)	u	'duɾo	*duro*	'hard'
a	'pa	*pa*	'shovel'				

Stress

Stress in Galician may fall on any of the last three syllables of a word. If a word has a closed syllable in final position, stress usually falls on that syllable, e.g. *final* [fiˈnal] 'end', *roncón* [roŋˈkoŋ] 'pipe in a bagpipe', *armar* [arˈmaɾ] 'to arm'. In certain loans and learned words stress may be on the penultimate syllable, as in *revólver* [reˈβolβeɾ] 'revolver', *dolmen* [ˈdɔlmẽŋ] 'dolmen', *útil* [ˈutil] 'useful'. If there is a final open syllable in a word, stress will normally fall on the penultimate syllable, e.g. *casa* [ˈkaşa] 'house', *home* [ˈɔme] 'man', *carballo* [karˈβaɟo] 'oak', *edificio* [ɛðiˈfiθjo] 'building'. However, some words end in a stressed vowel, e.g. *avó* [aˈβo] 'grandfather', *alá* [aˈla] 'over there'. This is true of the third person singular of the future tense in all verbs: *cantará* [kaṇtaˈra] 'will sing', *lerá* [leˈra] 'will read', *virá* [biˈra] 'will come'. There are in consequence some minimal pairs where stress placement is contrastive, e.g. *revólver* [reˈβolβeɾ] 'revolver' vs. *revolver* [reβolˈβeɾ] 'to mix'; *cantara* [kaṇˈtara] 'sang' (subj) vs. *cantará* [kaṇtaˈra] 'will sing'.

Some words ending in two open syllables bear the stress on the antepenultimate syllable, e.g. *cóbado* [ˈkoβaðo] 'elbow', *lóstrego* [ˈloştreɥo] 'lightning', *médico* [ˈmɛðiko] 'doctor', *lóxico* [ˈlɔʃiko] 'logical', *cálculo* [ˈkaɫkulo] 'calculation'.

Conventions

The consonants represented in the table above as /b d g/ are only realized as a plosive after a pause or after a nasal consonant (and also after a lateral in the case of [d]), whereas in other positions they have approximant variants [β ð ɰ] respectively. Thus in *veciño* [beˈθiɲo] 'neighbour', [um beˈθiɲo] 'a neighbour' a plosive is pronounced, while an approximant is found in *o veciño* [o βeˈθiɲo] 'the neighbour', *mal veciño* [mal βeˈθiɲo] 'bad neighbour', *ter veciños* [ˈteɾ βeˈθiɲoş] 'to have neighbours'.

Place of articulation in syllable-final nasals is non-contrastive, and assimilates to that of a following syllable-initial consonant, e.g. *inferno* [iɱfɛrno] 'hell', *enredar* [enreˈðaɾ] 'to entangle', *ancho* [ˈanʲtʃo] 'broad, wide', *nunca* [ˈnũŋka] 'never'; before a pause or before a word beginning with a vowel the realization is always velar [ŋ]: *non* [nõŋ] 'no, not', *son un home* [ˈşoŋ ũŋ ˈõme] 'I am a man'. The velar nasal also occurs intervocalically in a small number of words, for instance *unha* [ˈuŋa] 'a, one', *algunha* [aɫˈɥuŋa] 'some' (fem), *ningunha* [nĩŋˈguŋa] 'no, none', where the place of articulation is distinctive: *unha* [ˈuŋa] 'a, one' vs. *una* [ˈuna] 'joins' (subj), *uña* [ˈuɲa] 'nail' (Álvarez, Regueira and Monteagudo 1995: 33). Nevertheless, some authors do not include [ŋ] among the phonemes of Galician, suggesting that in cases such as those above the velar place of articulation is conditioned by the location of the syllable break: [ˈuŋ.a] vs. [ˈu.na] (Veiga 1976: 105–7; Castro 1989: 144–55). The present description prefers to regard /ŋ/ as a distinct phoneme.

As with the nasals, the place of articulation of the lateral approximant in syllable-final positions is also affected by a following dental, palatal or velar consonant: *alto* ['al̪to] 'tall', *colcha* ['kolʲt͡ʃa] 'bedspread', *algo* ['aɫ̪ɰo] 'something'. Elsewhere the lateral approximant is articulated as an alveolar [l].

Fricatives /θ/ and /s̺/ may become partially or fully voiced in syllable-final position before a voiced consonant: *dez meses* ['deθ̬ 'mes̺es̺] ~ ['deð 'mes̺es̺] 'ten months', *tres meses* ['tres̬ 'mes̺es̺] 'three months'. Elsewhere they remain voiceless. The open central vowel /a/ is realized as an open back [ɑ] in contact with velar consonants.

Transcription of recorded passage

o 'β̞en̪to ð̞o 'nɔrte ɛ majlo 's̺ol | porfi'aβ̞ãŋ s̺oβ̞re kɑl̪ 'deles̺ 'ɛra o majs̺ 'fɔrte
| kãn̪do kɑ'ð̞row ð̞e pa's̺ar ũm bia'ʃejro m'bɔl̪to nũŋa 'ãmpla 'kɑpa ‖
kõmbi'ɲeroŋ ẽŋ ke o ke 'an̪tes̺ kõŋs̺e'ɰiʃe fa'θerʝe ki'tala 'kɑpa ɔ β̞ia'ʃejro
s̺e'ria kõŋs̺ið̞erað̞oː majs̺ 'fɔrte ‖ o 'β̞en̪to ð̞o 'nɔrte s̺o'prow kõŋ grãɱ 'furja |
ɛ 'kɑn̪to majs̺ s̺o'praβ̞a majs̺ s̺e mbol'β̞i ɔ β̞ia'ʃejro na 's̺ua 'kɑpa ‖
final'mẽn̪te | o 'β̞en̪to ð̞o 'nɔrte aβ̞an̪do'now o 's̺ew ẽm'peɲo ‖ en̪'toŋ o 's̺ol
ken̪'tow kõɱ 'forθa | ɛ ĩŋmeð̞jata'mẽn̪te o β̞ia'ʃejro s̺a'kow a 'kɑpa ‖ ɛ
ð̞a'kela | o 'β̞en̪to ð̞o 'nɔrte 'tiβ̞o ke rekoɲe'θela s̺uperjori'ð̞að̞e ð̞o 's̺ol ‖

Orthographic version

O vento do norte e mailo sol porfiaban sobre cál deles era o máis forte, cando cadrou de pasar un viaxeiro envolto nunha ampla capa. Conviñeron en que o que antes conseguise facerlle quita-la capa ó viaxeiro sería considerado o máis forte. O vento do norte soprou con gran furia, e canto máis sopraba máis se envolvía o viaxeiro na súa capa; finalmente o vento do norte abandonou o seu empeño. Entón o sol quentou con forza e inmediatamente o viaxeiro sacou a capa. E daquela o vento do norte tivo que recoñece-la superioridade do sol.

Acknowledgements
I should like to thank Xosé Ramón Varela for his initiative in this description and for his help and comments. I am also grateful to him and to John Barlow for the translation of this text.

References
ÁLVAREZ, R., REGUEIRA, X. L. AND MONTEAGUDO, H. (1995). *Gramática galega,* 6th edition. Vigo: Galaxia.

CASTRO, O. (1989). *Aproximación a la fonología y morfología gallegas.* Dissertation, Georgetown University. Ann Arbor: University Microfilms International, 1991.

FERNÁNDEZ REI, F. (1991). *Dialectoloxía da lingua galega,* 2nd edition. Vigo: Xerais.

VEIGA, A. (1976). *Fonología gallega.* Valencia: Bello.

German

KLAUS KOHLER

Institut für Phonetik, Olshausenstraße 40, D-2300 Kiel, Germany

The style of speech illustrated is that of many educated Germans in the North. The accompanying recording is of a 62-year-old speaker reading in a colloquial style.

Consonants

	Bilabial	Labio-dental	Dental	Alveolar	Post-alveolar	Palatal	Velar	Uvular	Glottal
Plosive	p b			t d			k ɡ		ʔ
Nasal	m			n			ŋ		
Fricative		f v		s z	ʃ ʒ	ç		χ ʁ	h
Approximant						j			
Lateral Approximant				l					

The table of consonants lists phonemes with the exception of [ç] and [χ] as well as [ʔ]. Their distributions can be predicted from context, as stated below under conventions, provided morpheme boundaries are marked. *Frauchen* 'little woman' and *rauchen* 'to smoke' are differentiated as ['fʁaʊçən] and ['ʁaʊχən] because in the former [ç] is initial in the diminutive suffix *-chen*, but in the latter [χ] is final after a back vowel in the stem morpheme *rauch-*. So [ç] and [χ] can be said to be allophones of a phoneme /x/ with reference to different positions and contexts within morphemes. In the absence of such morphemic information, as is usually the case in IPA transcription, the difference between these consonant segments has to be symbolized. Similarly [fɐ'ʔaɪzən] *vereisen* 'to freeze over' and [fɐ'ʁaɪzən] *verreisen* 'to travel' show a paradigmatic opposition of [ʔ] and [ʁ] in the same segmental context. If the morpheme structure of the stems *-eis-* vs. *-reis-* after the prefix *ver-* is taken into consideration the occurrence of [ʔ] can be automatically inferred; if not, [ʔ] needs to be transcribed.

p	*passe*	'skip' (1 sg)	t	*Tasse*	'cup'	k	*Kasse*	'cash desk'	
b	*Baβ*	'bass'	d	*das*	'that'	ɡ	*Gasse*	'lane'	
m	*Masse*	'mass'	n	*nasse*	'wet'	ŋ	*lange*	'long'	
f	*fasse*	'catch' (1 sg)	s	*reiβe*	'rip' (1 sg)	ʃ	*rasche*	'quick'	
v	*Wasser*	'water'	z	*reise*	'travel' (1 sg)	ʒ	*Garage*	'garage'	

ç	*dich*	'you'	χ	*Dach*	'roof'	h	*hasse*	'hate' (1 sg)
j	*ja*	'yes'	ʁ	*Rasse*	'race'	l	*lasse*	'let' (1 sg)

Vowels

Monophthongs   Diphthongs

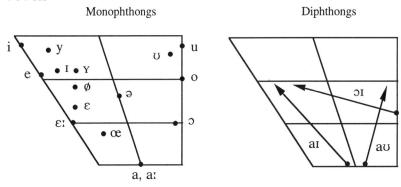

i	*bieten*	'to offer'	y	*hüten*	'to guard'	u	*sputen*	'to hurry'
ɪ	*bitten*	'to request'	ʏ	*Hütten*	'huts'	ʊ	*Butter*	'butter'
e	*beten*	'to pray'	ø	*Goethe*	(name)	o	*boten*	'offered' (1 pl)
ɛ	*Betten*	'beds'	œ	*Götter*	'gods'	ɔ	*Botten*	'clogs'
ɛː	*bäten*	'if they requested'						
			a	*hatten*	'had' (1 pl)			
			aː	*baten*	'requested' (1 pl)			
			ə	*Beute*	'booty' (sg)			
aɪ	*beiden*	'both' (1 pl)	ɔɪ	*Beuten*	'booty' (pl)	aʊ	*bauten*	'built'

Stress

ˈ (primary stress) and ˌ (secondary stress), as in compounds, e.g. [ˈʃɔɐnʃtainˌfegɐ] *Schornsteinfeger* 'chimney sweep'.

Conventions

/p, t, k/ are aspirated when not preceded by a fricative within the same word (e.g. [ˈʃtat] *Stadt* 'town'), nor followed by a syllabic nasal (e.g. [ˈlaitn̩] *leiten* 'to guide'); the aspiration is strongest before a stressed vowel, weakest in unstressed function words.

/ʁ/ can be an approximant intervocalically (e.g. *Herren* 'gentlemen'); after voiceless plosives and fricatives, especially those within the same word, it is devoiced (in e.g. *trat* 'kicked' it is completely voiceless [χ]); postvocalically before a consonant or word-finally it is vocalized to [ɐ], which results in diphthongs (e.g. [ˈhaɐt] *hart* 'hard', [ˈoɐ] *Ohr* 'ear', see the vowel chart below); the ending *-er* is realized as [ɐ] (e.g. [ˈbʊtɐ] *Butter* 'butter'); the place of articulation of the consonant varies from uvular in e.g. *rot* 'red' to velar in e.g. *treten* 'kick', depending on back or front vowel contexts.

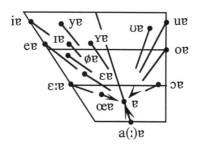

[ɐ] Diphthongs

Except for unstressed function words, word and stem initial vowels are prefixed by glottal stops (e.g. [ʔɛɐˈʔaɐbaɪtn] *erarbeiten* 'achieve through work').

[ç] occurs after front vowels and consonants within the same morpheme, as well as morpheme initially (e.g. [çeˈmi] *Chemie* 'chemistry', [çən] *-chen* = diminutive suffix). [χ] occurs after low back vowels (e.g. [ˈbaχ] *Bach* 'brook', [ˈdɔχ] *doch* 'yet'); [x] is used instead of [χ] after high and mid back tense vowels (e.g. [ˈbux] *Buch* 'book', [ˈhox] *hoch* 'high').

The closer vowels in a close/open pair are always longer under the same conditions of stress and environment; in unstressed position the close vowels are shortened and may keep their close vowel quality, as in [moˈʁaːl] *Moral* 'moral', [fyˈzik] *Physik* 'physics', but the latter constraint does not apply to unstressed function words (e.g. [ʏbɐ] *über* 'over').

Transcription of recorded passage

aɪns ˈʃtʁɪtn zɪç ˈnɔɐtvɪnt ʊn ˈzɔnə, vɛɐ fən im ˈbaɪdn vol dɐ ˈʃtɛɐkəʁə vɛʁə, als aɪn ˈvandəʁɐ, dɛɐ ɪn aɪn ˈvaɐm ˈmantl gəˌhʏlt vaɐ, dəs ˈvegəs daˈheɐkaːm. zɪ vʊɐdn ˈaɪnɪç, das ˈdeɐjenɪgə fyɐ dən ˈʃtɛɐkəʁən ˌgɛltn zɔltə, dɛɐ dən ˈvandəʁɐ ˈtsvɪŋŋ vʏɐdə, zaɪm ˈmantl ˈaptsuˌnemm. dɛɐ ˈnɔɐtvɪm ˈblis mɪt ˈalɐ ˈmaχt, abɐ je ˈmeɐ ɛɐ ˈblis, desto ˈfɛstɐ ˈhʏltə zɪç dɐ ˈvandəʁɐ ɪn zaɪm ˈmantl aɪn. ˈɛntlɪç gaɐp dɐ ˈnɔɐtvɪn dəŋ ˈkampf ˈaʊf. nun ɛɐˈvɛɐmtə dɪ ˈzɔnə dɪ ˈlʊfp mɪt iɐn ˈfʁɔɪntlɪçn ˈʃtʁaːln, ʊn ʃɔnaχ ˈvenɪgŋ ˈaʊgŋˌblɪkŋ tsok dɐ ˈvandəʁɐ zaɪm ˈmantl aʊs. da mʊstə dɐ ˈnɔɐtvɪn ˈtsugebm, das dɪ ˈzɔnə fən im ˈbaɪdn dɐ ˈʃtɛɐkəʁə vaɐ.

Orthographic version

Einst stritten sich Nordwind und Sonne, wer von ihnen beiden wohl der Stärkere wäre, als ein Wanderer, der in einen warmen Mantel gehüllt war, des Weges daherkam. Sie wurden einig, daß derjenige für den Stärkeren gelten sollte, der den Wanderer zwingen würde, seinen Mantel abzunehmen. Der Nordwind blies mit aller Macht, aber je mehr er blies, desto fester hüllte sich der Wanderer in seinen Mantel ein. Endlich gab der Nordwind den Kampf auf. Nun erwärmte die Sonne die Luft mit ihren freundlichen Strahlen, und schon nach wenigen Augenblicken zog der Wanderer seinen Mantel aus. Da mußte der Nordwind zugeben, daß die Sonne von ihnen beiden der Stärkere war.

Hausa

RUSSELL G. SCHUH AND LAWAN D. YALWA

Department of Linguistics, UCLA, 405 Hilgard Avenue, Los Angeles, CA 90095-1543, USA

The following description of Hausa is based on the variety of the language spoken in Kano, Nigeria. The sample text is transcribed from a recording of a male native of Kano in his late thirties. This variety of Hausa is considered 'standard'. Though Kano is a large urban center with some internal variation in speech, the sound inventory is relatively homogeneous within the city and surrounding area. Kano Hausa is the variety most commonly heard on national and regional radio and television broadcasts in Nigeria as well as most international broadcasting, such as the BBC, Deutsche Welle, Radio Moscow, and Voice of America. Kano Hausa is therefore familiar throughout the Hausa speaking areas of Nigeria as well as Hausa speaking communities in Niger, Ghana, and other areas outside northern Nigeria. Hausa has a standard orthography, in use since the 1930's and also based on the Kano variety. It is familiar to all Hausa speakers literate in the Romanized orthography. (Many Hausas are also literate in Arabic orthography, a variety of which has been used to write Hausa, probably for several centuries. The Arabic orthography for Hausa is less standardized than the Roman orthography and has little formally published literature.)

Vowels

Phonologically, Hausa has a 10-vowel system comprising five vowels, each with a long and a short counterpart. The five long vowels occupy roughly the five canonical vowel positions [i, e, a, o, u]. Their pronunciation is relatively stable regardless of environment, and they are consistently longer in duration than their short counterparts. Before pause, the five short vowels also fall roughly into the respective canonical positions, but medially (both word-medial and word-final when not followed by pause), they are strongly influenced by environment, including both preceding and following consonants and vowels in contiguous syllables. Short /i/ may thus range across [i ~ ɪ ~ ɨ] and short /u/ may range across [u ~ ʊ ~ ʉ]. In normal conversational speech, medial short high vowels are probably frequently neutralized to a high, centralized vowel, with rounding or lack of rounding determined by environment. The placement of the short high vowels in the vowel chart below is a compromise for their variant pronunciations. Short /a/ is a fairly low, central(ized) vowel, with fronting, backing, and rounding determined by environment. In the sample text below, short /a/ has been consistently transcribed as [ə], but it should be understood that this represents a range of pronunciation in the low to mid area. Medial short /e/ and /o/ are neutralized with short /a/. Thus, the words [zoːbèː] 'ring' and [reːʃèː] 'branch' in their plural forms (formed by lengthening the second consonant and changing the final vowel to [aː]) are, respectively, [zə̂bbaː] and [rə̂ssaː]. See Parsons (1970) for a discussion of vowel variability in Hausa. See notes introducing the illustrative text below for the marking of tone. Orthographic forms are in italics:

iː	kʲʼiːɽàː	*ƙira*	'forging'
eː	kʲʼeːɽàː	*ƙera*	'to forge'
aː	kʼaːɽàː	*ƙara*	'to increase'
oː	kʷoːɽàː	*kora*	'to chase'
uː	kʷʼùːɽaː	*ƙura*	'dust'
i	kʲiɽàː	*kira*	'calling'
e	tàːɽe	*tare*	'together'
a	kaɽaː	*kara*	'stalk'
o	gʷoːrò	*goro*	'kola nut'
u	kʷʼuɽàː	*ƙura*	'to stare'

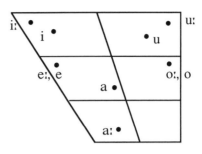

Consonants

	Bilabial	Alveolar	Post-alveolar	Palatal	Palatalized Velar	Velar	Labialized Velar	Glottal
Plosive & Affricate	b	t d	tʃ dʒ		kʲ gʲ	k g	kʷ gʷ	ʔ
Implosive & Ejective Stop & Affricate	ɓ	ts' ɗ	(tʃ')	j'	kʲʼ	k'	kʷʼ	
Nasal	m	n						
Fricative	ɸ	s z	ʃ					h
Tap/Trill		r ɾ						
Approximant	w			j				
Lateral Approximant		l						

Plosives and affricates: Word-initial voiceless plosives and affricates are moderately aspirated. We have no information on voicing onset time for the voiced counterparts. Among the velars, the plain/palatalized/labialized distinction is neutralized to labialized before rounded vowels, e.g. [kʷoːɽaː] *kora* 'ringworm' but no contrasting *[koːɽaː] or *[kʲoːɽaː]. The plain/palatalized distinction is neutralized to palatalized before front vowels, e.g. [kʲiːʃìː] *kishi* 'jealousy' but no contrastive *[kiːʃìː]. Labialized velars contrast with the plain/palatalized counterparts before front vowels, e.g. [kʷiːɓìː] 'side of body'. The glottal stop contrasts with other consonants medially. It also occurs predictably before words written in the standard orthography with initial vowels, e.g. [ʔaːjàː] *aya* 'verse of the

Koran', and as a terminator of short vowels before pause, e.g. [gʷoːròʔ] *goro* 'kola nut'.
See Carnochan (1952) for a discussion of these and other glottal phenomena.

			t	taːɾàː	'to gather'		k	kaːɾàː	'to screen off'
b	bàːɾa	'last year'	d	daːɾàː	'to laugh'		g	gaːɾaː	'wedding gifts'
			ts'	ts'aːɾàː	'to arrange'		k'	k'aːɾàː	'to increase'
ɓ	ɓaːɾàː	'to peel'	ɗ	ɗaːnàː	'to measure'				
m	maːɾàː	'belly'	n	naːmàː	'meat'				
ɸ	ɸaːɾàː	'to begin'	s	saːɾàː	'to excavate'				
			z	zaːnàː	'to draw'				
			r	raːɗàː	'to flog'				
			ɾ	ɾaːnaː	'sun'				
			l	laːkaː	'mud'				
			tʃ	tʃaːɾaː	'crowing'		kʲ	kʲaːwùː	'goodness'
			dʒ	dʒaːrìː	'assets'		gʲ	gʲaːɾàː	'to repair'
			(tʃ'	tʃ'àːda	'expensive')		kʲ'	kʲ'aːɾa	'grass' (sp.)
			ʃ	ʃàːɾaː	'sweeping'				
w	waːɾàː	'to select out'	j	jâːɾa	'children'				
			j'	j'aːj'aː	'offspring'				
							kʷ	kwaːɾàː	'to pour much'
							gʷ	gʷàːnoː	'stink-ant'
							kʷ'	kʷ'aːɾàː	'shea-nuts'
							ʔ	saːʔàː	'time'
							h	haːdʒàː	'goods'

Implosive and ejective stops and affricates: The sounds [ɓ, ɗ] have glottal vibration.
Ladefoged (1968: 16) transcribes these sounds as [ʔb, dʔ] respectively and notes that 'these
sounds may be incidentally implosive on some occasions; but they are always distinguished
from their voiced counterparts by being laryngealized'. Unpublished instrumental studies
which we have done showed consistent and strong implosion with these consonants. One
can therefore only conclude that the production of these consonants varies depending on
speaker and probably rate of speech. The sound represented here as [ts'] ranges from an
ejective alveolar affricate with clear plosive component to an ejective fricative [s'] – in the
Kano dialect, it tends to be realized as the affricate. Some dialects, though not that of Kano,
have a post-alveolar ejective affricate [tʃ'] in contrast with the alveolar affricate or fricative.
The velar ejectives [k', kʲ', kʷ'] show the same distribution with respect to following
vowels as do the pulmonic velars discussed in the preceding paragraph. Finally, a broad
range of dialects, including that of Kano, have a sound described here as a palatalized glottal
stop, [ʔʲ]. Historically, this represents a contraction of the sequence [ɗij], as can be seen in
dialects which preserve the original pronunciation, e.g. Sokoto dialect [ɗijaː] 'daughter',
Kano dialect [j'aː] (orthographic *ɗiya* and '*ya* respectively).

Nasals: Hausa has only two contrastive nasals, /m, n/. Phonetically there are also [ɲ, ŋ]. The palatal nasal [ɲ] is orthographically *ny*, which represents the correct phonemic analysis, shown, for example, by the fact that in a word like *hanya* 'road', the phonemic syllable boundary falls between *n* and *y* (cf. plural *hanyoyi*, where only the *y* is reduplicated, not *ny* as would be expected in this plural type if *ny* represented a unit phoneme). The velar nasal [ŋ] is the predictable form of /n/ before velar and glottal consonants and the labial-velar approximant [w], e.g. [səŋkˈoː] 'baldness', [səŋhòː] a type of basket, [kəŋwaː] 'potash' (orthographic *sanƙo, sanho, kanwa* respectively). The velar nasal is also a frequent variant (probably universal for some speakers) of any nasal before pause, e.g. [wənnə̀ŋ] 'this one', [mùtôŋ] 'person' (orthographic *wannan, mutum* respectively).

Fricatives: In the Kano and many other dialects, the only voiceless labial consonant phoneme is phonetically a bilabial fricative [ɸ], represented as *f* in the orthography. However, there is much dialectal and individual variation in the pronunciation of this phoneme. Some speakers tend to pronounce it as a bilabial plosive [p]. A labiodental variant of the fricative, [f], as well as bilabial variants of varying degrees of constriction are also heard. Some dialects, particularly in the north and west, have no voiceless labial consonant at all, instead having plain glottal fricative before front vowels, e.g. [hi] 'to exceed' (cf. Kano [ɸi, fi, pi]) and a labialized glottal [hʷ] elsewhere, e.g. [hʷaːɽàː] 'to begin' (cf. the Kano example in the list above).

Tap/trill: Most Hausa speakers distinguish two tap sounds in the alveolar region, [r, ɽ]. The first is the 'canonical trilled r' sound, found in many of the world's languages. It can be realized minimally as a single tap, but often has multiple taps, especially word-initially or finally, and obligatorily when geminated for morphological purposes. The [ɽ] is a retroflex flap, realized by flipping the tongue forward across the alveolar ridge. Newman (1980) provides the most extensive discussion of the status, distribution, and history of these sounds in Hausa. Ladefoged (1968: 30) was the first to investigate the sounds instrumentally, and though he notes the distinct articulations, he states, 'Indeed I have not been able to find any consistent acoustic difference between the two sounds'. The two are clearly contrastive as shown by the oft-cited though far from unique minimal pair, [bəràː] 'begging' vs. [bəɽàː] 'servant' (both orthographic *bara*), but in the one tap mode illustrated by a pair such as this, they are often difficult to distinguish. However, when they are lengthened through one of several morphological processes, the long variants share little articulatory or acoustic similarity. In pairs such as [jaː rərrə̀bkeː ʃi] 'he flogged him' vs. [ʃàːɽəɽɽeː] 'swept' (orthographic *ya rarrabke shi* and *shararre* respectively), the long [rr] is an alveolar trill whereas the long [ɽɽ] is a prolonged retroflex approximant (see Ladefoged and Maddieson (1996) for instrumental data and discussion). It should be noted that in the sample text below, the distinction between the two r's is not indicated. The speaker for this text is among the minority of Hausa speakers who have only the single r sound, [r].

Transcription of recorded passage

The transcriptional style adopted in this illustration is a relatively narrow one, which reflects the particular pronunciation used in the recording of the passage made for the illustration. Note the following features of transcription: (1) *Tone*: Hausa has two distinctive tones, high, which is unmarked here, and low, which is marked with a grave accent (ˋ) over the vowel of the syllable bearing the tone. There is also a phonetic falling tone, occurring only on heavy (CV: or CVC) syllables and analyzed by most Hausa specialists as high followed by low on a single syllable. This falling tone is marked with a circumflex accent (^) over the vowel of the syllable bearing the tone. Aside from the normal high and low tones, certain classes of words, particularly interjections and ideophones, are pronounced with an extra-high tone, which falls above the normal pitch register. These are marked with an acute accent (ˊ). Hausa has a downdrift intonation pattern, i.e. in a sequence high-low-high-low, each subsequent high is somewhat lower in pitch than the preceding high, and likewise for succeeding lows, but with less pitch declination than for the highs. (2) *Punctuation*: In the transcription here, I = a significant pause at a fairly large syntactic boundary but with the downdrift intonation carried on after the pause; , = a significant pause at a fairly large syntactic boundary with the intonation level reset to a higher register after the pause; . = sentence level boundary, after which a new intonation register always begins. (3) *Glottal stop*: As noted in the section on Consonants, [ʔ] contrasts with other consonants intervocalically, it occurs predictably at the beginning of words written in the standard orthography with initial vowels, and before pause, it terminates words with final short vowels. In the transcription here, word-initial and medial glottal stops are all written. Word-final glottal stops are indicated in those cases where the speaker paused and pronounced a clearly audible [ʔ]. (4) *Short vowels*: As noted above, the pronunciation of short vowels is heavily influenced by consonantal context as well as vowels in contiguous syllables. The transcription of the short vowels in the text attempts to roughly approximate the phonetic variability.

ʔɪskàː də̀ raːnaː

wətə raːnaː, də̀ ʔɪskə̀r hòntuːrù: tə ʔərèːwəʔ I də̀ raːnaː sʊkə̀ ji gə̀rdəmàː ʔə̀ kə̂n koːwàːtʃeːtʃèː də̀gə̀ tʃikɪnsù tə ɸi k'ərɸiː. tò sʊnàː tʃikɪn wənnə̀ŋ gə̀rdəmàː I səj gàː wənɨ mətə̀fɪjiː, jaː zoː sə̀ɲɛʔ də̀ ɲ̀ːgər səɲiː. tò ʃiːkèːnən, səj ʔɪskə̀r hòntuːrù: də̀ raːnaː sʊkə̀ ji jə̀rdʒeːdʒeːɲìjaː, ʔə̀ kə̂n jə̂w, zaːʔə̀ ji kʷ'ʊreʔ, dɔn ʔə̀ gə koː wàː zə̂j ʔijə̀ sâː mətə̀fɪɟɪn jə̀ tuːɓèː ɲ̀ːgərsə̀ʔ ʔə̀ kə̂n tiːlə̀s. tò ʃiːkèːnən, səj ʔɪskə̀r hòntuːrù: tə buːsoː sə̀pɪntə̀ʔ, də̀ k'ərɸi I ʔijə̀ jɪntə̀ I ə̀mmaː ìnâː. səj tə kaːsə̀ sâː ʃiː wənnə̀m mətə̀fɪji I jə̀ kʷ'əɓèː ɲ̀ːgərsə̀ʔ, dɔn kʷʊ̀wa, jaː də̀ndə̀nneː ɲ̀ːgə̂r gə́mgə́m ʔə̀ jɪkɪnsə̀ʔ. tò də̀gə̀ k'ə̀rʃeː dəj, səj ʔɪskàː tə səllə̀maː, də̀gə̀ nən nèː kʷʊma, ʔɪtə raːnaː I tə ʃɨgə naːtə̀ ʔajkɪ̀ŋ. ʔaj kòː raːnaː I səj tə buːɗoː həskʲə̀ntə̀ də̀ zaːfɪntə̀ wə̀rwə́r. hə́bə̀ː I kə̂n kə̀ tʃê: mèː, səj gàː ʃi wənnə̀m mùtûm I mətə̀fɪji: I jaː kʷ'əɓèː ɲ̀ːgərsàː, bâː gʲɪrmaː də̀ ʔərʒ̀kiː. gənɨ̀ŋ həkə̀ kʷʊ̀wa I səj ʔɪskàː dóːlè tə ʔəmɨ̀ntʃeʔ ʔə̀ kə̂n tʃêːwaː, ləlleː I raːnaː taː fiː tə̀ k'ərɸiː.

Orthographic version

Iska da Rana

Wata rana, da iskar hunturu ta arewa da rana suka yi gardama a kan kowace ce daga cikinsu ta fi ƙarfi. To, suna cikin wannan gardama, sai ga wani matafiyi ya zo sanye da rigar sanyi. To, shi ke nan, sai iskar hunturu da rana suka yi yarjejeniya a kan yau, za'a yi ƙure don a ga ko wa zai iya sa matafiyin ya tuɓe rigarsa a kan tilas. To, shi ke nan, sai iskar hunturu ta buso sanyinta da ƙarfi iya yinta, amma ina?! Sai ta kasa sa shi wannan matafiyi ya kwaɓe rigarsa, don kuwa ya dandanne rigar gamgam a jikinsa. To daga ƙarshe dai, sai iska ta sallama, daga nan ne kuma, ita rana ta shiga nata aikin. Ai ko, rana sai ta buɗo haskenta da zafinta warwar. Haba! Kan ka ce me, sai ga shi wannan mutum, matafiyi, ya kwaɓe rigarsa, ba girma da arziki. Ganin haka kuwa, sai iska dole ta amince a kan cewa, lalle rana ta fi ta ƙarfi.

References

CARNOCHAN, J. (1952). Glottalization in Hausa. *Transactions of the Philological Society* 78–109. London.

LADEFOGED, P. (1968). *A Phonetic Study of West African Languages*, 2nd edition. Cambridge University Press.

LADEFOGED, P. AND MADDIESON, I. (1996). *The Sounds of the World's Languages.* Oxford: Blackwells.

NEWMAN, P. (1980). The two R's in Hausa. *African Language Studies* 17, 77–87.

PARSONS, F. W. (1970). Is Hausa really a Chadic language? Some problems of comparative phonology. *African Language Studies* 11, 272–88.

Hebrew

ASHER LAUFER

The Phonetics Laboratory, Hebrew Language Department, The Hebrew University,
Mount Scopus, Jerusalem 91905, Israel

There are two main pronunciations in Modern native Israeli Hebrew: Oriental and Non-Oriental. The Oriental pronunciation is usually spoken by people with a Near Eastern origin, who have some sort of Arabic or Aramaic in their own or their parents' background. These speakers may have been born in Israel, and by now most of them do not know any Arabic or Aramaic. The Non-Oriental pronunciation is spoken by the rest of the population. It should be noted that, for various reasons, there are 'Oriental Israelis' who use the Non-Oriental pronunciation, and 'Non-Orientals' who use the Oriental pronunciation.

The Oriental pronunciation was chosen by the 'Va'ad Hallashon' (the committee preceding the Academy of the Hebrew Language) to be the representative and the prestigious speech in Israel. This pronunciation was selected to be the preferred one for the official broadcasting services. However, this decision is not always followed nowadays.

The recordings for this illustration were taken from two Israeli-born informants, whose education was in Hebrew. The Oriental informant was a 61-year-old woman whose parents were also born in Israel. The Non-Oriental informant was a 49-year-old man born to parents of East European origin; Hebrew and Yiddish were spoken at their home.

The main difference between these pronunciations is in the consonants; the Oriental pronunciation has two pharyngeal phonemes, which the Non-Oriental lacks. In the Non-Oriental pronunciation, /ʕ/ merges with /ʔ/ and /ħ/ with /χ/.

Consonants

	Bilabial	Lab-dent.	Alveolar	Postalv.	Palatal	Velar	Uvular	Pharyng.	Glottal
Plosive	p b		t d			k ɡ			ʔ
Nasal	m		n						
Trill			r				χ		
Fricative		f v	s z	ʃ ʒ				ħ	h
Approximant					j			ʕ	
Lateral			l						

The phonemes /ħ/ and /ʕ/ occur only in the Oriental pronunciation.

p	par	'bull'	t	tar	'tours'	k	kar	'cold'
b	bar	'wild'	d	dar	'dwelt'	g	gar	'lives, lived'
						ʔ	ʔor	'light'
m	gam	'also'	n	gan	'garden'			
f	tsaf	'floats'	s	sar	'minister'	ʃ	ʃar	'sings, sang'
			χ	ma'χar	'sold'	h	har	'mountain'
v	tsav	'turtle'	z	zar	'stranger'	ʒ	ʒa'ket	'jacket'
r	ram	'high'	l	gal	'wave'	j	jam	'sea'

Oriental pronunciation only

	ħ	ma'ħar	'tomorrow'		ʕ	ʕor	'skin'

Affricates might be regarded as phonological units, but they can be treated as sequences of stops followed by homorganic fricatives: /ts/ as in /tsar/ 'narrow'; /tʃ/ as in /tʃips/ 'chips' and /dʒ/ as in /dʒip/ 'jeep'.

Vowels

i	ħil	'fear'
e	ħel	'army of'
a	ħal	'occurred'
o	ħol	'sand, workaday'
u	ħul	'abroad'

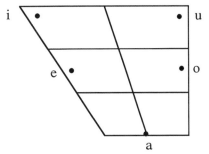

Diphthongs can be treated as sequences of vowels. If one of the vowels in such a sequence is an /i/ it can be interpreted as /j/. Thus, [ei] can be interpreted as /ej/.

Stress
Stress is distinctive

/'bereχ/ 'knee'
/be'reχ/ 'he blessed'.

Differences between the Oriental and the Non-Oriental pronunciations
The Oriental pronunciation has the two pharyngeals /ħ, ʕ/. Some of the Oriental speakers, especially in liturgical reading, have also pharyngealized sounds [sˤ, tˤ, kˤ]. Most of the speakers of the Oriental pronunciation have gemination, especially in careful and slow pronunciation (/'danu/ 'they discussed' vs. /'dannu/ 'we discussed'). They also preserve the traditional 'mobile schwa' more than the Non-Oriental speakers. Usually the Oriental-Hebrew speakers pronounce /r/ as an alveolar trill (or tap [ɾ]), and in the Non-Oriental

pronunciation it is usually a uvular approximant [ʁ] (still, some Non-Oriental speakers pronounce it as a trill). Some occurrences of the front-mid vowel /e/ are diphthongized by Non-Orientals as [ei], but most of the Oriental speakers retain a monophthong [e]. Years ago this distinction marked a distinct difference between these two pronunciations: while the Non-Orientals differentiated between pairs like [moˈre ˈdereχ] 'guide' vs. [moˈrei ˈdereχ] 'guides', the Orientals produced both as [moˈre ˈdereχ]. It seems that this difference is gradually disappearing, as more and more Oriental speakers acquire the diphthong [ei] in specific words.

Conventions

/k/ is aspirated and /p, t/ are slightly aspirated. /b, d, g/ are voiced throughout. In a normal style of speech /ʕ/ is a pharyngeal approximant. /ʔ/, especially in unstressed syllables, can be elided. /r/ in the Oriental dialect is usually an alveolar trill [r], but it is usually a uvular approximant [ʁ] for Non-Orientals. /χ/ is usually a voiceless uvular fricative trill. /n/ is usually [ŋ] before a velar plosive, and [ɲ] before /j/. Especially in unstressed syllables, the glottal stop, the glottal fricative and the pharyngeal approximant /ʔ, h, ʕ/ may be omitted (though their frequencies seem to depend on the personality, on the style and on the rapidity of speech). When intervocalic /h/ is pronounced, it is voiced [ɦ]. Vowels and consonants are long in stressed syllables. They are even longer at the end of sense groups. Vowels are centralized and shorter if they are unstressed.

Phonemic transcriptions of recorded passages

1 Oriental Hebrew

ˈruaħ hattsaˈfon, vehaʃˈʃemeʃ, hitvakeˈhu beneˈhem, ˈmi meˈhem ħaˈzak joˈter. gameˈru, ki ʔet hannitsaˈhon, jinˈhal, ˈmi ʃejjatsˈlijah lifˈʃot meˈʕal ʕoˈver ˈʔorah ʔet begaˈdav. paˈtah ˈruah hattsaˈfon venaˈʃav behozˈka. hidˈdek haʔaˈdam ʔet begaˈdav ʔel guˈfo. ˈʔaz, histaˈʕer ʕaˈlav haˈruah, beˈjeter ʕoz, ˈʔaχ haʔaˈdam, miʃʃehoˈsif hakˈkor leʕannoˈto, laˈvaʃ meˈʕil ʕelˈjon ʕal begaˈdav. noˈʔaʃ mimˈmennu haˈruah, umesaˈro biˈde haʃˈʃemeʃ. tehilˈla, zaˈrah ʕaˈlav haʃˈʃemeʃ berakˈkut. vehaʔaˈdam heˈsir ʔet bigˈdo haʕelˈjon meʕaˈlav. higˈbir haʃˈʃemeʃ ʔet ħumˈmo, ˈʕad ʃelˈlo jaˈχol haʔaˈdam laʕaˈmod bifˈne haʃʃaˈrav, ufaˈʃat ˈʔet begaˈdav, veniχˈnas leˈtoχ hannaˈhar, ʃehaˈja bekirˈvat maˈkom, keˈdei lirˈhots bemeiˈmav.

2 Non-Oriental Hebrew

ˈruaχ hatsaˈfon, vehaˈʃemeʃ, hitvakˈχu beineˈhem, ˈmi meˈhem χaˈzak joˈter. gamˈru, ki ʔet hanitsaˈχon, jinˈχal, ˈmi ʃejatsˈliaχ lifˈʃot meˈʔal ʔoˈver ˈʔoraχ ʔet begaˈdav. paˈtaχ ˈruaχ hatsaˈfon, venaˈʃav beχozˈka. hiˈdek haʔaˈdam ʔet begaˈdav ʔel guˈfo. ˈʔaz, histaˈʔer ʔaˈlav haˈruaχ, beˈjeter ˈʔoz, ˈʔaχ haʔaˈdam, miʃehoˈsif haˈkor leʔanoˈto, laˈvaʃ meˈʔil ʔelˈjon ʔal begaˈdav. noˈʔaʃ miˈmenu haˈruaχ, umsaˈro bijˈdei haˈʃemeʃ. teχiˈla, zaˈraχ ʔaˈlav haˈʃemeʃ

beraˈkut, vehaʔaˈdam, heˈsir ʔet bigˈdo haʔelˈjon meʔaˈlav. higˈbir haˈʃemeʃ
ʔet χuˈmo, ˈʔad ʃeˈlo jaˈχol haʔaˈdam laʔaˈmod bifˈnei haʃaˈrav, ufaˈʃat ˈʔet
begaˈdav, veniχˈnas leˈtoχ hanaˈhar, ʃehaˈja bekirˈvat maˈkom, kedei lirˈχots
bemeiˈmav.

Orthographic version

רוּחַ-הַצָּפוֹן וְהַשֶּׁמֶשׁ הִתְוַכְּחוּ בֵּינֵיהֶם מִי מֵהֶם חָזָק יוֹתֵר. גָּמְרוּ, כִּי אֶת הַנִּצָּחוֹן יִנְחַל מִי
שֶׁיַּצְלִיחַ לִפְשֹׁט מֵעַל עוֹבֵר-אֹרַח אֶת בְּגָדָיו. פָּתַח רוּחַ-הַצָּפוֹן וְנָשַׁב בְּחָזְקָה. הִדֵּק
הָאָדָם אֶת בְּגָדָיו אֶל גּוּפוֹ. אָז הִסְתָּעֵר עָלָיו הָרוּחַ בְּיֶתֶר עֹז, אַךְ הָאָדָם, מִשֶּׁהוֹסִיף
הַקֹּר לְעַנּוֹתוֹ, לָבַשׁ מְעִיל עֶלְיוֹן עַל בְּגָדָיו. נוֹאַשׁ מִמֶּנּוּ הָרוּחַ וּמְסָרוֹ בִּידֵי הַשֶּׁמֶשׁ.
תְּחִלָּה זָרַח עָלָיו הַשֶּׁמֶשׁ בְּרַכּוּת, וְהָאָדָם הֵסִיר אֶת בִּגְדוֹ הָעֶלְיוֹן מֵעָלָיו. הִגְבִּיר הַשֶּׁמֶשׁ
אֶת חֻמּוֹ, עַד שֶׁלֹּא יָכֹל הָאָדָם לַעֲמֹד בִּפְנֵי הַשָּׁרָב, וּפָשַׁט אֶת בְּגָדָיו וְנִכְנַס לְתוֹךְ הַנָּהָר,
שֶׁהָיָה בְּקִרְבַת מָקוֹם, כְּדֵי לִרְחֹץ בְּמֵימָיו.

Hindi

MANJARI OHALA

Department of Linguistics and Language Development and Department of English,
San Jose State University, San Jose, CA 95192, USA

The variety described here is Standard Hindi used in everyday casual speech by educated speakers in cities such as Varanasi, Lucknow, Delhi, etc. Although there are a few differences in pronunciation among speakers of these cities, the differences are minimal. The transcription is based on a recording of a female third-generation speaker of Standard Hindi who grew up mostly in Uttar Pradesh before moving to Delhi. For a detailed analysis of Hindi segments, see Dixit (1963) and Ohala (1983).

Consonants

	Bilabial	Labio-dental	Dental	Alveolar	Post-alveolar	Retroflex	Palatal	Velar	Glottal
Plosive	p b ph bɦ		t̪ d̪ t̪ʰ d̪ɦ			ʈ ɖ ʈʰ ɖɦ		k g kʰ gɦ	
Affricate					tʃ dʒ tʃʰ dʒɦ				
Nasal	m			n				ŋ	
Tap or Flap				ɾ		ɽ ɽɦ			
Fricative		f		s z	ʃ				h
Approximant		ʋ					j		
Lateral Approximant				l					

p	pal	'nurture'	t̪	t̪al	'beat' (n)	k	kal	'span of time'
b	bal	'hair'	d̪	d̪al	'lentil'	g	gal	'cheek'
pʰ	pʰal	'knife blade'	t̪ʰ	t̪ʰal	'platter'	kʰ	kʰal	'skin' (n)
bɦ	bɦal	'brow'	ɖɦ	ɖɦaɾ	'knife edge'	gɦ	gɦan	'bundle'
m	mal	'goods'	n	nala	'drain' (n)	ŋ	ʋaŋməj	'literature'
f	faɾsi	'Persian'	s	sal	'year'	h	hal	'condition'
ʋ	ʋala	'pertaining to'	z	zəmin	'ground'	j	jaɾ	'buddy'
			ɾ	ɾal	(tree species)			
			l	lal	'red'			

tʃ	tʃɑl	'gait'		t̪	t̪ɑl	'postpone'
dʒ	dʒɑl	'net'		ɖ	ɖɑl	'branch'
tʃʰ	tʃʰɑl	'tree bark'		t̪ʰ	t̪ʰɑl	'lumber shop'
dʒɦ	dʒɦəl	'glimmer'		ɖɦ	ɖɦɑl	'shield'
ʃ	ʃɑl	(tree species)				
				ɽ	bəɽɑ	'big'
				ɽɦ	bəɽɦɑ	'increase' (imp)

[f, z, ʃ] only occur in loans (from Perso-Arabic, English, or Sanskrit). They are, however, well established in Modern Standard Hindi. Some authors also include [ɽ̃] which occurs only in a few Sanskrit loans; in casual speech it is usually replaced by [n]. Sounds such as [x, ɣ, q], etc., do not occur in the variety of Hindi described here although they would be found in some varieties of Urdu, the form of the language used as the official language of Pakistan and by many Indian Muslims. [lɦ, rɦ, mɦ, nɦ] are considered clusters of a liquid or nasal and /h/ in the analysis adopted here.

Geminates

All consonants can also occur with distinctive length (i.e. as 'geminates') except the following: [bɦ, ɽ, ɽɦ, h]. Geminates occur only medially and are always preceded by the non-peripheral vowels [ɪ, ə, ʊ]. Although the orthography preserves a few geminates in final position, in all but the most formal speech they are pronounced as singletons. All the geminates occur monomorphemically except [ʃː] which occurs only in a few Sanskrit loans where a morpheme boundary could be posited in between: [nɪʃːil] 'without shame' < /nɪʃ + ʃil/. Geminates are longer than singletons by a ratio of about 2:1. Some illustrative examples of the geminate contrasts are given below.

t̪	pət̪ɑ	'address' (n)		tʃ	bətʃɑ	'save'
t̪ː	pət̪ːɑ	'leaf'		tʃː	bətʃːɑ	'child'
t̪ʰ	kət̪ʰɑ	'narrative'		t̪	pət̪ɑ	'to make someone agree'
t̪ʰː	kət̪ʰːɑ	'red powdered bark'		t̪ː	pət̪ːɑ	'a fold' (in cloth)
ɖ	gəɖɑ	'mace' (weapon)		k	pəkɑ	'cook' (v)
ɖː	gəɖːɑ	'mattress'		kː	pəkːɑ	'firm'

Vowels

There are eleven oral vowels in Hindi, as shown on the vowel chart. The vowel [æ] only occurs in English loans. All of these vowels except [æ] also have distinctively nasal counterparts. The sequences [əi] and [əu] also occur but are not listed separately because they are analyzed as vowel clusters and not as diphthongs.

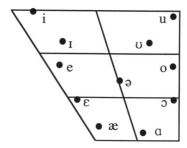

i	mil	'mile'				u	kul	'shore'
ɪ	mɪl	'meet'				ʊ	kʊl	'lineage'
e	mel	'harmony'	ə	məl	'rub' (imper)	o	bol	'speak'
ɛ	mɛl	'dirt'				ɔ	kɔl	(a name)
æ	bæʈ	'cricket bat'	ɑ	mɑl	'goods'			

i	sikʰ	'lesson'	ɑ	sɑs	'mother-in-law'	u	bʱukʰ	'hunger'
ĩ	sĩk	'twig'	ɑ̃	sɑ̃s	'breath'	ũ	bʱũk	'dog's bark'
ĩ	sĩtʃ	'be irrigated'				ʊ̃	kʊ̃ʋər	'prince'
ẽ	mẽ	'in'	ɔ̃	hɔ̃s	'laugh' (imp)	õ	jõ	'in this manner'
ɛ̃	mɛ̃	(1 sg pn)				ɔ̃	bʱɔ̃	'eyebrow'

Stress

Stress is not distinctive in Hindi. It is also controversial as to whether there is even phonetic word stress, other than for emphatic contrast. For details, see Ohala (1991).

Conventions

The velar nasal by and large only occurs before homorganic consonants except in a few Sanskrit loans such as the word for 'literature', cited above. Although palatal and retroflex nasals followed by homorganic consonants also occur phonetically and have been included in the list of phonemes by some authors, they have not been treated as phonemes in the analysis presented here (and thus are not listed in the consonant chart). [ʋ] is in free variation with [v] (and can also be pronounced as [w]). [ɾ] can vary with [r]. The geminate [ɾ] is always an alveolar trill [r]. Stops in final position are not released.

Vowels are nasalized before nasal consonants. The schwa is often pronounced with the same value as the vowel in the English word 'cut', i.e. the vowel that has traditionally been transcribed with [ʌ]. However, this vowel is central and not back, and thus perhaps a more appropriate IPA symbolization would be [ɐ]. As in many other languages, vowel length varies as a function of the voicing of the following consonant with vowels being longer before voiced ones, at least before stops (Ohala and Ohala 1992).

Transcription of recorded passage

This translation of 'The North Wind and the Sun' is a modified version of that presented in the 1949 version of the *Principles of the International Phonetic Association*.

ʊt̪ːəɾi həʋa ɔɾ suɾədʒ ɪs bət̪ pəɾ dʒʰəgəɾ ɾəhe t̪ʰe ki həm d̪onõ mẽ zjaɖa bəlʋan kɔn he. ɪt̪ne mẽ gərəm tʃoga pɛhne ek mʊsafɪɾ ʊd̪ʰəɾ a nɪkla. həʋa ɔɾ suɾədʒ d̪onõ ɪs bət̪ pəɾ ɾazi ho gəje ki d̪onõ mẽ se dʒo pɛhle mʊsafɪɾ ka tʃoga ʊt̪əɾʋa dega ʋəhi zjaɖa bəlʋan səmdʒʰa dʒajega. ɪs pəɾ ʊt̪ːəɾi həʋa əpna puɾa zor ləgakəɾ tʃəlne ləgi lekɪn ʋo dʒɛse dʒɛse əpna zor bəɽʰat̪i gəji ʋɛse ʋɛse mʊsafɪɾ əpne bəd̪ən pəɾ tʃoge ko ɔɾ bʰi zjaɖa kəs kəɾ ləpeʈʈa gəja. ənt̪ mẽ həʋa ne əpni koʃɪʃ bənd̪ kəɾ d̪i. pʰɪɾ suɾədʒ t̪ezi ke sət̪ʰ nɪkla ɔɾ mʊsafɪɾ ne t̪ʊɾənt̪ əpna tʃoga ʊt̪aɾ d̪ɪja. ɪs lɪje həʋa ko mənna pəɽa ki ʊn d̪onõ mẽ suɾədʒ hi zjaɖa bəlʋan he.

Orthographic version

उत्तरी हवा और सूरज इस बात पर झगड़ रहे थे कि हम दोनों में ज़्यादा बलवान कौन हैं। इतने में गरम चोगा पहने एक मुसाफ़िर उधर आ निकला। हवा और सूरज दोनों इस बात पर राज़ी हो गये कि दोनों में से जो पहले मुसाफ़िर का चोगा उतरवा देगा वही ज़्यादा बलवान समझा जायेगा। इस पर उत्तरी हवा अपना पूरा ज़ोर लगाकर चलने लगी लेकिन वह जैसे जैसे अपना ज़ोर बढ़ाती गई वैसे वैसे मुसाफ़िर अपने बदन पर चोगे को और भी कस कर लपेटता गया। अन्त में हवा ने अपनी कोशिश बन्द कर दी। फिर सूरज तेज़ी के साथ निकला और मुसाफ़िर ने तुरन्त अपना चोगा उतार दिया। इस लिये हवा को मानना पड़ा कि उन दोनों में सूरज ही ज़्यादा बलवान है

Acknowledgements

I thank John Ohala for his help with the software implementation of the IPA transcription. I also thank Usha Jain for her comments on the translation and for her assistance with the software for the Devanagari.

References

DIXIT, R. P. (1963). *The Segmental Phonemes of Contemporary Hindi*. M. A. thesis, University of Texas, Austin.

OHALA, M. (1983). *Aspects of Hindi Phonology*. Delhi: Motilal Banarsidass.

OHALA, M. (1991). Phonological areal features of some Indo-Aryan languages. *Language Science* 13, 107–24.

OHALA, M. AND OHALA, J. J. (1993). Phonetic universals and Hindi segment durations. *Proceedings of the Second International Conference on Spoken Language Processing*, 831–4. Edmonton: University of Alberta.

Hungarian

TAMÁS SZENDE

Institute of Linguistics, Hungarian Academy of Sciences,
P.O. Box 19, H-1250 Budapest, Hungary

The style of speech illustrated is that of Educated Colloquial Hungarian of the 1990s as spoken in Budapest. Historically, Standard Hungarian is based on the Eastern dialect, which became a supra-dialectal high prestige variety during the eighteenth century. The speech on the recording is that of a male speaker in his fifties with an academic background, using a somewhat advanced style of speech as spoken in a formal communicative situation.

Consonants

	Bilabial	Labiodental	Dental	Post-alveolar	Palatal	Velar	Glottal
Plosive	p b		t d			k ɡ	
Affricate			ts dz	tʃ dʒ	cç ɟʝ		
Nasal	m		n		ɲ		
Fricative		f v	s z	ʃ ʒ			h
Trill			r				
Approximant					j		
Lateral Approximant			l				

p	pipɑ	*pipa*	'pipe'	t	tolː	*toll*	'feather'	k	keːp	*kép*	'picture'
b	bot	*bot*	'stock'	d	dob	*dob*	'throw'	ɡ	ɡeːp	*gép*	'machine'
m	mɑ	*ma*	'today'	n	nɛm	*nem*	'no'	ɲ	ɲaːr	*nyár*	'summer'
f	fɑ	*fa*	'tree'	s	soː	*szó*	'word'	ʃ	ʃoː	*só*	'salt'
v	vaːɡ	*vág*	'cut'	z	zøld	*zöld*	'green'	ʒ	ʒɛb	*zseb*	'pocket'
ts	tseːl	*cél*	'goal'	tʃ	tʃɑk	*csak*	'only'	cç	cçuːk	*tyúk*	'hen'
dz	dzeːtɑ	*dzéta*	'zeta'	dʒ	dʒɛsː	*dzsessz*	'jazz'	ɟʝ	ɟʝaːr	*gyár*	'factory'
l	loː	*ló*	'horse'	r	roː	*ró*	'carve'				
h	hoː	*hó*	'snow'	j	joː	*jó*	'good'				

Consonant length is distinctive in Hungarian, cf. *hal* '(s)he/it is dying' vs. *hall* '(s)he/it hears' and *hal* 'fish' vs. *hall* 'hall'. Short/long opposition extends over the whole system of consonants functioning in (at least a limited number of) word forms. Accordingly, the full system consists of *short C : long C* pairs at all positions of the pattern. However, these long consonants are commonly analyzed as clusters of identical consonants. The phonemic analysis underlying the present chart reflects this second view.

Vowels

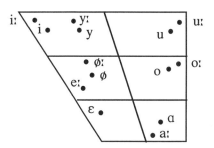

i	vis	*visz*	'carry'	iː	viːz	*víz*	'water'
y	yt	*üt*	'hit'	yː	tyːz	*tűz*	'fire'
u	u	*ujj*	'finger'	uː	uːt	*út*	'road'
ɛ	ɛz	*ez*	'this'	eː	eːl	*él*	'live'
ø	øl	*öl*	'kill'	øː	løː	*lő*	'shoot'
o	ok	*ok*	'cause'	oː	toː	*tó*	'lake'
ɑ	hɑt	*hat*	'six'	aː	vaːr	*vár*	'castle'

The seven basic vowel qualities occur in distinctively long and short quantities. Except for the low pair, the short vowels are a little lower and less peripheral than their long counterparts and the same symbol can be used for long and short members of each pair. However, the short vowel corresponding to long /aː/ is higher and backer than its long counterpart. To show its departure from the usual pattern it is transcribed as [ɑ]; in fact, this vowel has some rounding and might be transcribed [ɒ]. As for the [eː/ɛ] pair, mid front unrounded long [eː] is considerably higher and more peripheral than its lower mid front unrounded short counterpart [ɛ].

In addition to the seven basic vowel pairs three additional length/quality combinations, shown below, are phonemically distinctive in a limited number of minimal pairs only, for example /aː/ *A* 'the letter A' as opposed to /ɑ/ *a* (definite article). The marginal existence of both a long /aː/ and a short /a/ in the sound pattern of Hungarian provide further reason for transcribing /ɑ/ and /aː/ differently. The third marginal vowel, here written /ɛː/ is similar to a lengthened version of the short vowel /ɛ/.

(ɛː)	ɛː	*E*	(name of the letter E)
(a)	pasː	*passz*	'no bid' (in cards)
(ɑː)	ɑː	*A*	(name of the letter A)

Hungarian has two co-existent vowel systems, one of which does not distinguish two different heights among its mid front unrounded short vowels. However, a major segment (some 50 per cent) of the Hungarian-speaking population uses a vowel system with the distinction of /e/ and /ɛ/. In this Regional Standard version of Hungarian, orthographic *mentek* – i.e. Budapest Standard [mɛntɛk] – represents four different words: [mentek] 'go (2 pl., pres.)', [mentɛk] 'go (3 pl., past)', [mɛntek] 'save (1 sg., pres.)', or [mɛntɛk] 'be exempt from (3 pl., pres.)'.

Stress

Word-level stress is nondistinctive, and is fixed on the first syllable of the morpheme.

Conventions

/p, t, k/ are unaspirated, /b, d, g/ are fully voiced. /t, d, n, l, r/ are laminal dental, /s, z, ts, dz/ are laminal dentialveolar, /ʃ, ʒ/ are laminal postalveolar, /tʃ, dʒ/ are predorsal and postalveolar, and /tɕ, dz/ are mediodorsal and palatal. In formal style /cɕ, ɟj/ are realized mostly as palatal stops, i.e. [c] and [ɟ].

/r/ is a trill. /h/ is voiced [ɦ] in intervocalic position, [ç] in syllable-final position after front vowels, and [x] word-finally after back rounded vowels; word-final /h/ is often deleted.

Short vowels are to some extent reduced (lax) in unstressed position; their long counterparts are realized as full (tense) vowels. Long vowels, especially high ones, shorten in unstressed syllables with a consonant in the coda. The resulting vowel can be half-long or as short as a short vowel. A postvocalic /n/ usually nasalizes the preceding vowel and deletes before a following consonant, especially a continuant. (When the following consonant is a nasal, this process can be viewed as a coalescence of the two nasals.)

Transcription of recorded passage

ˌɛtsːɛr az ˈɛːsɑki ˈseːl eˈʃ ɑ ˌnɑp ˈvɛteˑlkɛtːɛk hoɟj ˈmɛjikyk az ˈɛrøːʃɛbː ‖ ˈeˑpː ɑːrɑ jøtː ɛɟj ˈvãːdor ˌvɑʃtɑk ˌkøpøɲɛgbɛ burkoloˑdzvɑ ‖ az ˌɛːsɑki ˌseːl eˈʃ ɑ ˌnɑp ˈɲombãˑ ˈmɛgɛɟjːɛstɛk hoɟj ˈaz lɛsː ɑ ˈɟjøːsteʃ ɑki ˈɦɑmɑrɑb ˌrɑːbiˑrjɑ ɑ ˌvãːdort hoɟj ˈlɛvɛɟjɛ ɑ ˈkøpøɲɛgeˑt ‖ ɑkːɔr az ˌɛːsɑki ˌseˑl ˌɛːkɛzdɛt ˈʃyvøltɛni ˌɑɦiotʃːɑk ˈbiːrt ‖ dɛ ɑ ˌvãːdor ˈɑnːaˑl ˈsoroʃɑbːɑɱ võtɑ ˌmɑgɑ køreˑ ɑ ˌkøpɛɲt ˌmineˑl ˈɛrøˈʃɛbːɛɱ ˌfujt ‖ ˌiːɟj ɑstɑˑn az ˌɛˈsɑki seˑl ˌɛl iʃ ˈvɛsitɛtːɛ ɑ ˌvɛrʃɛɲt ‖ ɑ ˌnɑp mɛg ˌɛːkɛstɛ ˈõtɑni ˈtyːzøˑ ʃugɑrɑit ˌmire ɑ ˌvãːdɔr ˈɛtsːɛribẽ ˈkibujt ɑ ˌkøpøɲɛgeˑbøl ‖ az ˌɛːsɑki ˈseːl ˈkeˑɲtɛlẽ vot ˈmɛgɑdni hoɟj ˌbizoɲ ɑ ˈnɑp az ˌɛrøːʃɛbː

Orthographic version

Egyszer az északi szél és a nap vetélkedtek, hogy melyikük az erősebb. Épp arra jött egy vándor, vastag köpönyegbe burkolódzva. Az északi szél és a nap nyomban megegyeztek, hogy az lesz a győztes, aki hamarabb rábírja a vándort, hogy levegye a köpönyegét. Akkor az északi szél elkezdett süvölteni, ahogy csak bírt. De a vándor annál szorosabban vonta maga köré a köpenyt, minél erősebben fújt. Így aztán az északi szél el is veszítette a versenyt. A nap meg elkezdte ontani tűző sugarait, mire a vándor egyszeriben kibújt a köpönyegéből. Az északi szél kénytelen volt megadni, hogy bizony a nap az erősebb.

Igbo

CLARA I. IKEKEONWU

Department of Linguistics and Nigerian Languages, University of Nigeria,
Nsukka, Enugu State, Nigeria

The style of speech illustrated is that of many educated speakers of Standard Igbo. Standard Igbo can be seen as a fusion of aspects of Central Igbo and Onitsha Igbo. In its present form, Standard Igbo cannot be localized in any particular region or area of Igboland (Ikekeonwu 1985).

Consonants

	Bilabial	Labio-dental	Dental	Alveolar	Post-alveolar	Palatal	Velar	Labialized Velar	Glottal	Labial-Velar
Plosive	p b		t d				k g	kʷ gʷ		k͡p g͡b
Nasal	m			n		ɲ	ŋ	ŋʷ		
Fricative		f		s z	ʃ		ɣ		ɦ	
Affricate					tʃ dʒ					
Approx.					ɹ	j				w
Lateral Approx.					l					

p	àpà	àpà	'scar'	ɲ	ɲṹ	nyṹ	'defecate'
b	ụ̀bá	ụ̀bá	'wealth'	ŋ	ŋṹ	ńṹ	'drink'
t	tá	tá	'chew'	ŋʷ	ŋʷṹ	nwṹ	'die'
d	dà	dà	'fall'	f	fé	fé	'fly'
tʃ	tʃá	chá	'ripen'	s	sá	sá	'wash'
dʒ	á⁺dʒá	ájā	'sand'	z	zá	zá	'swell'
k	ká	ká	'older, more'	ʃ	áʃà	áshà	'weaver bird'
g	gá	gá	'go'	ɣ	áɣá	ághá	'war'
kʷ	àkʷà	àkwà	'bed'	ɦ	áɦà	áhà	'name'
gʷ	àgʷà	àgwà	'behaviour'	w	wá	wá	'split'
k͡p	àk͡pà	àkpà	'bag'	ɹ	ɹí	rí	'eat'
g͡b	àg͡bà	àgbà	'fame'	j	jí	yí	'resemble'
m	mṹ	mṹ	'me'	l	lì	lì	'bury'
n	nṹ	nṹ	'hear'				

Vowels

i	ísí	*ísí*	'head'
ị	ị̀bọ̀	*ị̀bọ̀*	'dissect'
ụ	ụ́mụ̀	*ụ́mụ̀*	'children'
u	émù	*émù*	'derision'
o	ékò	*ékò*	'gizzard'
e	ùkó	*ùkó*	'rafter, roof'
ọ	ọ̀mị̀	*ọ̀mị̀*	'marrow'
a	ákụ́	*ákụ́*	'kernel'

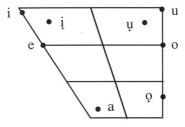

Conventions

Both dental and alveolar plosives [t̪, d̪] and [t, d] are found in the language. The alveolar plosive allophones occur mainly in the environment of /u/ and /ụ/. The voiced post-alveolar approximant /ɹ/ is realized as a flap [ɾ] intervocalically, e.g. *árá* [áɾá] 'madness'.

The labial-velar plosives /k͡p, g͡b/ involve double articulation; the velar and labial closures are made and released simultaneously. The airstream used is pulmonic egressive. However, in some dialects, e.g. Enu-Onitsha Igbo, the voiced bilabial-velar plosive /g͡b/ may be realized as a voiced bilabial implosive [ɓ] and in the Owerri dialect /k͡p/ may be realized as a voiceless bilabial implosive [ɓ̥]. Aspirated and nasalized consonants are not used in Standard Igbo. They are, however, used distinctively in some Igbo dialects, e.g. Ụmụahia and Owerri, within Inland East Igbo (Inland East Igbo incorporates what was known as Central Igbo in earlier writings). A voiced labiodental fricative [v] occurs in some Igbo dialects but not in Standard Igbo; the Ụmụahia dialect has [ɱ́vọ́] for 'fingernail' where Standard Igbo has [m̀bọ́].

There is vowel harmony in Igbo. The eight vowels fall into two sets distinguished by pharyngeal cavity size (Lindau 1975), with 'expanded' vs. 'unexpanded' pharynx. The sets are shown below. Vowels from different sets do not normally co-occur in a word. This distinction is often discussed in terms of an ATR (Advanced Tongue Root) parameter, since fronting the tongue root contributes to pharyngeal expansion. One of the diacritics [˔] or [˕] can be used to distinguish one set of vowels from the other. In this illustration, the unexpanded (-ATR) set are marked, except that since separate letters are used for /e/ and /a/ it is unnecessary to use a diacritic to distinguish this pair. The older tradition of using symbols that suggest the auditory height differences of the vowels, as indicated by their locations on the accompanying vowel chart, can be used as an alternative. The suggested symbols would be:

[+Exp] / [+ATR]		[-Exp] / [-ATR]	
i	u	ɪ	ʊ
e	o	a	ɔ

Two distinctive tones are often recognized in Igbo; in addition, there is a third tone, a downstepped high. The tones may be marked as follows:

['] = high   [`] = low   [ᵛ] = downstep.

In our text illustration, we have left the low tone unmarked. In the orthography, however, the downstep is usually indicated with a macron [⁻] on the affected segment. In the illustration of the passage in the Ọnwụ orthography (the current orthography for Igbo), we have marked all the tones.

There is the tonal phenomenon of downdrift in Igbo: each succeeding high tone is lower than the preceding one, especially when there is an intervening low tone. In a sequence H – L – H, the second high is on a lower pitch than the first. Low tones are also affected by downdrift. This phenomenon, of course, is of no phonemic significance.

Transcription of recorded passage

ikuku ụ́gụụ na á⁺ŋwụ́ naaɹụ́ɹ́tá ụ́⁺kà óɲé ⁺ká íbe já íké mgbe ɦá ɦụɹụ ótu óɲé ídʒe ka ó ji uwé ụ́gụụ já náabịá. ɦá kwekọɹ̣itaɹa na óɲé ⁺buɹu ụ́zọ mèé ka óɲé ídʒe áɦụ jípụ uwé ⁺ja ka á ga éwe dị ka oɲé ka íbe já íké. ikuku ụ́gụụ wéé malíté féé, féé, féé, otu íké ⁺já ɦa; ma ka ọ́ na efé ka óɲé ídʒe áɦụ na edʒidési ⁺úwé ⁺já ⁺íké na afị́ ⁺já. já fékatá ɦápụ. mgbe áɦụ a⁺ŋwú́ wéé tʃápụtá, tʃásí⁺ké mèé ka ebe níí⁺lé kpoɹó ọ́⁺kụ ná⁺átufuɣi óge oɲé ídʒe áɦụ jipụɹụ uwé ⁺já ŋké a meɹe ikuku ụ́gụɹụ kweɹe na a⁺ŋwụ́ ka já íké.

Orthographic version

Ìkùkù ụ́gừrừ nà Ánwū nà-arứŕtá ụ́kà ónyé kā ībè yá íké m̀gbè há hừrừ ótù ónyé íjè kà ó yì ùwé ụ́gừrừ yá nà-àbịá. Há kwèkọ̀ŕtàrà nà ónyé būrū ụ́zọ̀ mèé kà ónyé íjè áhừ yípừ ùwé yā kà á gà-éwè díkà ónyé ka íbè yá íké. Ìkùkù ụ́gừrừ wéé màlíté féé, féé, òtù íké yā hà; mà ka ọ́ nà-èfé kà ónyé íjè áhừ nà-èjídésí ūwē yā īkē nà àhú yā. Yá fékàtá hápừ. M̀gbè áhừ Ánwū wéé chápừtá, chásíkē, méé kà ébé níílē kpòró ọ́kụ̄; ná-àtùfūghì ógè ónyé íjè áhừ yìpừrừ ùwé yā. Ǹké à mèrè ìkùkù ụ́gừrừ kwèrè nà Ánwū kà yá íké.

References

IKEKEONWU, C. I. (1985). Aspects of Igbo dialectology. *Journal of West African Languages* 15, 93–109.

LINDAU, M. (1978). Vowel features. *Language* 54, 541–63.

Irish

AILBHE NÍ CHASAIDE

Centre for Language and Communication Studies, Trinity College, Dublin 2, Ireland

Irish, or Gaeilge, is a Celtic language which is spoken as a mother tongue in certain parts of Ireland, known as Gaeltacht regions. It is closely related to Scottish Gaelic and Manx, and more distantly to Breton, Welsh and Cornish. There are three main dialects of Irish, and although there is a written standard form there is no spoken standard accent. Written records in Gaeilge date back to the eighth century, with a literary tradition continuing in manuscript until the mid-nineteenth century, when published books became commonplace. The spelling system remained relatively unchanged from around the twelfth century until a government-sponsored reform in the mid twentieth century, but even so, orthographic forms can be rather archaic. There is on the whole a poor correspondence of letter to sound, as will be evident from the orthographic version of the text below. This phonetic opacity, however, confers the advantages of morphophonological transparency, and helps the written form bridge divergences between the modern-day dialects, being relatively equidistant from the spoken forms. The description and sample text given here is based on the speech of a native of Na Doirí Beaga, Gaoth Dobhair, one of the Gaeltacht areas in County Donegal, situated in the north west of the country. She is a teacher in her thirties, working in Dublin.

Consonants

Consonant quality: The most striking feature of the consonantal system is the phonological opposition of a series of palatalized and velarized segments. This is accommodated in the table by subdividing the rows and placing the velarized series above the palatalized. Consonants which do not enter into the opposition, such as [h], are placed in the middle of a cell. The palatalized-velarized opposition serves not only for lexical differentiation, but may also express certain grammatical functions, such as case and number marking on nouns, e.g. [ɔl̪ˠ] *ól* 'drink' (nom. sg.) [ɔl̪ʲ] *óil* 'drink' (gen. sg.); [bˠæd̪ˠ], *bád* 'boat' (nom. sg.) [bˠæd̪ʲ] *báid* 'boat' (gen. sg., and in some dialects, nom. plur.). Word internally, consonants in a cluster typically agree in terms of quality. The customary term velarization is used although the secondary articulation may be further back (in the uvular or upper pharyngeal regions) than strictly implied by the term velarization.

The phonetic distinctions between palatalized and velarized pairs of consonants may involve more than secondary palatalization and velarization. In the case of the labial consonants, the velarized segments are additionally labialized. For pairs such as /t̪ʲ, t̪ˠ/, both primary and secondary features are involved. The former is a palatalized laminopostalveolar, which will here be referred to as alveolopalatal, and the latter is a velarized apico-dental with contact extending onto the alveolar ridge. In the case of palatals and velars, for example /c, k/, where the primary place of articulation coincides with the secondary articulation characterizing the phonological series, the realizations are transcribed in terms of primary articulation differences alone.

	Labial	Dental	Alveolar	Alveolo-palatal	Palatal	Velar	Glottal
Plosive	pˠ bˠ pʲ bʲ	t̪ˠ d̪ˠ		t̪ʲ d̪ʲ	c ɟ	k ɡ	
Fricative/ Approximant	fˠ w fʲ vʲ		sˠ	ç	ç j	x ɣ	h
Nasal	mˠ mʲ	n̪ˠ	n	n̪ʲ	ɲ	ŋ	
Tap			ɾˠ ɾʲ				
Lateral Approximant	l̪ˠ		l	l̪ʲ			

pˠ	pˠiɾˠah	*Paorach*	(family name)	pʲ	pʲin̪ʲ	*píghin*	'penny'
bˠ	bˠi	*buí*	'yellow'	bʲ	bʲi	*bí*	'be' (imp)
t̪ˠ	t̪ˠid̪ʲə	*taoide*	'tide'	t̪ʲ	t̪ʲi	*(ar) tí*	'about to'
d̪ˠ	d̪ˠin̪ʲi	*daoine*	'people'	d̪ʲ	d̪ʲi	*dí*	'drink' (gen)
k	kil̪ˠ	*caol*	'thin' (masc)	c	cial̪ˠ	*ciall*	'sense'
ɡ	ɡil̪ˠ	*gaol*	'relative'	ɟ	ɟial̪ˠ	*giall*	'hostage'
fˠ	fˠi	*faoi*	'under'	fʲ	fʲi	*fí*	'weaving'
w	wi	*mhaoigh*	'boasted'	vʲ	vʲi	*bhí*	'was'
sˠ	sˠi	*suí*	'sit'	ç	çi	*'sí*	'she is'
x	xil̪ˠ	*chaol*	'thin' (fem)	ç	çial̪ˠ	*(mo) chiall*	(my) 'sense'
ɣ	ɣil̪ˠ	*(mo) ghaol*	(my) 'relative'	j	jial̪ˠ	*(mo) ghiall*	(my) 'hostage'
h	hil̪ˠ	*(le) haol*	(with) 'lime'				
mˠ	mˠi	*maoigh*	'boast' (imp)	mʲ	mʲi	*mí*	'month'
n̪ˠ	n̪ˠi	*naoi*	'nine'	n̪ʲ	n̪ʲih	*nigh*	'wash' (imp)
	l̪ʲen̪ˠ	*léann*	'education'		l̪ʲen̪ʲ	*léinn*	'education' (gen)
				n	en	*éan*	'bird'
ŋ	ŋil̪ˠ	*(a) ngaol*	(their) 'relative'	ɲ	ɲial̪ˠ	*(a) ngiall*	(their) 'hostage'
l̪ˠ	l̪ˠe	*lae*	'day' (gen)	l̪ʲ	l̪ʲej	*léigh*	'read' (imp)
	ɡal̪ˠ	*Gall*	'foreigner'		kal̪ʲ	*caill*	'lose' (imp)
				l	lej	*leí*	'with her'
					ɡɪl	*(ag) gail*	'boiling'
ɾˠ	mˠæɾˠah	*'márach*	'tomorrow'	ɾʲ	kæɾʲah	*cáireach*	'dirty'

Since both velarization and palatalization are generally indicated, the symbolization in the chart is over-specified, except for palatals and velars (as mentioned above) where primary and secondary features coincide, and /ɕ/ and /w/ where the secondary articulation is also implicit in the symbol. In phonological terms, it would be sufficient to mark only one member of the opposition (traditionally the palatalized one), but this over-specification draws attention to the auditorily striking presence of phonetic velarization in the non-palatalized series. Strong on/off glides are generally found between velarized consonants and adjacent front vowels.

Alveolar laterals and nasals, and glottal fricatives, are a potentially problematic area in this dialect. Here it appears that an earlier opposition of palatalized/velarized segments has been lost, or at least is in the process of being lost. As produced by the present informant, these segments have a rather neutral quality and take their colouring from the adjacent segments. The case of the nasals and laterals is discussed more fully below.

In some phonological treatments, a separate series of voiceless nasals and liquids has been posited. As such sounds occur only in certain grammatical morphemes, they are probably best treated as sequences of nasal (or liquid) plus /h/, an analysis suggested by Sommerfelt (1964).

Plosives: The voiceless series is strongly postaspirated and devoicing of the voiced series is fairly widespread, especially in non-intervocalic contexts. The voiceless series are slightly preaspirated. Nasals and liquids before and after voiceless plosives are devoiced. The alveolopalatal plosives /t̪ʲ, d̪ʲ/ are affricated, as are the palatal plosives /c, ɟ/, though to a lesser degree.

Fricatives: /vʲ, w, j, ɣ/ may be realized as approximants or as fricatives. The fricatives and approximants are grouped together because of their close relationship with their stop congeners. An important morphophonological alternation between word-initial stops and fricatives/approximants in Irish expresses certain grammatical functions such as present vs. past tense, gender marking on adjectives, and case marking in certain noun phrases. In the Gaoth Dobhair dialect, the voiceless velar fricative /x/ tends to occur only in initial position. Where it occurs non-initially in other dialects, Gaoth Dobhair usually has /h/.

Laterals and Nasals: Historically, there was a four-way opposition of laterals and nasals in the dental to alveolopalatal region. This system is widely reported in the dialect literature for Ulster (e.g. Quiggin 1906; Sommerfelt 1922; Ó Searcaigh 1925) and seems to have involved an opposition of palatalized and velarized alveolar segments, contrasting with a velarized dental and a palatalized alveolopalatal segment. However the present-day situation, particularly among the younger generation in Gaoth Dobhair, is that one of the alveolar segments has more or less disappeared, leaving a robust three way contrast, with the possibility for some speakers of a marginal fourth phoneme. The latter was not reliably produced by this informant. In the case of the laterals, the velarized alveolar has tended to merge with the velarized dental /l̪ˠ/ (see Ní Chasaide 1977, 1979). In the case of the nasals, the situation is more fluid: the palatalized alveolar has tended to merge with the palatalized alveolopalatal nasal /n̠ʲ/. In lexical items which have retained the (original) alveolar pronunciation, there does not appear to be a contrast with the (originally) velarized alveolar.

The remaining single alveolar lateral and nasal consonants have a fairly neutral or slightly clear quality, and tend to coarticulate freely with the quality of adjacent segments (see Ní Chasaide 1977). In prepausal position, the alveolar lateral and nasal segments tend to be devoiced, and to clip a preceding short vowel making it over-short. As the alveolar nasal does not occur in initial position, illustrations of the dental, alveolar, and alveolopalatal nasals and laterals in word-final position are included in the consonant word list.

Rhotics: An older four-way distinction among rhotics has been reduced to a two-way distinction in Gaoth Dobhair. Initially, the /rˠ, rʲ/ distinction has been neutralized to a voiced post-alveolar approximant [ɹ], which takes its colouring from the following vowel. In non-initial position, the velarized member can be realized as either [rˠ] or [ɹˠ]. The historical palatalized /rʲ/, which in most other dialects is a palatalized tap or apico-postalveolar fricative, may also appear in Gaoth Dobhair as a voiced palatal fricative [ʝ] in non-initial position. For both palatalized and velarized taps, there is often incomplete closure with considerable frication.

Vowels

Vowels fall into long and short sets, with long vowels (/i, e, æ, ɔ, o, u/) typically shown in the orthography with an acute accent. Since long and short pairs of vowels are qualitatively distinct, the transcription does not mark length explicitly. Long vowels have short allophones in unstressed syllables and before /h/. Schwa occurs only in unstressed position. The close rounded vowel is often realized with only weak lip rounding.

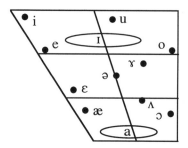 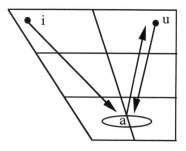

Allophonic realizations: The locations of vowels marked on the charts represent a fairly high degree of abstraction, since consonantal quality exerts major influences on the quality of adjacent vowels. For all vowels, clearly audible on/off glides appear when their frontness or backness conflicts with the secondary articulation of the consonant with which they co-occur. Thus, a velarized consonant preceding a front vowel gives rise to a strong diphthongal glide of velar origin, and conversely, a strong palatal glide is audible between a palatalized consonant and a following back vowel. The wide range of steady state realizations of short /ɪ/ and /a/ are illustrated by large ellipses.

i	bˠilˠah	*baolach*	(to be) 'feared'		ɪ	ɪlə	*uile*	'all'
e	elˠi	*éalaigh*	'escape' (imp)		ɛ	ɛlə	*eile*	'another'
æ	ælˠɪnʲ	*álainn*	'beautiful'		a	alˠah	*eallach*	'cattle'
ɔ	ɔlˠən̪ˠ	*ólann*	(he) 'drinks'		ʌ	ʌlˠə	*ola*	'oil'
o	orˠan	*amhrán*	'song'		ɤ	ɤlˠu	*Uladh*	'Ulster'
u	ulˠi	*úllaí*	'apples'					

ia	ialˠahə	*iallacha*	'laces'
ua	ualˠah	*ualach*	'burden'
au	auwɪn̪ʲ	*Eamhain*	(place)

Suprasegmentals

Primary lexical stress is located on the first syllable of most words. The stress marks in the transcription indicate the syllables accented by the speaker in the reading of the passage. ‖ and | indicate the ends of major and minor intonational phrases respectively.

Transcription of recorded passage

vʲi ən 'ɣi ə'd̪ˠuaj ɪsˠ ən 'jrʲian əɟ 'arˠəgal lə çɛlə lə fˠal ə'mˠah 'caku d̪ˠən 'vʲɛrʲtʲ əbˠə 'çrʲɛçə | n̪ˠərˠə hanɪɟ 't̪ˠact̪ʲalˠˠi ən 'bʲalˠah | əgəsˠ 'kl̪ˠɔkə 't̪ʲeh a xaçu ɛɟə ‖ 'd̪ˠen̪ˠt̪ˠi çəd̪ˠ gərˠ ən d̪ˠɪn̪ʲə bˠə 'çrʲɛçə | ən d̪ˠɪn̪ʲə bˠə 'l̪ˠuaçə ə 'horˠhu ərˠ ən 't̪ˠact̪ʲalˠˠi ə 'xl̪ˠɔkə wˠɪn̪ʲt̪ʲ 'd̪ˠɔ ‖ ɪn'çɪn 'hed̪ʲ ən 'ɣi ə'd̪ˠuaj xɤh 't̪ʲrʲen̪ˠ ɪsˠ ə 'hɤku leçə | ah a 'vʲed̪ʲ ɪsˠ ə 'hed̪ʲ çi | ça bˠə 'l̪ˠuçə ə 'han̪ˠ an 't̪ˠact̪ʲalˠˠi ə 'xl̪ˠɔkə 'harˠt̪ˠ fˠa 'd̪ˠu d̪ˠʌ ‖ əgəsˠ sˠə 'd̪ʲɛrʲu 'd̪ʲirʲi ən 'ɣˠi ə'd̪ˠuaj əsˠ ən 'iarˠarˠt̪ˠ ‖ ən'çɪn 'l̪ˠɤn̪ˠrʲi ən 'jrʲian gə 't̪ʲeh | əgəsˠ wˠɪn̪ʲ ən 't̪ˠact̪ʲalˠˠi 'd̪ˠɔ ə 'xl̪ˠɔkə 'l̪ˠæhrʲah 'bˠɤn̪ˠ ‖ əgəsˠ ərˠ ə 'd̪ˠɔj çɪn | bʲɛɟən d̪ˠən 'ɣi ə'd̪ˠuaj ə 'ad̪ˠwal | gɤrˠəbʲ i n 'jrʲian ə bˠə 'l̪ˠæd̪ʲrʲə d̪ˠən 'vʲɛrʲtʲ ‖

Orthographic version

Bhí an ghaoth aduaidh 's an ghrian ag aragáil le chéile le fáil amach cé acu den bheirt a ba threise nuair a tháinig taistealaí an bealach agus clóca te á chaitheamh aige. D'aontaigh siad gur an duine 'ba threise an duine 'ba luaithe a thabhairfeadh ar an taistealaí a chlóca a bhaint dó. Ansin shéid an ghaoth aduaidh comh tréan is a thiocfadh léithe, ach dá mhéid a shéid sí 'sea ba dhlúithe a theann an taistealaí a chlóca thart fá dtaobh dó, agus sa deireadh d'éirigh an ghaoth aduaidh as an iarracht. Ansin lonnraigh an ghrian go te agus bhain an taistealaí dó a chlóca láithreach bonn. Agus ar a' dóigh sin b'éigean don ghaoth aduaidh a admháil gurbh í 'n ghrian a ba láidre den bheirt.

Acknowledgements

I am very grateful for suggestions and assistance in the preparation of this illustration to Cathair Ó Dochartaigh and Prionnsias Ó Nualláin.

References

NÍ CHASAIDE, A. (1977). *The Laterals of Donegal Irish and Hiberno-English: An Acoustic Study*. M.A. thesis, University of Wales, Bangor.

NÍ CHASAIDE, A. (1979). The laterals of Donegal Irish and Hiberno-English. In Ó Baoill, D. P. (editor), *Papers in Celtic Phonology*. Coleraine: New University of Ulster.

Ó SEARCAIGH, S. (1925). *Foghraidheacht Ghaedhilge an Tuaiscirt*. Béal Feirste (Belfast): Brún & Ó Nualláin.

QUIGGIN, E. C. (1906). *A Dialect of Donegal*. Cambridge University Press.

SOMMERFELT, A. (1922). *The Dialect of Torr, Co. Donegal*. Cristiania (Oslo): Jacob Dybwad.

SOMMERFELT, A. (1964). Consonant clusters or single phonemes in Northern Irish? In Abercrombie, D., Fry, D. B., MacCarthy, P. A. D., Scott, N. C. and Trim, J. L. M. (editors), *In Honour of Daniel Jones: Papers Contributed on the Occasion of his Eightieth Birthday 12 September 1961*, 368–73. London: Longmans.

Japanese

HIDEO OKADA

6-29-22 Sakuradai, Nerima-ku, Tokyo 176-0002, Japan

The style of speech illustrated is that of many educated Japanese brought up in Tokyo or other areas with similar pitch accent systems. The transcription is based on a recording of a 25-year-old student whose speech is typical of speakers of his age group with this background.

Consonants

	Bilabial	Labio-dental	Dental	Alveolar	Post-alveolar	Palatal	Velar	Uvular	Glottal
Plosive	p b		t d				k ɡ		
Affricate				tˢ					
Nasal	m		n					N	
Flap					ɾ				
Fricative				s z					h
Approximant						j	w		

p	páN	'bread'	t	táijoː	'the sun'
b	báN	'(one's) turn'	d	daNdaN	'gradually'
			tˢ	tˢuːtˢi	'notice'
m	mázu	'first'	n	náni	'what'
			ɾ	ɾáN	'orchid'
			s	suːsi	'numeral'
			z	zátˢuzi	'chores'
			j	jamá	'mountain'
				mjakú	'pulse'

k	kaze	'wind'
ɡ	gaitoː	'cloak, overcoat'
	íɡaku	'medicine'
N	zéNi	'goodwill'
	(See also /b, p, d, ɾ/.)	
h	hana	'nose'
w	wa	(particle)

Vowels

i	ími	'meaning'
e	éme	'smile!' (archaic imperative)
a	áma	'woman diver (for abalone)'
o	ómo	'(sur)face' (archaic)
u	úmu	'suppurate'

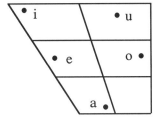

Vowel length

ozisántatˢi	'uncles'	oziːsántatˢi	'grandfathers'
hodo	'degree, extent'	hodoː	'sidewalk'

Pitch accent

hási	'chopsticks'	hási o nuɾu	'paint chopsticks'
hasí	'bridge'	hasí o nuɾu	'paint a bridge'
hasi	'end'	hasi o nuɾu	'paint the end'

Conventions

/p, t, tˢ, k/ are only moderately aspirated. Syllable-final (moraic) forms of these and other voiceless obstruents occur as the first part of geminates, e.g. /happoː/ 'firing', /jatto/ 'at last', /gakkoː/ 'school', /hossa/ 'attack (of disease)'. The geminate form of /tˢ/ is /ttˢ/, as in /kuttˢukemásita/ 'pressed, attached'. /b/ is normally [b], but in rapid speech it may become [v̞] or [β]. /g/ tends to become [ɣ] between vowels. Older and otherwise conservative speakers use [ŋ] in all medial positions, except mainly for the element /góↄ/ 'five' in number designations, as e.g. /nízjuː-góↄ/ [ɲízuːgóↄ] 'twenty-five'. /ɾ/, which corresponds to 'r' in Romanization, is postalveolar in place rather than retroflex and mainly occurs medially. Initially and after /N/, it is typically an affricate with short friction, [d̠ɺ̈]. A postalveolar [l̠] is not unusual in all positions. Approximant [ɹ] may occasionally occur in some environments. /tˢ/ is normally [ts] but becomes [tɕ] before /i/. /n/ before /i/ is prepalatal [ɲ]. Before /u/, it may be alveolar with some speakers. Consonants generally are strongly palatalized before /i/, as /mi/ [mʲi] 'body'. /N/ represents a moraic nasal with very variable pronunciation. Word-finally before a pause, it is typically a uvular nasal with a loose tongue contact or a close to close-mid nasalized vowel. Such a nasalized vowel is also the normal realization before a vowel or approximant, or before /h/ or /s/, as e.g. /zéNi/ [ᵈzéĩi] 'goodwill', /hoNjaku/ [hoĩjaku] 'translation', /zeNhaN/ [ᵈzeɣ̃haN] 'first half'. Before other consonants, it is homorganic with that following consonant, as e.g. /síNpo/ [ɕímpo] 'progress', /síNni/ [ɕíɲɲi] 'truly', /síNɾi/ [ɕíɲd̠ɺ̈i] 'truth'. /s/ and /z/ are [ɕ] and [ʑ] before /i/. /z/ tends to be [ᵈz] initially ([ᵈʑ] before /i/) and after /N/. /h/ tends towards [ç] and [ɸ] before /i/ and /u/ respectively. /hh/ is realized as [çç], [xx] or [ɸɸ] depending on the (normally identical) surrounding vowels. /j/ affects the preceding consonant as /i/ does, and is itself absorbed, thus: /mjakú/ [mʲakú] 'pulse', /tˢja/ [tɕa] 'tea', /sjóↄ/ [ɕóↄ] 'prize', /kanjuː/ [kaɲuː] 'joining'. /w/ has very slight or no rounding (except after /o/), but involves no spreading either.

/u/, resembling [ɯ] auditorily, has compressed lips, so that it is unrounded but without spreading; it could be transcribed narrowly as [ü̜] or [ɯ̈]. The slit between the lips may be very narrow vertically and is generally much shorter in the horizontal plane than for [i]. A very advanced variety in the [i] area may occur among the younger age groups. Except in accented or lengthened syllables, /i, u/ tend to be devoiced [i̥, u̥] between voiceless consonants. As often as not, preceding fricatives replace them altogether. Final unaccented /su/ is very often reduced to [s].

There are two lexically relevant pitch levels: high and low. Within a word, if the first mora is high-pitched, the second is inevitably low-pitched, and vice versa. A mora transcribed with an acute accent, á, is said to be accented and is high. If more than one mora precedes it, the high pitch extends towards the beginning of the word up to the second mora. A word with no accent mark begins low and continues high from the second mora onwards. All moras following the accent are low until another accented or polysyllabic word is reached, when these accentuation rules reapply. Note that word pairs such as /hasí/ 'bridge' and /hasi/ 'end' are both low-high when spoken in isolation, but will be distinguished when something else follows. What follows will be low after the accent, but otherwise high. When a long (two-mora) vowel is transcribed with an accent, only the first mora is high, and a pitch drop occurs between the two moras.

Transcription of recorded passage

áɽutoki kitakaze to táijoː ga tˢikaɽakúɽabe o simásita. tabibito no gaitoː o nugáseta hóː ga katˢí to juː kotó ni kimete, mázu, kitakaze kaɽa hazimemásita. kitakaze wa, náni, hitomákuɽi ni site misejóː, to, hagésiku hukitatemásita. suɽuto tabibito wa, kitakaze ga hukéba hukúhodo gaitoː o sikkáɽito kaɽada ni kuttˢukemásita. kóɴdo wa táijoː no báɴ ni naɽimásita. táijoː wa kúmo no aida kaɽa jasasii kao o dásite, atatákana hikaɽí o okuɽimásita. tabibito wa daɴdaɴ jói kokoɽomotˢi ni nátte, simai nî wa gaitoː o nugimásita. sokode kitakaze no make ni naɽimásita.

Romanization (Hepburn system)

Arutoki Kitakaze to Taiyō ga chikara-kurabe o shimashita. Tabibito no gaitō o nugaseta hō ga kachi to yū koto ni kimete, mazu Kitakaze kara hajimemashita. Kitakaze wa, 'Nani, hitomakuri ni shite miseyō', to, hageshiku fukitatemashita. Suruto tabibito wa, Kitakaze ga fukeba fukuhodo gaitō o shikkarito karada ni kuttsukemashita. Kondo wa Taiyō no ban ni narimashita. Taiyō wa kumo no aida kara yasashii kao o dashite, atatakana hikari o okurimashita. Tabibito wa dandan yoi kokoromochi ni natte, shimai ni wa gaitō o nugimashita. Sokode Kitakaze no make ni narimashita.

Orthographic version

ある時、北風と太陽が力くらべをしました。旅人の外套を脱がせた方が勝ちとい うことに決めて、まず北風から始めました。北風は、『なに、一まくりにして見せ よう』と、激しく吹き立てました。すると旅人は、北風が吹けば吹くほど外套を しっかりと体にくっつけました。今度は太陽の番になりました。太陽は雲のあい だから優しい顔を出して暖かな光を送りました。旅人は段々よい心もちになって、 しまいには外套を脱ぎました。そこで北風の負けになりました。

Korean

HYUN BOK LEE

Phonetics Laboratory, Department of Linguistics, Seoul National University,
Seoul 151–742, Korea

The variety of Korean spoken in and around Seoul, on which the following phonetic description is based, is widely recognized as the standard language of the Korean peninsula. It differs from the speech of Pyongyang in North Korea, however, in phonetic features such as vowel and consonant qualities, vowel length, accent, rhythm and intonation.

Consonants

	Bilabial	Labio-dental	Dental	Alveolar	Post-alveolar	Palatal	Velar	Glottal
Plosive	p pʰ b			t tʰ d			k kʰ g	
Nasal	m			n			ŋ	
Fricative				s z				h
Affricate					c cʰ ɟ			
Lateral Approximant				l				

p	pal	'sucking'	t	tal	'daughter'	k	kal	'spreading'
pʰ	pʰal	'arm'	tʰ	tʰal	'riding'	kʰ	kʰal	'knife'
b	bal	'foot'	d	dal	'moon'	g	gal	'going'
m	mal	'horse'	n	nal	'day'	ŋ	baŋ	'room'
			s	sal	'rice'	h	hal	'doing'
			z	zal	'flesh'			
			c	cal	'squeezing'			
			cʰ	cʰal	'kicking'			
			ɟ	ɟal	'well'			
			l	balam	'wind'			

Vowels

a) Monophthongs

Korean can be considered as having nine vowel qualities, which occur distinctively long or short. The vowel /ø(ː)/ is usually pronounced as [we] in Seoul speech although there are also words with /we/ not derived from /ø/. In view of the overwhelming tendency of Seoul speakers to pronounce a diphthong instead of /ø/, it may be more appropriate to postulate a system of only eight vowel qualities in modern standard Korean. Vowel qualities are affected to a great extent by vowel quantity. Long vowels are pronounced with a more peripheral quality than the corresponding short ones, which are centralized or lowered. Long and short /ʌ(ː)/ show the greatest quality difference: short /ʌ/ is a mid-open back unrounded vowel but long /ʌː/ is realized as a central vowel [əː].

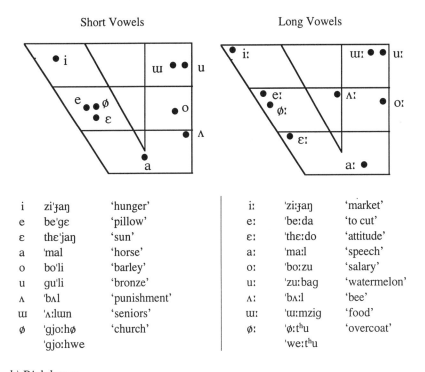

Short Vowels   Long Vowels

i	ziˈʝaŋ	'hunger'	iː	ˈziːʝaŋ	'market'
e	beˈgɛ	'pillow'	eː	ˈbeːda	'to cut'
ɛ	theˈjaŋ	'sun'	ɛː	ˈtheːdo	'attitude'
a	ˈmal	'horse'	aː	ˈmaːl	'speech'
o	boˈli	'barley'	oː	ˈboːzu	'salary'
u	guˈli	'bronze'	uː	ˈzuːbag	'watermelon'
ʌ	ˈbʌl	'punishment'	ʌː	ˈbʌːl	'bee'
ɯ	ˈʌːlɯn	'seniors'	ɯː	ˈɯːmzig	'food'
ø	ˈgjoːhø	'church'	øː	ˈøːtʰu	'overcoat'
	ˈgjoːhwe			ˈweːtʰu	

b) Diphthongs

/ j, w/ are considered to be components of diphthongs rather than separate consonants.

			/wi /	dwi	'back'	/ɰi /	ˈɰiza	'doctor'
/je/	ˈjeːzan	'budget'	/we/	gwe	'box'			
/jɛ/	ˈjeːgi	'story'	/wɛ/	wɛ	'why'			
/ja/	ˈjaːgu	'baseball'	/wa/	gwaːˈil	'fruits'			

/jo/	'gjoːza	'teacher'				
/ju/	ju'li	'glass'				
/jʌ/	jʌ'gi	'here'		/wʌ/	mwʌ	'what'

Stress

Stress placement is predictable in Korean. In words of more than one syllable it is initial when the first syllable is a heavy syllable, i.e. one which either contains a long vowel or has a syllable-final consonant because of the presence of an intervocalic consonant sequence. All other words of more than one syllable are accented on the second syllable. An accented syllable is longer and louder than an unaccented one.

1) Words with accent on the first syllable:

a) long vowel in the first syllable:

/ˈgaːɟaŋ/ 'disguise', /ˈzʌːli/ 'acting head'

b) closed first syllable:

/ˈzanzu/ 'landscape', /ˈcʰulgu/ 'exit'

c) long vowel and closed first syllable:

/ˈzaːnzu/ 'arithmetic', /ˈgaːmza/ 'thanks'

2) Words with accent on the second syllable:

/gaˈɟaŋ/ 'most', /zʌˈli/ 'frost', /zaˈdali/ 'ladder'

Conventions

/b, d, g/ are voiceless unaspirated (or slightly aspirated) lenis plosives [b̥, d̥, g̊] syllable-initially, but are regularly realized as voiced sounds in intervocalic position. /ɟ/ shows the same voicing variation. /z/ is a lenis voiceless alveolar fricative. It is sometimes realized as voiced [z] intervocalically, especially when preceded by a nasal as in /gaːmza/ 'thanks' and /inza/ 'greetings' spoken in an informal style. /p, t, k, c, s/ are voiceless unaspirated fortis sounds syllable-initially, produced with a partially constricted glottis and additional subglottal pressure. /pʰ tʰ, kʰ, cʰ/ are strongly aspirated voiceless sounds syllable-initially.

In syllable-final position /b, p, pʰ/ are realized as a voiceless bilabial stop without plosion, [p˺], /d, t, tʰ, ɟ, c, cʰ/ are realized as a voiceless alveolar stop without plosion, [t˺], and /g, k, kʰ/ are realized as a voiceless velar stop without plosion, [k˺]. The four sonorants /m, n, ŋ, l/ are the only other consonants which can occur syllable-finally.

/ɟ, c, cʰ/ are voiceless postalveolar affricates syllable-initially. /z/ and /s/ are realized as alveolopalatal fricatives [cʰ], [ç] when followed by /i/ or a diphthong beginning with [j]. /h/ is [ç] before /i/ and [j], [x] before /ɯ/, [ɦ] between voiced sounds and [h] elsewhere. /n/ is [ɲ] before /i/ and [j], and [n] elsewhere. /l/ is [ɾ] intervocalically, but [l] or [ɭ] syllable-finally, and [ʎ] before /i/ or [j]; /ll/ is [ll] or [lʎ], according to the vowel context.

Broad transcription of recorded passage

baˈlamgwa ˈhɛnnimi zʌˈlo hiˈmi ˈdʌ ˈzeːdago daˈtʰugo iˈsɯl tɛ, ˈhan naˈgɯnega taˈtɯtʰan ˈweːtʰulɯl ˈibgo ˈgʌːlʌ waˈsɯmnida. gɯˈdɯlɯn nuˈgudɯnɟi naˈgɯnewi ˈweːtʰulɯl ˈmʌnɟʌ ˈbʌdginɯn niga hiˈmi ˈdʌ ˈzeːdago haˈgilo ˈgjʌlɟʌŋhɛsɯmnida. bugpʰuŋɯn ˈhimkʌd buˈlʌsɯna ˈbuːlmjʌn ˈbuːlsulog naˈgɯnenɯn ˈweːtʰulɯl ˈdandanhi jʌˈmjʌsɯmnida. gɯ ˈtɛe ˈhɛnnimi tɯˈgʌun ˈhɛdbicʰɯl gaˈmanhi nɛˈljʌ ˈcweːni naˈgɯnenɯn ˈweːtʰulɯl ˈʌllɯn bʌˈzʌsɯmnida. iˈlihajʌ ˈbugpʰuŋɯn ˈhɛnnimi ˈduːlɟuŋe hiˈmi ˈdʌ ˈzeːdago ˈinɟʌŋhaji aˈnɯl zu ˈʌːbzʌsɯmnida.

Narrow transcription of recorded passage

b̥aˈramgwa ˈhɛnɲimi z̥ʌˈro çiˈmi ˈdʌ ˈz̥eːdago d̥aˈtʰugo iˈsɯl̥ tɛ, ˈhan naˈgɯnega taˈtɯtʰan ˈweːtʰurɯl̥ ˈib̥ko ˈg̊əːrʌ waˈsɯmɲida. g̊ɯˈdɯrɯn nuˈgudɯnɟi naˈgɯnewi ˈweːtʰurɯl̥ ˈmʌnɟʌ ˈb̥ʌd̥kinɯn ɲiga çiˈmi ˈdʌ ˈz̥eːdago haˈgiɾo ˈg̊jʌl̥cʌŋhɛsɯmɲida. b̥ug̊pʰuŋɯn ˈçimkʌd̥ b̥uˈrʌsɯna ˈb̥uːl̥mjʌn ˈb̥uːl̥suɾog̊ naˈgɯnɛnɯn ˈweːtʰurɯl̥ ˈd̥andanfi jʌˈmjʌsɯmɲida. g̊ɯ ˈtɛe ˈhɛnɲimi tɯˈgʌun hɛd̥ˈpicʰɯl̥ g̊aˈmanfi nɛˈrjʌ ˈcweːɲi naˈgɯnenɯn ˈweːtʰurɯl̥ ˈʌl̥lɯn b̥ʌˈzʌsɯmɲida. iˈrihajʌ ˈb̥ug̊phuŋɯn ˈhɛnɲimi ˈd̥uːl̥cuŋe çiˈmi ˈdʌ ˈz̥eːdago ˈinɟʌŋhaɟi aˈnɯl̥ su ˈəːb̥sʌsɯmɲida.

Orthographic version

바람과 햇님이 서로 힘이 더 세다고 다투고 있을 때, 한 나그네가 따뜻한 외투를 입고 걸어 왔습니다. 그들은 누구든지 나그네의 외투를 먼저 벗기는 이가 힘이 더 세다고 하기로 결정했습니다. 북풍은 힘껏 불었으나 불면 불수록 나그네는 외투를 단단히 여몄습니다. 그 때에 햇님이 뜨거운 햇빛을 가만히 내려쬐니, 나그네는 외투를 얼른 벗었습니다. 이리하여 북풍은 햇님이 둘중에 힘이 더 세다고 인정하지 않을 수 없었습니다.

Korean phonetic transcription

ㅂㅏㄹㅏㅁㄱㅘ ㅎㅐㄴㄴㅣㅁㅣ ㅅㅓㄹㅗ ㅎㅣㅁㅣ ㄷㅓ ㅅㅔːㄷㅏㄱㅗ ㄷㅏㅌㅜㄱㅗ ㅣㅆㅜㄹ ㄸㅐ. ㅎㅏㄴ ㄴㅏㄱㅜㄴㅔㄱㅏ ㄸㅏㄸㅜㅌㅏㄴ ㄷㅔːㅌㅜㄹㅜㅂ ㅣㅂㄲㅗ ㄱㅓː ㄹㅓㄷㅏㅆㅜㅁㄴㅣㄷㅏ. ㄱㅜㄷㅜㄹㅜㄴ ㄴㅜㄱㅜㄷㅜㄴㅈㅣ ㄴㅏㄱㅜㄴㅔㅜㅣ ㄷㅔːㅌㅜㄹㅜㅂ ㅁㅓㄴㅈㅓ ㅂㅓㄷㄲㅣㄴㅜㄴ ㄴㅣㄱㅏ ㅎㅣㅁㅣ ㄷㅓ ㅅㅔːㄷㅏㄱㅗ ㅎㅏㄱㅣ ㄹㅗ ㄱㄴㅓㄹㅉㅓㅇㅎㅐㅆㅜㅁㄴ ㅣㄷㅏ. ㅂㅜㄱㅍㅜㅇㅜㄴ ㅎㅣㅁㄲㅓㄷ ㅂㅜㄹㅓㅆㅜㄴㅏ ㅂㅜː ㄹㅁㅕㄴ ㅂㅜː ㄹㅆㅜㄹㅗㄱ ㄴㅏㄱㅜㄴㅔㄴㅜㄴ ㄷㅔːㅌㅜㄹㅜㅂ ㄷㅏㄴㄷㅏㄴㅎㅣ ㄴㅕㅁㅕㅆㅜㅁㄴㅣㄷㅏ. ㄱㅜㄸㅐㅇㅔ ㅎㅐㄴㄴㅣㅁㅣ ㄸㅜㄱㅓㄴ ㅎㅐㄷㅃㅣㅊㅜㅂ ㄱㅏㅁㅏː ㄴㅎㅣ ㄴㅐㄹㅕㄴㅕ ㅉㅜㄷㅔːㄴ ㅣ, ㄴㅏ ㄱㅜㄴㅔㄴㅜㄴ ㄷㅔːㅌㅜㄹㅜㅂ ㅓㄹㄹㅜㄴ ㅂㅓㅅㅓㅆㅜㅁㄴㅣㄷㅏ. ㅣㄹㅣㅎㅏㄴㅓ ㅂㅜㄱㅍ ㅜㅇㅜㄴ ㅎㅐㄴㄴㅣㅁㅣ ㄷㅜː ㄹ ㅉㅜㅇㅔ ㅎㅣㅁㅣ ㄷㅓ ㅅㅔːㄷㅏㄱㅗ ㅣㄴㅈㅓㅇㅎㅏㅈㅣ ㅏ ㄴㅜㅂ ㅆㅜ ㄲㅓː ㅂㅆㅓㅆㅜㅁㄴㅣㄷㅏ.

Persian (Farsi)

MOHAMMAD-REZA MAJIDI AND ELMAR TERNES

*Institut für Phonetik, Allgemeine Sprachwissenschaft und Indogermanistik, Universität Hamburg,
Bogenallee 11, D-20144 Hamburg, Germany*

The style of speech illustrated is that of many educated Persian speakers in the area of Tehran. It is based on a recording of a 45-year-old male speaker.

Consonants

	Bilabial	Labiodent.	Dental	Postalv.	Palatal	Velar	Glottal
Plosive	p b		t d			k g	ʔ
Nasal	m		n				
Fricative		f v	s z	ʃ ʒ		x ɣ	h
Affricate				tʃ dʒ			
Trill			r				
Approximant					j		
Lateral Approximant			l				

p	pær	'feather'	t	tir	'arrow'	k	kur	'blind'
b	bær	'fruit'	d	dir	'late'	g	gur	'grave'
m	nɒm	'name'	n	nɒn	'bread'	x	xæm	'bend'
f	nɒf	'navel'	s	sir	'garlic'	ɣ	ɣæm	'sorrow'
v	nɒv	'warship'	z	zir	'below'	ʔ	tæʔsir	'impression'
r	siri	'satiety'	ʃ	ʃɒʃ	'urine'	h	kuh	'mountain'
l	sili	'slap'	ʒ	ʒɒʒ	'idle talk'	j	jek	'one'
			tʃ	tʃire	'victorious'			
			dʒ	dʒire	'ration'			

Vowels

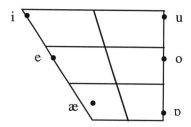

i	dir	'late'
e	del	'heart'
æ	dær	'door'
ɒ	dɒr	'gallows'
o	por	'full'
u	dur	'far'

Stress

Stress is distinctive:

	['mærdi]	mærdi	'a man'
	[mær'di]	mærdi	'manhood'

Conventions

/p, t, k/ are strongly aspirated in word-initial position, in other positions slightly aspirated. /b, d, g/ and /v, z, ʒ, ɣ/ are slightly devoiced in word-final position. /ɣ/ is [ɢ] in word-initial position, after nasals, and when geminated; otherwise it is postvelar [ɣ]. /m, n/ are voiceless in word-final position after a voiceless consonant. /m/ is [ɱ] before /f, v/ and /n/ is [ŋ] before /k, g/, and [ŋ̱] before /ɣ/. /r/ varies between [r] and [ɹ]. /v/ is [w] after /o/, otherwise it is [v].

Vowel length is not distinctive, but all vowels are rather long in stressed position. /i, ɒ, u/ are, in general, somewhat longer than /e, æ, o/. /e, æ, o/ are long or half-long before consonant clusters. Before or after nasal consonants, vowels are nasalized. Word-initial vowels are preceded by [ʔ], vowels in hiatus are separated by [ʔ]. /ɒ/ is underrounded. Articulatory positions of the other vowels are as on the chart.

Transcription of recorded passage

'jek 'ruzi 'bɒde ʃo'mɒl bɒ xor'ʃid bɒhæm dæʔ'vɒ 'mikærdænd, ke 'ɒjɒ ko'dɒmjeki ɣævi'tæræst. dær 'ɒn 'hin mosɒ'feri re'sid, ke læbbɒ'deje ko'lofti be 'dovre 'xodeʃ pitʃi'de bud. ɒn'hɒ ɣæ'rɒr 'gozɒʃtænd, 'hærko'dɒmeʃɒn, ke 'ævvæl 'betævɒnæd mosɒ'ferrɒ mædʒ'bur konæd læbbɒ'deæʃrɒ 'bekænæd, mæʔ'lum 'miʃævæd, ke 'zuræʃ biʃ'tæræst. 'bɒde ʃo'mɒl tɒ tævɒnest væ'zid, 'æmmɒ 'hærtʃe biʃ'tær væ'zid, mosɒ'fer læbbɒ'deæʃrɒ biʃ'tær 'dovre 'xodeʃ 'dʒæm? kærd. ɒɣe'bæt 'bɒde ʃo'mɒl xæs'te ʃod væ 'dæst 'bærdɒʃt. 'bæʔd xor'ʃid tɒ'bid, væ hæ'vɒ in'ɣædr 'gærm ʃod ke fov'ri mosɒ'fer læbbɒ'deæʃrɒ 'dærɒværd. pæs 'bɒde ʃo'mɒl mædʒ'bur ʃod eɣ'rɒr konæd ke xor'ʃid 'zuræʃ biʃ'tæræst.

Orthographic version

يك روزى باد شمال با خورشيد با هم دعوا مى‌كردند كه آيا كدام يكى قوى‌تر است. در آن حين مسافرى رسيد، كه لبّادهٔ كلفتى به دور خودش پيچيده بود. آنها قرار گذاشتند، هركدامشان كه اوّل بتواند مسافر را مجبور كند لبّاده‌اش را بكند، معلوم مى‌شود كه زورش بيشتر است. باد شمال تا توانست وزيد. امّا هرچه بيشتر وزيد، مسافر لبّاده‌اش را بيشتر دور خودش جمع كرد. عاقبت باد شمال خسته شد و دست برداشت. بعد خورشيد تابيد، و هوا اينقدر گرم شد كه فورى مسافر لبّاده‌اش را در آورد. پس باد شمال مجبور شد اقرار كند كه خورشيد زورش بيشتر است.

Portuguese (European)

MADALENA CRUZ-FERREIRA

Department of English Language and Literature, National University of Singapore,
10 Kent Ridge Crescent, Singapore 119260

The following illustration of European Portuguese is based on the Lisbon dialect. The text is transcribed from a recording made by a female native speaker of Lisbon in her mid-forties, speaking in a style that may be described as educated colloquial. All phonemes of European Portuguese are illustrated in the passage unless otherwise noted.

European Portuguese comprises several regional accents, including those of the archipelagos of Madeira and the Azores. The Lisbon accent is one of the two national standard varieties in mainland Portugal, the second being that spoken in the area of the city of Coimbra.

The language is characterized by a velarized resonance superimposed on both vowels and consonants, in that the usual posture of the tongue body is retracted and raised. In addition, an overall rather lax articulation further affects vowel quality and voicing, as well as the articulation and voicing of voiced consonants. These features are not, it should be pointed out, exclusive to informal or careless speech and, together with specific prosodic patterns, they constitute the most striking characteristic distinguishing European from Brazilian accents of Portuguese.

Consonants

	Bilabial	Labio-dental	Dental	Alveolar	Palato-alveolar	Palatal	Velar	Uvular
Plosive	p b		t d				k ɡ	
Nasal	m		n			ɲ		
Fricative		f v		s z	ʃ ʒ			ʁ
Tap				ɾ				
Lateral Approximant			l			ʎ		

p ˈpatu *pato* 'duck' (m)	t ˈtatu *tacto* 'tact'	k ˈkatu *cacto* 'cactus'
b ˈbatu *bato* 'I strike'	d ˈdatu *dato* 'I date'	ɡ ˈɡatu *gato* 'cat' (m)
m ˈmatu *mato* 'I kill'	n ˈnatu *nato* 'innate' (m)	ɲ ˈpiɲɐ *pinha* 'pine cone'
f ˈfatu *fato* 'costume'	s ˈkasu *caço* 'I hunt'	ʃ ˈʃatu *chato* 'flat' (m)
v ˈviɲɐ *vinha* 'vine'	z ˈkazu *caso* 'I marry'	ʒ ˈʒatu *jacto* 'jet'

ɾ	'piɾɐ	*pira*	'pyre'		ʁ	'ʁatu	*rato*	'mouse' (m)
l	'liɲɐ	*linha*	'line'		ʎ	'piʎɐ	*pilha*	'battery'

Vowels

European Portuguese has 14 monophthongs, 9 oral and 5 nasalized. These vowels are usually described using four values for height and three for backness. Their positions are shown on the chart below according to the values widely agreed on in the literature, with the exception of the vowel /ɯ/. This vowel, which occurs only in unstressed syllables, is often represented as /ə/ but does not correspond to the mid central quality associated with *schwa*. It is a fronted and lowered high back unrounded vowel; hence the symbol chosen here for its transcription. The chart represents target articulations of the vowels, which are normally 'undershot' in connected speech, resulting in more centralized qualities.

Oral vowels

i	vi	*vi*	'saw' (1 sg)
e	ve	*vê*	'see' (3 sg)
ɛ	sɛ	*sé*	'cathedral'
a	va	*vá*	'go' (3 sg)
ɔ	sɔ	*só*	'alone'
o	so	*sou*	'I am'
u	'mudu	*mudo*	'mute' (m)
ɐ	pɐ'gaɾ	*pagar*	'to pay'
ɯ	pɯ'gaɾ	*pegar*	'to grip'

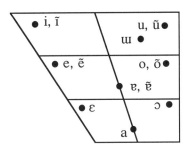

Nasalized vowels

ĩ	vĩ	*vim*	'came' (1 sg)
ẽ	'ẽtɾu	*entro*	'enter' (1 sg)
ɐ̃	'ɐ̃tɾu	*antro*	'den'
õ	sõ	*som*	'sound' (n)
ũ	'mũdu	*mundo*	'world'

Diphthongs

There are 14 diphthongs, 10 oral and 4 nasalized, as shown below. The diphthongs /ɛi, ɔi, ui, ɛu/ do not occur in the transcribed passage.

ɛi	ɐ'nɛiʃ	*anéis*	'rings' (n)
ai	sai	*sai*	'go out' (3 sg)
ɐi	sɐi	*sei*	'know' (1 sg)
ɔi	mɔi	*mói*	'grind' (3 sg)
oi	'moitɐ	*moita*	'thicket'

ui	ɐ'nuiʃ	*anuis*	'agree' (2 sg)
iu	viu	*viu*	'saw' (3 sg)
eu	meu	*meu*	'mine' (poss m)
ɛu	vɛu	*véu*	'veil'
au	mau	*mau*	'bad' (m sg)
ɐ̃i	sɐ̃i	*cem*	'hundred'
õi	ɐ'nõiʃ	*anões*	'dwarves' (m)
ũi	'mũitɐ	*muita*	'much, many' (f)
ɐ̃u	mɐ̃u	*mão*	'hand' (n)

Conventions

Except in word-initial position (and after nasalized vowels), the voiced plosives /b, d, g/ are normally pronounced as the fricatives [β, ð, ɣ]. /ʃ, ʒ/ are weakly fricated in syllable-final position. Syllable-final /ʃ/ occurs as [ʒ] before a voiced consonant (except before /ʒ/ itself, where it is deleted), and as [z] before a syllable-initial vowel both within and across word boundaries, as in [ku̯al duʒ doiz 'ɛɾɔ] *qual dos dois era o* 'which of the two (m) was the (m)' in the transcribed passage. /l/ is velarized in all its occurrences.

/ɾ/ does not occur in word-initial position, and /ɲ, ʎ/ only occur initially in a few borrowed words, and in the case of /ʎ/ also in the clitic pronoun /ʎɯ/ *lhe* 'to him/her/it' and all the forms in its paradigm.

All vowels have lower and more retracted allophones before /l/, and higher and more advanced allophones before alveolar, palato-alveolar or palatal consonants. /ɯ/ and unstressed /ɐ, u/ are voiceless in word-final position.

The end-points of the diphthongs, although transcribed [i] and [u], tend to be more central and, in the case of [u], less strongly rounded than these symbols suggest. The diphthong /ɐi/ in the Lisbon accent is tending towards a retracted onset [ɐ̠i̯] or [ʌi̯]. In some words the offglide has been altogether lost, as in the pronunciation of the word /'pɐiʃɯ/ *peixe* 'fish (n)' as [pɐʃ].

In a vowel sequence in which the first vowel is an unstressed /i/ or /u/ and the second a stressed vowel, the first vowel may lose it syllabicity, e.g. /ʁi'al/ *real* 'real' can be pronounced as a monosyllable, [ʁi̯al], and /mu'idɐ/ *moída* 'ground' (adj, f) as ['mu̯idɐ].

Prosody

Lexical stress

Lexical stress is distinctive. Stress provides very productive class-changing contrasts, such as those between nouns and verbs in pairs like ['duvidɐ] *dúvida* 'doubt (n), [du'vidɐ] *duvida* 'doubt (v, 3 sg)'. Less frequently, words in the same class contrast in stress, e.g. the nouns ['tunɛl] *túnel* 'tunnel', [tu'nɛl] *tonel* 'wine cask'.

Most Portuguese words are stressed on the penultimate syllable, although lexical stress may fall on any of the last three syllables of the word, and even on the fourth from last in the case of verbal forms with enclitic personal pronouns such as [ʃɐˈmavɐmuʃtɯ], *chamávamos-te* 'we called you (sg)', [ɐkɐˈbavɐsɯʎtɯ] *acabava-se-lhe* 'he/she/it ran out of'. Syllables with diphthongs not bearing primary stress are assigned a secondary stress, e.g. [ˌauˈtẽtiku] *autêntico* 'authentic (m sg)'.

Rhythm, vowel reduction and devoicing
European Portuguese is a stress-timed language with vowel reduction in unstressed syllables. In connected speech, unstressed vowels are either centralized or altogether omitted, and consonants and vowels in unstressed positions may be devoiced (Mateus 1975; Willis 1971). Examples in the transcribed passage include /ẽˈvoltu/, phonetically [ũ̩ˈvolt], *envolto* 'wrapped (m)' and /dɯziʃˈtiu/ [d̥z̥ʃtiu] *desistiu* 'gave up' (3 sg), where a potentially trisyllabic word is reduced to a monosyllable with a complex onset.

Intonation
Portuguese intonation can be analyzed as a set of nuclear tones associated with phrase-length intonation groups. The nuclear tones fall on a stressed syllable, typically the last stressed syllable in the intonation group. If the nuclear syllable is not the last syllable in the group, the nuclear pitch movement continues on any following weak syllables. Normally, such weak syllables are only pronounced when required for completion of an intonational pattern.

    There are six main nuclear tones in Portuguese, three falling, two rising, and a rise-fall. They are transcribed here with 'tone letters' placed before the nuclear syllable. The low fall (ˎ) is the neutral tone for statements and question-word questions; a high fall (ˋ) is generally associated with emphasis; an extra-low fall is used in exclamations and commands. The low rise (ˏ) is the typical tone for yes/no questions, and marks continuation or incompleteness in discourse. The high rise (ˊ) is associated with echo questions or with questions requiring repetition of a previous utterance. The rise-fall (ˆ) typically marks implication and reserve. Only the low fall and low rise occur in the transcribed passage. Cruz-Ferreira (1998) provides a more comprehensive outline of the prosodic system.

Transcription of recorded passage
The transcription provided below is narrow in certain respects, and includes the representation of sandhi phenomena (Herslund 1986), for example, in line 1 where ['ɛrɔ] is the contraction of /ˈɛrɐ u/, and of pitch excursions. Unstressed syllables which maintain their target vowel qualities are not transcribed with a secondary stress; secondary stress is shown only with diphthongs. Upstepped syllables are followed by low or falling syllables, downstepped syllables by low or rising syllables. Since upstep and downstep do not necessarily occur on a stressed syllable, all primary stresses not indicated by a tone mark are shown in the transcription.

u ᵗˈvẽtu ˈnɔɾt ᵗi u sɔl d̪ʃkuˈtiˌẽu ᵗku̪al duʒ doiz ᵗˈɛɾɔ maiʃ ⅃fɔɾtɯ | ᵗˈku̪ẽdu susɯˈdeu pɐˈsaɾ ũ viɐᵗˈʒẽtɯ u̪ᵗ·ˈvolt numɐ ⅃kapɐ ‖ au ⅃velu | ˈpõiᵗˌẽis diɐᶈˈkoɾdu ẽi ˈkomu ɐᵗˈkel kɯ pɾiᵗˈmɐiɾu kõsˈgis ɔbɾiˈgaɾ u viɐˈʒẽtɯ ɐ tiˈɾaɾ ɐ ⅃kapɐ | sɾiɐ kõsiduᵗˈɾadu u maiʃ ⅃fɔɾt ‖ u ᵗˈvẽtu ˈnɔɾtɯ kumɯˈso ɐ suˈpɾaɾ kõ ˈmũitɐ ⅃fuɾiɐ | mɐʃ ᵗˈku̪ẽtu maiʃ su⅃pɾavɐ | maiz ᵗu viɐᶈˈʒẽtɯ si ɐkõʃᶈˈgava suɐ ⅃kapɐ | ɐˈtɛ ᵗkiu ˈvẽtu ˈnɔɾtɯ ⅃d̪ʒʃtiu ‖ ᵗu sɔl bɾiˈʎo ẽˈtẽu kõ ˈtodu ʃplẽ⅃doɾ | i ᵗimɯdiatɐˈmẽt u viɐᵗˈʒẽtɯ tiˈɾo ɐ ⅃kapɐ ‖ u ᵗˈvẽtu ˈnɔɾtɯ tev ɐˈsĩ dɯ g̊kuɲɯᵗˈseɾ ɐ supɯɾiuɾiˈdad ᵗdu ⅃sɔl ‖

Orthographic version

O vento norte e o sol discutiam qual dos dois era o mais forte, quando sucedeu passar um viajante envolto numa capa. Ao vê-lo, põem-se de acordo em como aquele que primeiro conseguisse obrigar o viajante a tirar a capa seria considerado o mais forte. O vento norte começou a soprar com muita fúria, mas quanto mais soprava, mais o viajante se aconchegava à sua capa, até que o vento norte desistiu. O sol brilhou então com todo o esplendor, e imediatamente o viajante tirou a capa. O vento norte teve assim de reconhecer a superioridade do sol.

Acknowledgement

I am indebted to Professor Paroo Nihalani for his kind help in acquainting me with the implementation of the IPA font.

References

CRUZ-FERREIRA, M. (1998). Intonation in European Portuguese. In Hirst, D. and di Cristo, A. (editors), *Intonation Systems: A Survey of Twenty Languages*. Cambridge University Press.

HERSLUND, M. (1986). Portuguese sandhi phenomena. In Andersen, H. (editor), *Sandhi Phenomena in the Languages of Europe*, 505–18. Amsterdam: Mouton de Gruyter.

MATEUS, M. H. M. (1975). *Aspectos da Fonologia Portuguesa* (Publicações do Centro de Estudos Filológicos 19). Lisbon: Instituto de Alta Cultura.

WILLIS, R. C. (1971). *An Essential Course in Modern Portuguese*, revised edition. London: Harrap.

Sindhi

PAROO NIHALANI

Department of English Language and Literature
Oita University, 700 Dannoharu, Oita-City 870-1192, Japan

The variety of Sindhi described here is roughly representative of the Vicholi dialect, which is considered to be the 'Standard variety'. This variety has special prestige attached to it because the most celebrated poet of Sindhi, Abdul Latif, wrote the classic 'Shah jo Rasalo' in this dialect. The description, based on the author's own speech, has been kept fairly close to the colloquial style. The transcription is based on a recording of a male first generation speaker of Standard Sindhi who grew up in Sindh, Pakistan, before moving to India in 1947. For a detailed discussion of Sindhi segments see Khubchandani (1961).

Consonants

	Bilabial	Labio-dental	Dental	Alveolar	Post-alveolar	Palatal	Velar	Glottal
Plosive	p b pʰ bɦ		t d tʰ dɦ		ʈ ɖ ʈʰ ɖɦ		k g kʰ gɦ	
Implosive	ɓ			ɗ		ʄ	ɠ	
Affricate						c ɟ cʰ ɟɦ		
Nasal	m mɦ			n nɦ	ɳ ɳɦ	ɲ	ŋ	
Fricative		f		s z	ʂ		x ɣ	h
Tap				r	ɽ ɽɦ			
Approximant		ʋ				j		
Lateral Approximant			l lɦ					

p	pənʊ	'leaf'	t	təro	'bottom'	ʈ	ʈopi	'cap'
b	buʈʊ	'shoes'	d	dʊnʊ	'navel'	ɖ	ɖəpʊ	'fear'

pʰ	pʰuʈə	'rift'	tʰ	tʰali	'plate'	tʰ	ʈʰəɾʊ	'be cool'
bɦ	bɦʊlə	'mistake'	dɦ	dɦarə	'separate'	ɖɦ	ɖɦəkʊ	'cover' (n)
ɓ	ɓarʊ	'child'	ɗ	ɗarʊ	'crevice'			
m	məʈʊ	'pitcher'	n	nalo	'name'	ɳ	məɳi	'diamond'
mɦ	mɦē	'buffalo'	nɦ	sənɦi	'thin'	ɳɦ	maɳɦu	'person'
f	fərasi	'bed cover'	s	sufʊ	'apple'	ʂ	ʂe	'thing'
			z	zalə	'wife'			
			r	rolu	'wanderer'	ɽ	pʰoɽo	'sore' (n)
						ɽɦ	poɽɦo	'old man'
ʋ	ʋarʊ	'hair'	l	limo	'lemon'			
			lɦ	tʰʊlɦi	'fat' (adj, fem)			

c	calu	'cunning'	k	kano	'straw'
ɟ	ɟuto	'shoes'	g	gano	'song'
cʰ	cʰati	'breast'	kʰ	kʰano	'drawer'
ɟɦ	ɟɦəʈɪ	'immediately'	gɦ	gɦoɽo	'horse'
ʄ	ʄaro	'cobweb'	ɠ	ɠəro	'heavy'
ɲ	ʄəɲə	'marriage procession'	ŋ	cəŋo	'good'
			x	xɔfʊ	'fear'
			ɣ	ɣəmʊ	'sorrow'
j	jarʊ	'friend'	h	harʊ	'necklace'

Vowels

Sindhi has a system of ten oral vowels.

i	sirə	'midstream'
ɪ	sɪrə	'brick'
e	serə	(a measure of weight)
ɛ	sɛrə	'walks' (n)
a	sarə	'jealousy'
ə	sərə	'funeral'
ɔ	cəʋəndɔ	'you will say'
o	cəʋəndo	'he will say'
ʊ	sʊrə	'tunes'
u	surə	'aches and pains'

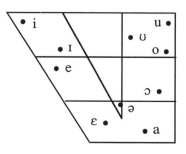

The vowels /ɛ/ and /ɔ/ tend to be diphthongized, as [ɛə] and [əʊ]. These vowels have a limited distribution, not occurring before aspirated stops, implosives, nasals or /ɣ/. Vowels are audibly nasalized preceding a nasal consonant, but, as in many other modern Indo-Aryan languages, there are a few words in Sindhi with distinctive nasalized vowels. Compare /əsi/ 'eighty', /əsĩ/ 'we'; /adⁱⁱi/ 'half-rupee', /ādⁱⁱi/ 'storm'; /dəhi/ 'yoghurt', /dɔ̃hi/ 'tenth'. For this reason, vowel nasalization must be regarded as phonemic, and it has been marked in the transcription of the passage below in positions where it is not predictable from a preceding nasal.

Stress
Word-level stress is nondistinctive, and is fixed on the first syllable of the morpheme. Contrastive stress may be used to give special emphasis to a word or to point to a contrast of ideas.

Conventions
The consonants in the post-alveolar column of the chart are pronounced as apical post-alveolars (Nihalani 1974b). They have been transcribed, following tradition, with symbols for retroflex sounds. The consonants in the palatal column are laminal post-alveolars. /c, cʰ, ɟ, ɟⁱⁱ/ have an affricated release of relatively short duration. The alveolar nasal /n/ occurs mostly before dental or alveolar consonants and is pronounced homorganic with the following consonant. [ʋ] is in free variation with [w] as the realization of /ʋ/.

Breathy-voiced consonants, transcribed with [ⁱⁱ], are produced with the vocal folds incompletely closed at the centre and with the arytenoid cartilages apart (Nihalani 1974a). Of the rhotics /r, ɽ, ɽⁱⁱ/, /r/ is realized most often as a tap but may be a trill with two or more contacts, /ɽ, ɽⁱⁱ/ are typically flaps.

Vowels in open syllables tend to be longer than those in closed syllables. /ə, ɪ, ʊ/ are shorter than other vowels. Stops in intervocalic position preceded by these vowels tend to be longer than those preceded by other vowels, e.g.:

[mʊdːo]	'period'	[mado]	'capability'
[pətːo]	'leaf'	[pato]	'worn'
[pɪʈːə]	'curse'	[moʈo]	'fat' (adj, male)

Transcription of recorded passage

ʊtərə ɟi həʋa ɛ̃ sɪɟʊ pāɳə mẽ ɟⁱⁱəɟɽo kəre rəhja hʊja tə ɓɪnⁱⁱi mẽ kerʊ ʋədⁱⁱikə takətʋaro ahe. etre mẽ hɪkʊ mʊsafɪrʊ gərəm koʈʊ pae ʊtā əci ləŋgⁱⁱjo. həʋa ɛ̃ sɪɟə ɓɪnⁱⁱi kəbul kəjo tə ɟeko mʊsafɪrə ɟo koʈʊ lahrae səgⁱⁱəndo uho i ʋədⁱⁱikə takətʋaro lekʰjo ʋendo. po ʊtərə ɟi həʋa ɗadⁱⁱo zorə sā ləɟi, pərə ɟetro ʋədⁱⁱikə zorə sā ləɟi otro ʋədⁱⁱikə zorə sā mʊsafɪrə pāɳə

kʰe d̤ʱəkɪɳə ɟi koʂɪʂ kəji. axɪr mẽ ʋtərə ɟe həʋa koʂɪʂ cʰədɛ d̥ɪni. po sɪɟə ɟi
ʋsə zorə sã nɪkti ẽ mʋsafɪrə pāhɪɳɟo koʈʋ ɟəldi lahe pəre pʰɪʈi kəjo. ɪnhiə
kəre ʋtərə ɟe həʋa məɳjo tə sɪɟʋ hi ɓɪnʱi mẽ ʋəd̤ʱikə takətʋaro ahe.

Orthographic version

References

KHUBCHANDANI, L. M. (1961). *The Phonology and Morphophonemics of Sindhi*. M.A.
dissertation, University of Pennsylvania, Philadelphia.
NIHALANI, P. (1974a). An aerodynamic study of stops in Sindhi. *Phonetica* 29, 193–224.
NIHALANI, P. (1974b). Lingual articulation of stops in Sindhi. *Phonetica* 30, 197–212.

Slovene

RASTISLAV ŠUŠTARŠIČ, SMILJANA KOMAR

Department of English, Faculty of Arts, University of Ljubljana,
Aškerčeva 2, 1000 Ljubljana, Slovenia

AND

BOJAN PETEK

Faculty of Natural Sciences and Engineering, University of Ljubljana,
Snežniška 5, 1000 Ljubljana, Slovenia

Slovene (or Slovenian) is the national language of the Republic of Slovenia and is also spoken in adjoining areas of Austria, Hungary and Italy. The variety described here is Standard Slovene as spoken by educated speakers in Slovenia. The transcription is based on a recording of two speakers, a female and a male, from Ljubljana, the capital.

Slovene has 21 consonants and 8 vowels. The orthography generally represents the segmental pronunciation quite faithfully. The main exceptions are that [u] can be represented by the letters 'l' and 'v' as well as 'u', and that 'e' is used to represent [e, ɛ, ə] and 'o' to represent [o, ɔ]. Note also that 'lj' and 'nj' are pronounced as [l] and [n] unless followed by a vowel.

Consonants

	Bilabial	Labio-dental	Dental	Alveolar	Palato-alveolar	Palatal	Velar
Plosive	p b		t d				k g
Affricate			ts	tʃ dʒ			
Nasal	m		n				
Tap				ɾ			
Fricative		f		s z	ʃ ʒ		x
Approximant		ʋ				j	
Lateral Approximant				l			

p	'piːti	*piti*	'to drink'	t	tiːsk	*tisk*	'print' (n)	k	kiːp	*kip*	'statue'
b	'biːti	*biti*	'to be'	d	diːsk	*disk*	'disk'	g	giːp	*gib*	'movement'
				ts	tsiːn	*tsin*	'tin' (metal)	tʃ	tʃiːn	*čin*	(army) 'rank'
								dʒ	dʒiːn	*gin*	'gin'

m	'miːti	*miti*	'myths'		n	'niːti	*niti*	'threads'				
f	fiːn	*fin*	'fine' (adj)		s	'siːniti	*siniti*	'to shine out'	ʃ	'ʃiːla	*šila*	'awls'
					z	'ziːniti	*ziniti*	'to open one's mouth'	ʒ	'ʒiːla	*žila*	'vein'
					ɾ	'riːti	*riti*	'to dig'	x	'xiːti	*hiti*	'rush' (imp)
ʋ	'ʋiːdiʃ	*vidiš*	'you see'		l	'liːti	*liti*	'to pour'	j	'jiːdiʃ	*jidiš*	'Yiddish'

Before voiceless obstruents and in word-final position (unless they are followed by a word-initial voiced obstruent) voiced obstruents are completely devoiced: [slaːt] *slad* 'malt', *sladkor* ['slaːtkɔr] 'sugar'. Compare: [graːd gɔ'riː] *grad gori* 'the castle is on fire'. Voiceless obstruents become voiced before voiced obstruents: [leːs] *les* 'wood', [leːz gɔ'riː] *les gori* 'wood burns'.

/s, z, ts/ when followed by /ʃ, ʒ, tʃ, dʒ/ assimilate or coalesce to [ʃ, ʒ, tʃ] respectively, e.g. prefix /s-/ in ['ʃtʃaːsɔma] *sčasoma* 'in the course of time'; /iz/ 'from' but [i'ʒːeːpa] *iz žepa* 'from the pocket'.

The nasal /n/ is pronounced as velar [ŋ] before /k, g, x/: ['baːŋka] *banka* 'bank', ['aːŋgɛl] *angel* 'angel', ['aːŋxoʋo] *Anhovo* (name of a town). The bilabial and alveolar nasals, /m, n/, are pronounced as labiodental [ɱ] before /f, ʋ/: [siɱfɔ'niːja] *simfonija* 'symphony', [səɱ'ʋeːdeu] *sem vedel* 'I knew', [iɱfɔr'maːtsija] *informacija* 'information', [iɱʋa'liːd] *invalid* 'invalid (n)'.

The sonorants /m, n, l, r, j, ʋ/ are normally voiced, but the approximant /ʋ/ has four allophonic variants: preceding a vowel it is pronounced as labiodental [ʋ]: ['ʋɔːda] *voda* 'water', in final position or preceding a consonant it is pronounced [u]: [siu] *siv* 'grey', ['brautsi] *bralci* 'readers', in syllable-initial position preceding a voiced consonant it is a voiced labial-velar approximant [w]: [wnuːk] *vnuk* 'grandson', [ɔd'wzeːti] *odvzeti* 'take away' and in syllable-initial position preceding a voiceless consonant it is a voiceless labial-velar approximant [ʍ]: [ʍsaːk] *vsak* 'every', [prɛt'ʍseːm] *predvsem* 'in particular'. Instead of [w] and [ʍ], the pronunciation can also be [u].

Vowels

Traditionally, the vowel system in Standard Slovene was described as including a vowel length distinction, with /i, a, u, ɛ, ɔ/ occurring both long and short, /eː, oː/ only long and /ə/ short (Toporišič 1984). Vowel length, however, can no longer be regarded as distinctive for most speakers, and it is generally accepted that long vowels occur in stressed, and short vowels in unstressed position (Srebot-Rejec 1988), giving a phonemic inventory of eight distinctive vowel qualities, /i, e, ɛ, ə, a, o, ɔ, u/, as shown on the chart. All vowels occur in stressed and unstressed syllables, but /e/ and /o/ occur in unstressed position in a few grammatical words only, e.g. the auxiliary *bo* ('will') in the recorded passage. Because of this restriction, some authorities consider that there are only six unstressed vowel qualities. What is meant by 'stress' will be discussed below.

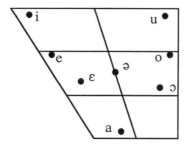

Stressed				Unstressed			
iː	miːt	*mit*	'myth'	i	'miːti	*miti*	'myths'
eː	meːt	*med*	'honey'	e	ʒe 'veː	*že ve*	'already knows'
ɛː	'peːta	*peta*	'heel'	ɛ	'peːtɛ	*pete*	'heel' (gen)
aː	maːt	*mat*	'checkmate'	a	'maːta	*mata*	'checkmate' (gen)
ɔː	'pɔːtən	*poten*	'sweaty'	ɔ	pɔ'teːm	*potem*	'then'
oː	poːt	*pot*	'path'	o	bo 'ʃloː	*bo šlo*	'will go'
uː	puːst	*pust*	'carnival'	u	'puːstu	*pustu*	'carnival' (dat)
əː	pəːs	*pes*	'dog'	ə	'doːbər	*dober*	'good'

Phonetic diphthongs arise when the approximants /ʋ/ and /j/ are preceded by a vowel and followed by a consonant or a word boundary. The labiodental /ʋ/ in these positions becomes a rounded second element of a diphthong, i.e. [u], and /j/ becomes [i]. These phonetic diphthongs do not occur with salient lengthening when they occur in stressed syllables. The degree of openness in the first element in /ei/ is between that of /e/ and /ɛ/, and for /ou/ it is between that of /o/ and /ɔ/.

				iu	piu	*pil*	'drank'
ei	glei	*glej*	'look' (imp)	eu	peu	*pel*	'sang'
				ɛu	leu	*lev*	'lion'
ai	dai	*daj*	'give' (imp)	au	pau	*pav*	'peacock'
oi	tʋoi	*tvoj*	'your' (masc sg)	ou	pou	*pol*	'half'
ɔi	bɔi	*boj*	'battle'				
ui	tui	*tuj*	'foreign'				
				əu	'tɔːpəu	*topel*	'warm'

Stress and accent

In the illustrative wordlists and the transcribed passage below, certain syllables have been marked as stressed. These stressed syllables are characterized by greater duration as well as by amplitude and pitch prominence. Non-compound words have no more than one stressed syllable. Stress placement is not predictable but is also rarely distinctive in Slovene, although in a few instances different forms of the same noun or verb differ only in stress placement, e.g.: ['stʋaːɾi], [stʋaˈɾiː], *stvari* ('things', dual vs. plural), ['noːsimɔ], [nɔˈsiːmɔ], *nosimo* ('carry' 1st p. pl. indicative and imperative).

Standard Slovene distinguishes two pitch accents, traditionally referred to as the 'acute' and the 'circumflex' accents, and these accents are tied to the location of stress. The pronunciations are variable, but in typical realizations, the 'acute' accent involves a step up in pitch and the 'circumflex' a step down in pitch (Toporišič 1984). In non word-final position, these patterns are distributed over a stressed syllable and the following unstressed syllable, so that the acute has a low-pitched stressed syllable and a high peak on the unstressed, whereas the circumflex has a high peak on the stressed syllable followed by a lower unstressed syllable. Hence the acute is also referred to as the low or rising toneme and the circumflex as the high or falling toneme. The accents are illustrated graphically on the words for 'mother' and 'grandfather' in the following sentences:

Acute: *Ma*^{*ma*} *je prišla.* 'Mother has come'.

Circumflex: *De*
dek je prišel. 'Grandpa has come'.

The accents are seldom lexically distinctive, although there are examples such as [ˈkìːlá] *kila* 'hernia' (acute) and [ˈkîːlà] *kila* 'kilo' (circumflex). Perhaps because of this, many words vary in which accent they are given, and some speakers, although they speak Standard Slovene, do not make any distinction between the two accents. In the transcription below, the different accents have not been marked, although both vowel length and stress are indicated despite the considerable redundancy involved. An intonation group boundary is marked by [|] and a pause by [||].

Transcription of recorded passage

'seːʋəɾni 'ʋeːtər in 'soːntsɛ sta sɛ prɛ'piːrala | kaˈteːɾi ɔd 'njiːju jɛ mɔtʃ'neiʃi |
kɔ jɛ 'miːmɔ priˈʃeu pɔ'poːtnik | zaˈʋiːt u 'tɔːpəu 'plaːʃtʃ. || dɔɡɔʋɔˈriːla sta sɛ
| da bo ʋɛlʲjau za mɔtʃ'neiʃega 'tiːsti | ki mu bo 'pəːɾʋɛmu u'speːlɔ | da bo
pɔ'poːtnik 'sleːkəu sʋoi 'plaːʃtʃ. || 'seːʋəɾni 'ʋeːtər jɛ za'piːxau z u'sɔː mɔ'tʃjoː ||
toda 'boːl kɔ jɛ 'piːxau | 'boːl tə'snːo jɛ pɔ'poːtnik | ɔ'ʋiːjau sʋoi 'plaːʃtʃ ɔkoli
'seːbɛ. || 'kɔːntʃnɔ | jɛ 'seːʋəɾni 'ʋeːtər pɔ'puːstiu. || na'toː jɛ 'soːntsɛ tɔ'ploː
pɔsi'jaːlɔ | in pɔ'poːtnik jɛ ta'koi 'sleːkəu sʋoi 'plaːʃtʃ. || in ta'koː jɛ 'seːʋəɾni
'ʋeːtər 'moːɾau priˈznaːti | da jɛ 'soːntsɛ mɔ'tʃneiʃɛ ɔd 'njeːga. ||

Orthographic version

Severni veter in sonce sta se prepirala, kateri od njiju je močnejši, ko je mimo prišel popotnik, zavit v topel plašč. Dogovorila sta se, da bo veljal za močnejšega tisti, ki mu bo prvemu uspelo, da bo popotnik slekel svoj plašč. Severni veter je zapihal z vso močjo, toda bolj ko je pihal, bolj tesno je popotnik ovijal svoj plašč okoli sebe. Končno je Severni veter popustil. Nato je Sonce toplo posijalo in popotnik je takoj slekel svoj plašč. In tako je Severni veter moral priznati, da je Sonce močnejše od njega.

Acknowledgements

The authors would like to thank Mr. Janez Oblak for technical assistance, and Dr. Beverley Collins (Leiden University, Holland) for his valuable advice and suggestions.

References

SREBOT-REJEC, T. (1988). *Word Accent and Vowel Duration in Standard Slovene: An Acoustic and Linguistic Investigation* (Slavistische Beiträge, 226). Munich: Otto Sagner.

TOPORIŠIČ, J. (1984). *Slovenska slovnica*. Maribor: Založba Obzorja.

Swedish

OLLE ENGSTRAND

Institute of Linguistics, University of Stockholm, S-106 91 Stockholm, Sweden

The style of speech illustrated is that of many educated speakers of Central Standard Swedish as spoken in the Stockholm area. The actual speech on the accompanying recording is that of a male speaker in his forties whose speech is typical of that variety of Swedish.

Consonants

	Bilabial	Labiodental	Dental	Alveolar	Palatal	Velar	Glottal
Plosive	p b		t d			k ɡ	
Nasal	m		n			ŋ	
Fricative		f v	s		ʝ		h
Approximant				ɹ			
Lateral Approximant			l				

ɧ (Voiceless dorso-palatal/velar fricative)   ɕ (Voiceless alveolo-palatal fricative)

p	*pol*	'pole'	t	*tok*	'fool'	k	*kon*	'cone'
b	*bok*	'book'	d	*dop*	'christening'	ɡ	*god*	'good'
m	*mod*	'courage'	n	*nod*	'node'	ŋ	*lång*	'long'
f	*fot*	'foot'	s	*sot*	'soot'	ɕ	*kjol*	'skirt'
v	*våt*	'wet'	ɧ	*sjok*	'chunk'	h	*hot*	'threat'
ɹ	*rov*	'prey'	l	*lov*	'tack'	ʝ	*jord*	'soil'

Vowels

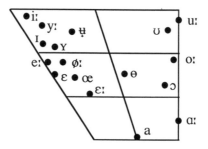

iː	*sil*	'strainer'	øː	*nöt*	'nut'
ɪ	*sill*	'herring'	œ	*nött*	'worn'
yː	*syl*	'awl'	ɑː	*mat*	'food'
ʏ	*syll*	'sleeper'	a	*matt*	'feeble'
ʉ	*ful*	'ugly'	oː	*mål*	'goal'
ɵ	*full*	'full'	ɔ	*moll*	'minor' (music)
eː	*hel*	'whole'	uː	*bot*	'penance'
ɛː	*häl*	'heel'	ʊ	*bott*	'lived' (perf)
ɛ	*häll*	'flat rock'			

Stress and accent
' (primary stress), ˌ (secondary stress), and ˋ (word accent) as in [ˈnùːɖanˌvɪndən] *nordanvinden* 'the north wind'.

Conventions
/p, t, k/ are aspirated in stressed position when not preceded by /s/ within the same morpheme. /t, d, n, s, l/ are dental. The retroflex sounds [ʈ, ɖ, ɳ, ʂ, ɭ] can be considered phonetic forms of /rt, rd, rn, rs, rl/; this is also reflected in the orthography (e.g. *nordanvinden*). They also arise at word and morpheme boundaries, e.g. *för+söket*. /ɹ/ can be approximant (e.g. *starkast*), voiced fricative (e.g. the first *r* in *vandrare*), or trilled; the trilled variant is restricted to emphatic stress in many speakers and does not appear in the recording. Open varieties of /ɛː, ɛ, øː, œ/ are used before /ɹ/ and the retroflex allophones (e.g. *först*). Long vowels are often diphthongized or fricativized, particularly the high ones: [ij, yɥ, uβ, ʉβ]. Lip rounding differs between /y, ø/ ('outrounded') and /u, ʉ/ ('inrounded'). /ɑː/ is slightly rounded. Consonants are long after short vowels in stressed position, and short elsewhere. Voiced consonants are frequently devoiced in voiceless context, e.g. [tʏ̥ɪstadə], [jɘst d̥o]. Compound words have the so-called grave tonal word accent (accent 2) with falling pitch on the primary stressed syllable and a strong secondary stress. Most bisyllabic and polysyllabic stems also have the grave accent but with a weaker secondary stress.

Transcription of recorded passage
ˈnùːɖanˌvɪndən ɔ ˈsuːlən ˈtʏ̀ɪstadə əŋ ˈgɔŋ ɔm vɛm av ˈdɔm sɔm va ˈstàɹkast. ˈjɘst ˈd̥oː kɔm ən ˈvàndɹaɹə ˈveːgən ˈfɹam, ˈɪnˌsveːpt i ən ˈvaɹm ˈkàpa. dɔm kɔm doː øvəˈɹɛns ɔm, at dɛn sɔm ˈfœ̨ʂ̣ț kəndə fo vàndɹaɹən at ta ˈɑːv sɛ̣j ˈkàpan, han skələ ˈànˌseːs vaɹa ˈstàɹkaɹə ɛn dɛn ˈàndɹa. doː ˈblòːstə ˈnùːɖanˌvɪndən so ˈhoːʈ han ˈnɔ̀nˌsɪn ˈkɘ̀ndə, mɛn jʉ ˈhòːɖaɹə han ˈblòːstə, dɛstʊ ˈtɛ̀ːtaɹə ˈsʏ̀ɛːptə ˈvàndɹaɹən ˈkàpan ˈɔm sɛ̣j, ɔ tɪ ˈsɪst gav ˈnùːɖanˌvɪndən ˈəp fœ̨ˈʂ̣øːkət. doː lɛːt ˈsuːlən sina ˈstɹòːlaɹ ˈfjiːna ˈheːlt ˈvaɹmt, ɔ ˈjɛ̀nast tug ˈvàndɹaɹən ˈɑːv sɛ̣j ˈkàpan, ɔ so va ˈnùːɖanˌvɪndən ˈtvɛ̀ŋən at ˈɛ̀ɹˌçɛna, at ˈsuːlən va dɛn ˈstàɹkastə av dɔm ˈtvoː.

Orthographic version

Nordanvinden och solen tvistade en gång om vem av dom som var starkast. Just då kom en vandrare vägen fram, insvept i en varm kappa. Dom kom då överens om, att den som först kunde få vandraren att ta av sig kappan, han skulle anses vara starkare än den andra. Då blåste nordanvinden så hårt han nånsin kunde, men ju hårdare han blåste desto tätare svepte vandraren kappan om sig, och till sist gav nordanvinden upp försöket. Då lät solen sina strålar skina helt varmt och genast tog vandraren av sig kappan, och så var nordanvinden tvungen att erkänna att solen var den starkaste av dom två.

Acknowledgement

Appreciation is extended to Ian Maddieson for the preparation of the vowel diagram.

Taba

JOHN BOWDEN AND JOHN HAJEK

Department of Linguistics and Applied Linguistics,
University of Melbourne, Parkville, VIC 3052, Australia

Taba (also known as 'East Makian' or 'Makian Dalam') is an Austronesian language spoken in northern Maluku province, Indonesia. It is spoken on Makian, Moti and Kayoa islands and also in a few villages on other nearby islands. The speech recorded here is from the village of Ngofakiaha on Makian island. Slight dialectal variations are to be found in most villages where the language is spoken.

Consonants

	Bilabial	Labio-dental	Dental	Alveolar	Post-alveolar	Palatal	Velar	Glottal
Plosive	p b			t d			k g	
Nasal	m			n			ŋ	
Fricative		f		s				h
Affricate					tʃ dʒ			
Trill				r				
Approximant						j	w	
Lateral Approximant				l				

The consonant table shows phonemic contrasts. Although /tʃ/ and /dʒ/ are relatively infrequent and originally borrowed, both can now be considered fully native.

p	pait	'moon'	t	top	'sugar cane'	k	kam	'I see'
b	bait	'wrestle'	d	dɔ	'couscous'	g	gah	'theft'
m	mai	'then'	n	nɔ	'there'	ŋ	ŋan	'sun'
f	fati	'to cover'	s	sɔ	'to ascend'	h	han	'to go'
			tʃ	tʃɔat	'firewood bundle'	j	jan	'fish'
			dʒ	dʒɔu	'good'	w	wah	'island'
			r	rɔrɛ	'stone'			
			l	lɔat	'to slice'			

Geminates

All of the Taba consonants except /j, w, r, dʒ/ can occur with distinctive length (i.e. as 'geminates'). Interestingly, although geminates are found word-medially, they are most common in word-initial position. Geminates are never found in word-final position. They may occur monomorphemically, but they also occur across morpheme boundaries where initial agreement markers are prefixed to verbs. Phrase-initial geminates are realized in careful speech with a greater degree of tension and more articulatory force; in more casual varieties of speech they can be realized with the same reduced tension and articulatory force as singletons. Some illustrative examples of geminate contrasts are given below.

t	tala	'to meet'	l	lɔ	'inside'
tt	ttala	'we (inclusive) meet'	ll	llɔ	'blood'
g	gɔwɔ	'place'	k	kut	'louse'
gg	ggɔwɔ	'neck'	kk	kku	'tail'
m	mul	'to return'	h	han	'to go'
mm	mmul	'you (sg) return'	hh	hhan	'you (pl) go'
ŋ	ŋan	'sun'			
ŋŋ	ŋŋɛ	'canarium nut'			

Vowels

Taba has a simple five vowel system, as shown on the chart. The phone [ɛ] is relatively rare. Notwithstanding the effects of predictable contextual conditioning (see below), vowels are normally realized as relatively short. Very rare examples of long vowels can be found, e.g. [kiː] 'vagina', but only one marginal example of a length contrast has been uncovered: [tɛ] 'no(t)' vs. [tɛː] 'if not'.

All possible sequences of unalike vowels occur in the corpus except for [ɛa] and [ɛɔ], but none are listed here because they are analysed as vowel clusters and not diphthongs.

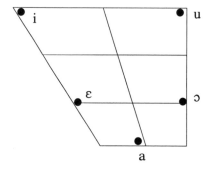

i	im	'fishing reel'
ɛ	hɛn	'turtle'
a	am	'to see'
ɔ	ɔm	'uncle'
u	um	'house'

Stress

Stress is indicated by a greater degree of force in the production of a syllable, a noticeably higher pitch than in unstressed syllables, and some degree of lengthening. In general, primary stress falls on the only syllable of monosyllabic words or on the penultimate syllable of polysyllabic words. Examples of antepenultimate stress are extremely rare, e.g. ['ttʃiɔtit] 'we defecate'. Final stress in polysyllables is more frequent, but is generally restricted to a few loan words, e.g. [a'had] 'Sunday, week' (< Arabic), and some polymorphemic verb forms with monosyllabic roots, e.g. [na'pɛ] 'he does' from ['pɛ] 'to do'.

Conventions

Stops are not released in final position, and [t] is usually slightly palatalized before [i]. The nasals [m] and [n] tend to assimilate towards a following labiodental [f] while [n] also tends to assimilate towards following bilabials and velars. [r] is always strongly trilled.

In addition to its use of initial geminates, Taba is also characterized by the appearance of a large set of unusual clusters, e.g. ['nmu] 'muddy water', ['mhonas] 'sick', ['nhik] 'bat', ['khan] 'I go', ['mtɔ] 'eye'. More common initially than medially, they are often the result of prefixing simple consonants to verb roots in order to mark person and number. In nasal consonant + [h] clusters, e.g. ['mhonas], the nasal starts off as fully voiced, with the latter portion devoiced without any concomitant increase in nasal airflow. The [h] offset is clear. Heterorganic clusters with initial [h] are also found, e.g. ['hkutan] 'you ask' vs. ['kutan] 'to ask'. The articulation of [h] in onset is also clear.

Initial geminate contrasts are generally stable, although there is a tendency for some speakers to reduce initial [hh] to [h], e.g. ['hhan] ~ ['han] 'you (pl) go'. Conversely, some non-geminate fricative clusters may be subject to optional metathesis or even complete assimilation, e.g. expected ['hsɔpaŋ] alongside ['shɔpaŋ] and ['ssɔpaŋ] 'you (pl) descend'.

There is not much allophonic variation in the vowels, apart from the kinds of variations seen in a great many languages: vowels tend to be nasalized before nasal consonants, and they tend to be lengthened slightly before voiced consonants and in stressed positions. Some dialects of Taba replace many instances of Ngofakiaha /ɔ/ with /a/, e.g. ['wɔg] vs. ['wag] 'canoe'.

Transcription of recorded passage

A riddle about being sick

'banda 'ni 'wɛ 'mhonas | 'nim 'wɛ na'lusa 'mhonas ‖ 'nim pap'pukɔ 'mɛ na'lusa 'mhonas ‖ 'biŋɔ namɔ'lam ‖ u'lɔn 'nmau 'nhan ‖ 'pɔtɔ 'pɔpɛ 'nmau 'nhan 'ntʃiwi ‖ 'sumɔ na'lusa 'khan ‖ 'mtɔ 'nujak | 'pɔjɔ 'mhonas | bai'bijɔ nma'lɔŋɔ ‖ u'lɔn 'nmau 'nhan | 'mtumɔ ɛ 'lɔ ɛ ‖ pap'pukɔ 'mai na'lusa 'mhonas ‖ 'biŋɔ na'lusa namɔ'lam ‖ u'lɔn 'jasɛ 'nmau mpa'rɛnta 'nhan ‖

ˈpɔtɔ ˈpɔpɛ naˈlusa taˈsiaki ‖ ˈmpili ɛ ˈlɔ ˈli ɛ ‖ ˈpɔlɔ ˈbanda taˈsiak | ˈnhan ˈtuli naˈhatɛs ‖ ˈmau ˈnhan ˈtuli sɛˈdaŋkan ˈbanda naˈpɛ taˈsiaki ‖ ˈmalɛ ˈsiɔ ˈmalai ˈhan ˈtuli ‖ ˈsiɔ ˈmul ˈmalai ˈhan ˈtuli aˈhan ‖ ˈmalɛ ˈttʃiɔtit ˈhu ˈmalai ˈthan ‖ ˈttʃiɔtit ˈɔkik ˈmalai ˈthan ˈtuli | ˈthan ˈtrɔnda ‖

Orthographic version

Banda ni we mhonas, nim we nalusa 'mhonas'. Nim pappuko me nalusa 'mhonas'. Bingo namolam. Ulon nmau nhan. Poto pope nmau nhan ncioi. Sumo nalusa 'khan'. Mto nuyak, poyo mhonas, baibiyo nmalongo. Ulon nmau nhan, mtumo e lo e? Pappuko mai nalusa mhonas. Bingo nalusa namolam. Ulon yase nmau nparenta nhan. Poto pope nalusa tasiaki. Mpili e lo li e? Polo Banda tasiak, nhan tuli nahates. Mau nhan tuli sedangkan Banda nape tasiaki. Male sio malai han tuli. Sio mul malai han tuli ahan. Male tciotit hu malai than. Tciotit okik malai than tuli, than tronda.

Thai

M. R. KALAYA TINGSABADH

Department of Linguistics, Faculty of Arts, Chulalongkorn University, Bangkok 10330, Thailand

AND

ARTHUR S. ABRAMSON

Haskins Laboratories, New Haven, CT, and Department of Linguistics, The University of Connecticut, Storrs, CT 06269-1145, USA

Standard Thai is spoken by educated speakers in every part of Thailand, used in news broadcasts on radio and television, taught in school, and described in grammar books and dictionaries. It has developed through the standardization of a socially prestigious variety of Central Thai, the regional dialect of Bangkok and the surrounding provinces.

The transcription of 'The North Wind and the Sun' is based on recordings made by three cultivated speakers of the language, who were asked to read the passage in a relaxed way. In fact, we find them all to have used a fairly formal colloquial style, apparently equivalent to Eugénie J. A. Henderson's 'combinative style' (Henderson 1949). In a more deliberate reading of the text, many words in the passage would be transcribed differently. The main features subject to such stylistic variation are vowel quantity, tone, and glottal stop. Thus, for example, /tὲ:/ 'but' is likely under weak stress to be /tὲ/ with a short vowel; the modal auxiliary /tɕàʔ/ 'about to' becomes /tɕā/, with change of tone from low to mid and loss of final glottal stop. The prosodic and syntactic factors that seem to be at work here remain to be thoroughly explored.

Consonants

	Bilabial	Labio-dental	Alveolar	Post-alveolar	Palatal	Velar	Glottal
Plosive	p pʰ b		t tʰ d			k kʰ	ʔ
Nasal	m		n			ŋ	
Fricative		f	s				h
Affricate				tɕ tɕʰ			
Trill			r				
Approximant					j	w	
Lateral Approximant			l				

p	pāːn	'birthmark'	t	tāːn	'sugar palm'	k	kāːn	'act'
pʰ	pʰāːn	'belligerent'	tʰ	tʰāːn	'alms'	kʰ	kʰāːn	'shaft'
b	bāːn	'to bloom'	d	dâːn	'calloused'	ŋ	ŋāːn	'work'
m	māːn	'demon'	n	nāːn	'long time'	w	wàːn	'to sow'
f	fǎːn	'to slice'	s	sǎːn	'court'	j	jāːn	'sagging'
			r	ráːn	'shop'	ʔ	ʔāːn	'saddle'
			l	láːn	'million'	h	hǎːn	'to divide'
			tɕ	tɕāːn	'dish'			
			tɕʰ	tɕʰāːn	'trash'			

Vowels

There are nine vowels. Length is distinctive for all the vowels. (In some phonological treatments, /Vː/ is analyzed as /VV/.) Although small spectral differences between short and long counterparts are psychoacoustically detectable and have some effect on vowel identification (Abramson and Ren 1990), we find the differences too subtle to place with confidence in the vowel quadrilateral. The vowel /a/ in unstressed position, including the endings of the diphthongs /ia, ɯa, ua/, is likely to be somewhat raised in quality. The final segments of the other two sets of phonetic diphthongs: (1) [iu, eu, eːu, ɛːu, au, aːu, iau] and (2) [ai, aːi, ɔi, ɔːi, ui, ɤːi, uai, ɯai] are analyzed as /w/ and /j/ respectively.

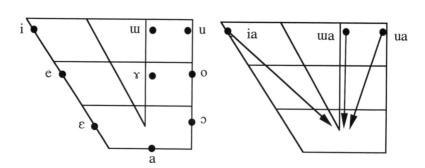

i	krìt	'dagger'	iː	krìːt	'to cut'	ia	riān	'to study'
e	ʔēn	'ligament'	eː	ʔēːn	'to recline'	ɯa	rɯān	'house'
ɛ	pʰɛ́ʔ	'goat'	ɛː	pʰɛ́ː	'to be defeated'	ua	rūan	'to be
a	fǎn	'to dream'	aː	fǎːn	'to slice'			provocative'
ɔ	klɔ̀ŋ	'box'	ɔː	klɔ̄ːŋ	'drum'			
o	kʰôn	'thick (soup)'	oː	kʰôːn	'to fell (a tree)'			
u	sùt	'last, rearmost'	uː	sùːt	'to inhale'			
ɤ	ŋɤ̄n	'silver'	ɤː	dɤ̄ːn	'to walk'			
ɯ	kʰɯ̂n	'to go up'	ɯː	kʰlɯ̂ːn	'wave'			

Tones

There are five tones in Standard Thai: high /ˊ/, mid /ˉ/, low /ˋ/, rising /ˇ/, and falling /ˆ/.

kʰāː	'to get stuck'		kʰáː	'to engage in trade'
kʰàː	'galangal'		kʰǎː	'leg'
kʰâː	'I'			

Stress

Primary stress falls on the final syllable of a word. The last primary stress before the end of a major prosodic group commonly takes extra stress.

Conventions

The feature of aspiration is manifested in the expected fashion for the simple prevocalic oral stops /pʰ, tʰ, kʰ/. The fairly long lag between the release of the stop and the onset of voicing is filled with turbulence, i.e. noise-excitation of the relatively unimpeded supraglottal vocal tract. In the special case of the 'aspirated' affricate /tɕʰ/, however, the noise during the voicing lag excites a narrow postalveolar constriction, thus giving rise to local turbulence. It is necessarily the case, then, that the constriction of the aspirated affricate lasts longer than that of the unaspirated one (Abramson 1989). Not surprisingly, it follows from these considerations that the aspiration of initial stops as the first element in clusters occurs during the articulation of the second element, which must be a member of the set /l, r, w/.

Only /p, t, k, ʔ, m, n, ŋ, w, j/ occur in syllable-final position. Final /p, t, k, ʔ/ have no audible release. The final oral plosives are said to be accompanied by simultaneous glottal closure (Henderson 1964; Harris 1992). Final /ʔ/ is omitted in unstressed positions. Initial /t, tʰ/ are often denti-alveolar. Initial /t/ and /f/ are velarized before close front vowels.

The consonant /r/ is realized most frequently as [ɾ] but also as [r]. Perceptual experiments (Abramson 1962: 6–9) have shown that the distinction between /r/ and /l/ is not very robust; nevertheless, the normative attitude among speakers of Standard Thai is that they are separate phonemes, as given in Thai script. This distinction is rather well maintained by some cultivated speakers, especially in formal speech; however, many show much vacillation, with a tendency to favour the lateral phone [l] in the position of a single initial consonant. As the second element of initial consonant clusters, both /l/ and /r/ tend to be deleted altogether.

In plurisyllabic words, the low tone and the high tone on syllables containing the short vowel /a/ followed by the glottal stop in deliberate speech, become the mid tone when unstressed, with loss of the glottal stop.

Transcription of recorded passage

kʰāˈnàʔ tʰî ˌlōmˈnŭa lé ˌpʰráʔāˈtʰit | kāmˈlāŋ ˈtʰiǎŋ kān ˈwâː | ˈkʰrāj tɕā ˈmīː pʰāˈlāŋ ˈmâːk kwà ˈkān | kɔ̂ ˈmīː ˈnákˌdɤ̄ːnˈtʰāːŋ ˈpʰûː ˈnŭŋ ˈdɤ̄ːn ˈpʰàːn ˈmāː | ˈsàj ˈsŭaˌkānˈnâːw ‖ ˌlōmˈnŭa lé ˌpʰráʔāˈtʰit ˈtɕūŋ ˌtòkˈlōŋ kān ˈwâː | ˈkʰrāj tʰî ˌsǎːmâːt ˈtʰām hâj ˈnákˌdɤ̄ːnˈtʰāːŋ ˈpʰûː ˈníː | ˈtʰɔ̂ːt ˈsŭaˌkānˈnâːw ʔòk ˈdâːj

ˌsǎmˈrèt ˈkɔːn | tɕā ˈtʰɯ̌ː ˈwâː | pēn ˈpʰûː tʰî ˈmīː pʰāˈlāŋ ˈmâːk ˈkwàː ‖ ˈlé? ˈlɛ́ːw |
ˌlōmˈnɯ̌a kɔ̂ krāˈpʰɯ̌ː ˈpʰát ˈjàːŋ ˈsùt ˈrēːŋ ‖ tè ˈjîŋ ˈpʰát ˈrēːŋ ˈmâːk ˈkʰɯ̂n ˈpʰīaŋ
ˈdāj | ˈnákˌdɤ̄ːnˈtʰāːŋ kɔ̂ ˈjîŋ ˈdɯ̄ŋ ˈsɯ̄aˌkān'nǎːw ˈhâj krāˈtɕʰáp kàp ˈtūa ˈmâːk
ˈkʰɯ̂n ˈpʰīaŋ ˈnán ‖ ˈlé? ˈnāj tʰî ˈsùt | ˌlōmˈnɯ̌a kɔ̂ ˈlɤ̄ːk ˈlóm ˈkʰwāːm
pʰājāˈjāːm ‖ ˈtɕàːk ˈnán | ˌpʰrá?āˈtʰít tɕɯ̄ŋ ˈsàːt ˈsɛ̌ːŋ ?ān ˈrɔ́ːn ˈrēːŋ ?ɔ̀k ˈmāː ‖
ˈnákˌdɤ̄ːnˈtʰāːŋ kɔ̂ ˈtʰɔ̀ːt ˈsɯ̄aˌkān'nǎːw ˈ?ɔ̀ːk ˈtʰān ˈtʰīː ‖ ˈnāj tʰî ˈsùt | ˌlōmˈnɯ̌a
tɕɯ̄ŋ ˈtɕām ˈtɔ̂ŋ ˈjɔ̄ːm ˈráp ˈwâː | ˌpʰrá?āˈtʰít mīː pʰāˈlāŋ ˈmâːk ˈkwàː ˈtōn ‖

Orthographic version

ขณะที่ลมเหนือและพระอาทิตย์กำลังเถียงกันว่าใครจะมีพลังมากกว่ากัน ก็มีนักเดินทางผู้
หนึ่งเดินผ่านมา ใส่เสื้อกันหนาว ลมเหนือและพระอาทิตย์จึงตกลงกันว่า ใครที่สามารถ
ทำให้นักเดินทางผู้นี้ถอดเสื้อกันหนาวออกได้สำเร็จก่อนจะถือว่าเป็นผู้ที่มีพลังมากกว่า และ
แล้วลมเหนือก็กระพือพัดอย่างสุดแรง แต่ยิ่งพัดแรงมากขึ้นเพียงใด นักเดินทางก็ยิ่งดึงเสื้อ
กันหนาวให้กระชับกับตัวมากขึ้นเพียงนั้น และในที่สุดลมเหนือก็เลิกล้มความพยายาม จาก
นั้นพระอาทิตย์จึงสาดแสงอันร้อนแรงออกมา นักเดินทางก็ถอดเสื้อกันหนาวออกทันที ในที่
สุดลมเหนือจึงจำต้องยอมรับว่าพระอาทิตย์มีพลังมากกว่าตน

Acknowledgements

We thank Dr. Chalida Rojanawathanavuthi, Dr. Kingkarn Thepkanjana, and Miss Surangkana Kaewnamdee, whose readings of the passage underlie our transcription. Dr. Theraphan Luangthongkum and Dr. Sudaporn Luksaneeyanawin read the manuscript and made helpful comments. Part of the work of the second author was supported by Grant HD01994 from the U.S. National Institutes of Health to Haskins Laboratories.

References

ABRAMSON, A. S. (1962). *The Vowels and Tones of Standard Thai: Acoustical Measurements and Experiments*. Bloomington: Indiana University Research Center in Anthropology, Folklore, and Linguistics, Publication 20.

ABRAMSON, A. S. (1989). Laryngeal control in the plosives of Standard Thai. *Pasaa* 19, 85–93.

ABRAMSON, A. S. AND REN, N. (1990). Distinctive vowel length: Duration vs. spectrum in Thai. *Journal of Phonetics* 18, 79–92.

HARRIS, J. G. (1992). The consonant sounds of 17th century Siamese. *Mon-Khmer Studies* 21, 1–17.

HENDERSON, E. J. A. (1949). Prosodies in Siamese: A study in synthesis. *Asia Major* New Series 1, 189–215.

HENDERSON, E. J. A. (1964). Marginalia to Siamese phonetic studies. In Abercrombie, D., Fry, D. B., MacCarthy, P. A. D., Scott, N. C. and Trim, J. L. M. (editors), *In Honour of Daniel Jones: Papers Contributed on the Occasion of his Eightieth Birthday 12 September 1961*, 415–24. London: Longmans.

Tukang Besi

MARK DONOHUE

Department of Linguistics, University of Sydney, NSW 2006, Australia

Tukang Besi is an archipelago in south-east Sulawesi, Indonesia, where an Austronesian language is spoken. The speech represented here is that of the northern coast of the island of Wanci. With mainly slight lexical variation it represents the speech of the two northernmost islands in the archipelago, Wanci and Kaledupa.

Consonants

	Bilabial	Labiodental	Dental	Alveolar	Velar	Glottal
Plosive	p b		t (d)		k g	ʔ
Implosive	ɓ		ɗ			
Nasal	m			n	ŋ	
Fricative	β			s (z)		h
Prenasalized Plosive	mp mb		nt nd		ŋk ŋg	
Prenasalized Fricative			ns			
Trill				r		
Lateral Approximant			l			

The consonant table represents phonemic contrasts, with the exception of [d] and [z] which are allophones of the loan phoneme /dʒ/; only borrowed words (or suspected loans) show this phoneme. /b/ is also a loan phoneme, present only in a few recently borrowed words, but contrastive with /ɓ/, as seen in [balɛ] 'turn around (walking only)' (< Malay *balik*) vs. [ɓalɛ] 'frond of coconut tree'.

p	apa	'up to'	t	titi	'breast'	k	kai	'hook'
ɓ	aɓa	'previous'	ɗ	piɗi	'rubbish'	g	gai	'pull out'
m	ama	'father'	n	ana	'child'	ŋ	aɲa	'gills'
β	ʔaβa	'obtain'	s	asa	'one'			
mp	kompa	'eel'	nt	tinti	'run'	ŋk	ɓaŋka	'ship'
mb	komba	'moon'	nd	pindi	'faeces'	ŋg	iŋgaβi	'yesterday'
			ns	pinsɛ	'squeeze'			
			r	ara	'if'	ʔ	ʔaɗa	'send'
			l	ala	'fetch'	h	haɗa	'imminent'

Vowels

i	ɓali	'turn around'
ɛ	ɓalɛ	'frond of a young coconut tree'
a	ɓala	(classifier for soap and small objects)
o	ɓalo	'answer'
ɯ	ɓalɯ	'buy'

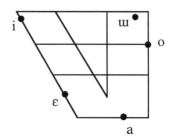

Stress/ accent

Stress, realized as a generally higher and level pitch on the whole syllable, is almost always on the penultimate syllable of the word. The definition of the word is sometimes extended to include the following (inherently stressless) absolutive article /tɛ/. Thus the sentence *nomanga te bae* 'he ate the rice' can be pronounced either as [nɔˈmaŋatɛˈɓae] or as [ˌnɔmaˈŋatɛˈɓae]. A secondary stress, consisting of a greater amplitude without the higher pitch that is the characteristic of the primary stress, is also found on every second syllable away from the primary stressed syllable.

Contrastive accent patterns have arisen from the introduction of loan words with final nasals; the final nasal is borrowed as a separate syllabic nucleus, with predictable effects on the penultimate accent, and then later dropped. This has produced at least one case of a lexical difference based solely on accent: [ˈkɛnta] 'fish' (archaic) vs. [kɛˈnta] 'potato' (loan, < Malay [kɛntaŋ]).

Conventions

Free variation is observed between [β], [ɸ] and [ʋ], with [β] being the most common phone except amongst children, who prefer [ɸ]; the implosives and /g/ are preglottalized following a stressed syllable ([ʔɓ], [ʔɗ] and [ʔg]). /h/ varies with [ɸ] before a high back vowel. The lateral /l/ is sometimes realized as a retroflex lateral flap [ɭ] after back vowels. The phoneme /r/ varies between [r], [ɾ], [ɻ] and [ɺ]; thus, after a back vowel, realizations of /r/ and /l/ overlap. The loan phoneme /dʒ/ varies idiolectally between [dʒ] (most common), [d] (contrasting with [ɗ]), and [z]. Thus: [ˌkaɺaˈdaː] ~ [ˌkaɺaˈdʒaː] *karajaa* 'work (for a wage)', [ˈdari] ~ [ˈzari] ~ [ˈdʒari] *jari* 'then, thus'.

Voiceless or sonorant consonants are often geminated in the stressed or post-stressed syllable, in a restrictive set of vocalic environments that depends on the consonant. Thus: [ˈaka] ~ [ˈakːa] 'root', [ˌmɔtʊˈtɯrɯ] ~ [ˌmɔtɯˈtːɯrɯ] 'sleepy'. The voiced prenasalized stops sometimes reduce to a geminate nasal in casual speech. Thus [ɓaˈmbai] ~ [ɓaˈmːai] 'comb', [ˈndaŋa] ~ [ˈnːaŋa] 'jackfruit', [iˈŋgaβi] ~ [iˈŋʲaβi] 'yesterday'. A glottal stop deletes or is replaced by [k] in a syllable adjacent to another glottal stop: thus /ʔɯ/ '2nd person singular possessive' and /ŋoʔo/ 'nose', but [ŋɔˈʔoɯ] 'your nose' (< /ŋoʔo + ʔɯ/), /ʔɛ/ '3rd person object' and /tɯʔo/ 'chop down', but [tɯˈʔoke] 'chop it down' (< /tɯʔo + ʔɛ/).

The high front vowel shows little variation in quality, nor does the low back vowel. The high back unrounded vowel /ɯ/ can round to [u] in a syllable immediately following the vowel /o/ or following /w/. In these and other environments it shows occasional variation with [ʊ]. The front mid vowel /ɛ/ tends to raise to [e] or even [ɪ] when not followed by a consonant (i.e. finally or before a syllable without an onset), with the notable exception of the core article *te*, which is invariably [tɛ]. The mid back vowel is higher than the mid front vowel, again tending to be higher when followed by a vowel, especially when the following syllable contains /o/ or /ɯ/. Following a bilabial consonant the height of the vowel is also more pronounced, and the closer the syllable to the end of the word, the higher the vowel. All the vowels tend to de-syllabify if they occur before the stressed syllable adjacent to another vowel, or in a stressless word; usually the highest of the vowels desyllabifies. When two vowels come together across a word boundary, the first of these often deletes. See the text for examples of these phenomena.

Transcription of recorded passage

sa'pajɾa sa'pajɾa 'ana, 'anɛ kɛ la 'ɓɛla βa'ndeṇsa'ŋia 'kɛnɛ la 'ɓɛla ʔo'lo:. tɛ a'm:ai 'ana ˌnɔpoˌɓʊsɯ'ɓʊsɯ̢ 'ako tɛ ɛ'mai na mɛ'ɓʊkɯ. mbe'aka mo'leŋo 'ʔumpa ˌnɔma'imo na 'mia ɸu'mila pʊ'make ʔɛ 'ɓadʒɯ mo'kɔʔɓa. ˌsaʔiˌtaʔa'kɔno, ˌnɔsɛ'tɯdʒɯ kɯ̢a tɛ ˌɓa:'ɓa:no pʊˌmaɭɯ'ɭɯʔe na 'mia βu'mila 'iso, tɛ 'ia naˌhopo'taɭɯ i poˌtaɟɯ'ʔano 'isŏ aj. 'maka tɛ la 'ɓɛla βa'ndeṇsa'ŋia 'ana nɔ'tɔp:a, nɔ'tɔp:a, nɔ'tɔp:a, 'tɔk:a ˌsamɛ'ɓʊkɯ nɔ'tɔp:a ˌsamɛ'ɓʊkɯ tɛ 'ia 'iso nɔ'kɔnta tɛ 'ɓadɯ ˌmokɔ'ɓano. ka'mɓea ˌmoni'nino. maˌkala'ʔamo ˌmbɛa'kamo nɔ'sɔʔɓa na la 'ɓɛla βaˌndeṇsa'ŋia 'ana. po'ʔoli 'iso, la 'ɓɛla ʔo'lo: noˌpasɔ'soa tɛ 'mia mɛ'ɓadʒɯ iso 'kɛnɛ ˌmbea'kamo ɔ'haʔɖa pa'ke tɛ ɓadʒɯno. 'dʒar ˌaβa'na:tɯ nɔˌhopo'taɭɯ na la 'ɓɛla ʔo'lo:, 'kɛnɛ ˌnomo'taɭɯ na ɭa 'ɓɛla βaˌndeṇsa'ŋia i ˌpota'ɾɯʔ ɯ ka'βasa 'iso aj. ˌsapa'ira ˌsapa'ira ˌtaŋka'nomŏ.

Orthographic version

Sapaira sapaira ana, ane ke La Bela Wandensangia kene La Bela 'Oloo. Te amai ana nopobusubusu ako te emai na mebuku. Mbeaka molengo 'umpa nomaimo na mia wumila pumake te baju mokoba. Sa'itaakono, nosetuju kua te baabaano pumalulu'e na mia wumila iso, te ia nahopotalu i potaru'ano iso ai. Maka te La Bela Wandensangia ana notopa, notopa, notopa, toka samebuku notopa samebuku te ia iso nokonta te baju mokobano. Kambea moninino. Maka la'amo mbeakamo nosoba na La Bela Wandensangia ana. Po'oli iso, La Bela 'Oloo nopasosoa te mia mebaju iso kene mbeakamo ohada pake te bajuno. Jari awana atu nohopotalu na La Bela 'Oloo, kene nomotalu na La Bela Wandensangia i potaru'a u kawasa iso ai. Sapaira sapaira tangkanomo.

Turkish

KARL ZIMMER AND ORHAN ORGUN

Department of Linguistics, University of California, Berkeley, CA 94720, USA

The speech is that of a 25-year-old native of Istanbul. This variety of the language is considered standard; most educated speakers of Turkish are familiar with this pronunciation as well as a regional variety.

Consonants

	Bilabial	Labio-dental	Dental	Alveolar	Post-alveolar	Palatal	Velar	Glottal
Plosive and Affricate	p　b		t　d		tʃ　dʒ	c　ɟ	k　ɡ	
Nasal	m		n					
Fricative		f　v	s　z		ʃ　ʒ		ɣ	h
Tap				ɾ				
Approximant						j		
Lateral Approximant			ɫ		l			

p	puɫ	'stamp'	t	tel	'wire'	c	caɾ	'profit'
b	buɫ	'find'	d	del	'pierce'	ɟ	ɟem	'bit (for a horse)'
						k	kaɾ	'snow'
						ɡ	ɡam	'grief'
			m	maɫ	'property'	n	naɫ	'horseshoe'
			ɾ	ɾej	'vote'			
f	faɾ	'headlight'	s	saɾ	'wrap'			
v	vaɾ	'exists'	z	zaɾ	'membrane'	ɣ	daɣ [daː]	'mountain'
						h	heɾ	'every'
			tʃ	tʃam	'pine'			
			dʒ	dʒam	'glass'			
						j	jeɾ	'place'
			ɫ	ɫaˈɫa	'servant'			
			l	laːˈle	'tulip'			

Vowels

i	kil	'clay'
y	kyl	'ashes'
e	kel	'bald'
œ	gœl	'lake'
a	kał	'stay'
ɯ	kɯł	'hair'
u	kuł	'slave'
o	koł	'arm'

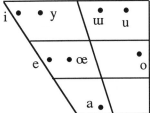

Long vowels are [iː], [eː], [uː] and [aː]. Diphthongs can be treated as sequences of vowel and /j/.

Stress
Word stress tends to be on the last syllable of the word. However, there are some unstressable suffixes which cause the main word stress to fall on the syllable preceding such a suffix, e.g. [jap-tɯr-maˈlɯ] 's/he must have (it) done' vs. [jap-ˈtɯr-ma-malɯ] 's/he must refrain from having (it) done', where the negative suffix [-ma] is an unstressable suffix. There are also some lexical exceptions to final stress, e.g. [ˈmasa] 'table'.

Conventions
The voiceless stops are usually aspirated in syllable-initial position and are always released in codas unless followed by a homorganic consonant. /c, ɟ/ do not contrast with /k, g/ in the native vocabulary, where [c] and [ɟ] appear only in syllables with front vowels, while [k] and [g] appear only in syllables with back vowels. There are, however, some loanwords in which there are unpredictable occurrences of [c] and [ɟ] with back vowels, e.g. /caɾ/ *kâr* 'profit' (cf. /kaɾ/ *kar* 'snow'). /l/ is a palatalized postalveolar lateral, /ł/ a velarized dental lateral; /ł/ does not occur after front vowels. /h/ in final position may be realized as a voiceless velar fricative. /ɾ/ is most commonly a single tap. /ɾ, ł, l/ are frequently devoiced in final position or when a voiceless consonant follows. [v] is frequently pronounced as a bilabial fricative or approximant when preceded by a vowel. /ɣ/ corresponds to the 'soft g' (ğ) in Turkish orthography; its use finds its main justification in accounting for morphological alternations. /ɣ/ between front vowels is pronounced as a weak front-velar or palatal approximant. When the /ɣ/ is word-final or followed by a consonant it is realized phonetically as a lengthening of the preceding vowel; elsewhere when intervocalic, it is phonetically zero. All vowels except /a, o/ have a lower variant in the final open syllable of a phrase, e.g. [kel] 'bald' but [kaˈlɛ] 'castle'.

Transcription of recorded passage

poj'razła ɟy'neʃ birbirlerin'den da'ha kuvvet'li ołdukłaruı'nuı ile'ri sy'rerec iddiaːła'ʃuıjorłarduı. 'dercen ka'łuın 'bir 'pałto ɟij'miʃ 'bir joɟ'dʒu ɟœrdy'ler. 'bu joldʒu'ja 'pałtosu'nu tʃuıˌkarttuırabile'nin da'ha kuvvet'li ołduɣu'nu ka'buːl etmi'je ka'rar verdi'ler. poj'raz 'var ɟy'dʒyle esmi'je baʃła'duı. 'andʒak joł'dʒu 'pałtosuˌna 'ɟitɟide da'ha suı'kuı saruı'nuıjordu. 'sonunda poj'raz uɣraʃmak'tan 'vazɟetʃti. 'bu se'fer ɟy'neʃ atʃ'tuı orta'łuık uısuı'nuındʒa joł'dʒu 'pałtosunu he'men tʃuıkar'duı. 'bœjledʒe poj'raz ɟyne'ʃin ˌkendisin'den da'ha kuvvet'li olduɣu'nu ka'buːl etmi'je medʒ'bur kał'duı.

Orthographic version

Poyrazla güneş, birbirlerinden daha kuvvetli olduklarını ileri sürerek iddialaşıyorlardı. Derken, kalın bir palto giymiş bir yolcu gördüler. Bu yolcuya paltosunu çıkarttırabilenin daha kuvvetli olduğunu kabul etmeye karar verdiler. Poyraz, var gücüyle esmeye başladı. Ancak, yolcu paltosuna gitgide daha sıkı sarınıyordu. Sonunda poyraz uğraşmaktan vazgeçti. Bu sefer güneş açtı; ortalık ısınınca yolcu paltosunu hemen çıkardı. Böylece poyraz, güneşin kendisinden daha kuvvetli olduğunu kabul etmeye mecbur kaldı.

PART 3

Appendices

Appendix 1

The Principles of the International Phonetic Association

From its earliest days (see appendix 4) the Association has tried to make explicit the principles which guide its work. The statement of these principles has been amended and updated from time to time; the current formulation (below) was approved at the 1989 Convention of the Association.

1   The International Phonetic Association has a standard alphabet which is usually referred to by the initials IPA, or, in a number of non-English-speaking countries, API. It is designed primarily to meet practical linguistic needs, such as putting on record the phonetic or phonological structure of languages, providing learners of foreign languages with phonetic transcriptions to assist them in acquiring the pronunciation, and working out roman orthographies for languages written in other systems or for languages previously unwritten. A large number of symbols and diacritics is also provided for representing fine distinctions of sound quality, making the IPA well suited for use in all disciplines in which the representation of speech sounds is required.

2   The IPA is intended to be a set of symbols for representing all the possible sounds of the world's languages. The representation of these sounds uses a set of phonetic categories which describe how each sound is made. These categories define a number of natural classes of sounds that operate in phonological rules and historical sound changes. The symbols of the IPA are shorthand ways of indicating certain intersections of these categories. Thus [p] is a shorthand way of designating the intersection of the categories voiceless, bilabial, and plosive; [m] is the intersection of the categories voiced, bilabial, and nasal; and so on. The sounds that are represented by the symbols are primarily those that serve to distinguish one word from another in a language.

3   In the construction of the IPA attention has been paid not only to the appropriateness of each symbol from a phonetic point of view, but also to the suitability of symbols from the typographical point of view. The non-roman symbols of the IPA have, as far as possible, been made to harmonize with the roman letters. For instance, the Greek letters included in the IPA are roman adaptations; as the ordinary shape of the Greek letter β does not harmonize with roman type, in the IPA it has been given the form β. The Association does not favour the use of italic forms of symbols as models for the design of new symbols.

4   The construction and use of the IPA are guided by the following principles:

(a)   When two sounds occurring in a given language are employed for distinguishing one word from another, they should wherever possible be represented by two distinct symbols without diacritics. Ordinary roman letters should be used as far as is practicable, but recourse must be had to other symbols when the roman alphabet is inadequate.

(b)   When two sounds are very similar and not known to be employed in any language for distinguishing meanings of utterances, they should, as a rule, be represented by the same symbol. Separate symbols or diacritics may, however, be used to distinguish such sounds when necessary.

(c) It is not possible to dispense entirely with diacritics. The International Phonetic Association recommends that their use be limited as far as possible to the following cases:

(i)   For denoting length, stress and pitch.

(ii)   For representing minute shades of sounds.

(iii)   When the introduction of a single diacritic obviates the necessity for designing a number of new symbols (as, for instance, in the representation of nasalized vowels).

5   The use of symbols in representing the sounds of a particular language is usually guided by the principles of phonological contrast. All languages use a limited number of vowels and consonants that are able to distinguish word meanings: the contrast between English **m** and **n** is used to distinguish the words *met* and *net*, and these two sounds should therefore be represented by different symbols. The three **k**-sounds of the English words *keep*, *cart*, *cool* can be heard and felt to be different, but from the linguistic or phonological point of view the differences are not distinctive and all may be represented by the same [k] symbol. The same applies to the French **k**-sounds in *qui*, *cas*, *cou*, though these differ phonetically from the corresponding English ones.

6   The Association recommends that a phonetic transcription should be enclosed in square brackets [ ]. A transcription that notes only phonological contrasts may be enclosed in slanted lines or slashes / /.

7   A transcription always consists of a set of symbols and a set of conventions for their interpretation. Furthermore, the IPA consists of symbols and diacritics whose meaning cannot be learned entirely from written descriptions of the phonetic categories involved. The Association strongly recommends that anyone intending to use the symbols should receive training in order to learn how to produce and recognize the corresponding sounds with a reasonable degree of accuracy.

Appendix 2

Computer coding of IPA symbols

This section is a revision of an article which first appeared in the *Journal of the International Phonetic Association* 23, 83–97 (1993), entitled 'Computer codes for phonetic symbols', by John H. Esling and Harry Gaylord. The chart of IPA Numbers and the coding tables in this section have been updated to 1998.

The process of assigning computer codes to phonetic symbols began when the 1989 Kiel Convention of the International Phonetic Association was called to revise the Association's alphabet. The Workgroup on Computer Coding formed at that time had the task of determining how to represent the IPA alphabet numerically, and of developing a set of numbers referring to IPA symbols unambiguously. This involved assembling phoneticians who work with computer representations of phonetic symbols, and communicating with specialists in computer coding to gauge the fit between the phonetician's perspective on symbol usage and the non-phonetician's understanding of how to identify and use phonetic symbols. Prior to the Kiel meeting, a collection of practical approaches to coded representations was outlined in *JIPA* (Esling 1988), which dealt mainly with keyboard assignments of characters.

At Kiel, after reviewing several submissions on current practice, the Workgroup concluded that each symbol used by the IPA should be assigned a unique, three-digit number known as its IPA Number. IPA Numbers were assigned in linear order following the new IPA Chart which resulted from the deliberations at Kiel (IPA 1989a). IPA Numbers were not only created for approved consonant, vowel, diacritic and suprasegmental symbols, but also for symbols often referred to in IPA deliberations or implied by IPA convention but which do not appear explicitly on the IPA Chart.

The conclusions and recommendations reached by the Workgroup at Kiel appeared in *JIPA* (IPA 1989b), followed by a supplementary report with an initial listing of IPA Numbers by symbol and by symbol name (Esling 1990). The comprehensive documentation of phonetic symbol usage and categorization in the *Phonetic Symbol Guide* by Pullum and Ladusaw (1986, 1996) assisted in this process. Several recommendations were made at Kiel, including the use of at least two levels of transcription when entering coded phonetic values to accompany data, but what is most important to point out about the process of associating each possible character with a discrete numerical entity is its comprehensive nature. No symbols could be ignored, and the application of diacritics had to be made explicit. The result is that the list of IPA Numbers includes more characters than are specified on the IPA Chart alone. Thus, in addition to the IPA Chart, an IPA Number Chart was also established to show the equivalent Number for each symbol; and a comprehensive list was drawn up that includes symbols cited by the IPA since 1949, as well as some non-IPA symbols, cross-referenced to their equivalent Numbers.

The reason for the comprehensive inclusion of all symbols is to anticipate the possibility that some symbols may be withdrawn while other symbols may be reintroduced into current usage; and a numerical listing of character shapes and types must be comprehensive enough to support slight revisions in symbol specification or diacritic placement as well as to be available to a wide spectrum of phonetic users of computer systems. The set of IPA Numbers also allows for the addition of new symbols, within the 100 series for consonants, the 200 series for extra symbols and cross-reference to other phonetic sets, the 300 series for vowels, the 400 series for diacritics, and the 500 series for suprasegmental symbols. Ligatures for affricates, for example, are included in the 200 series as formerly recognized IPA symbols although they do not occupy a specific location on the IPA Chart.

As the 1989 IPA Chart was subjected to review, several modifications emerged, resulting in the publication of the 1993 IPA Chart (IPA 1993) which was updated in 1996. No new Numbers were required to specify these symbols, even though a few symbols were revived and reinstated. Although the order of IPA Numbers is different from the 1989 order, because the original order was itself arbitrary, the changes on the 1993 Chart do not impinge on the IPA Number scheme as an effective numerical interface. In some small measure, the Numbers that accompany the symbols help to document the history of their development. The IPA Number Chart corresponding to the updated IPA Chart is shown as table 1.

The set of IPA symbols and their numbers were used to draw up an entity set within SGML by the Text Encoding Initiative (TEI). The name of each entity is formed by 'IPA' preceding the number, e.g. IPA304 is the TEI entity name of lower-case A. These symbols can be processed as IPA symbols and represented on paper and screen with the appropriate local font by modifying the entity replacement text. The advantage of the SGML entity set is that it is independent of the character set being used.

At the same time that this work was being done, two organizations were drawing up computer character sets for all world languages: the Unicode Consortium and ISO, the International Standards Organization. These projects were linked so that the code for each character is the same in Unicode and the ISO Universal Character Set (UCS), also known as ISO 10646. The IPA symbols were submitted for inclusion in these character sets and with a few exceptions have been incorporated. Character set 10646 was approved by the ISO and published on 1 May 1993. The full set, which comprises over 40,000 characters, undergoes periodic revision. A recent update can be found in *The Unicode Standard, Version 2.0* (Unicode Consortium 1996).

Tables 3, 4, 5 and 6 below contain the UCS Code position for each phonetic character. Unicode/UCS is a 16-bit character set, and is represented therefore as a four-character hexadecimal number. There are also some non-IPA phonetic symbols in Unicode/UCS which had been submitted by other groups than the IPA. A few IPA symbols, e.g. the Chao tone characters, have not yet been included in the Unicode/UCS character set. If the symbol is not included, this is indicated by '------' in the table. A few symbols have two possible encodings, e.g. IPA598 is encoded as 0316 if placed under the symbol and as

THE INTERNATIONAL PHONETIC ALPHABET (revised to 1993, updated 1996)

CONSONANTS (PULMONIC)   NUMBER CHART

	Bilabial	Labiodental	Dental	Alveolar	Postalveolar	Retroflex	Palatal	Velar	Uvular	Pharyngeal	Glottal
Plosive	101 102		103 104			105 106	107 108	109 110	111 112		113
Nasal		114 115	116			117	118	119	120		
Trill	121		122						123		
Tap or Flap			124			125					
Fricative	126 127	128 129	130 131	132 133	134 135	136 137	138 139	140 141	142 143	144 145	146 147
Lateral fricative			148 149								
Approximant		150	151			152	· 153	154			
Lateral approximant			155			156	157	158			

Where symbols appear in pairs, the one to the right represents a voiced consonant. Shaded areas denote articulations judged impossible.

CONSONANTS (NON-PULMONIC)

Clicks	Voiced implosives	Ejectives
176 Bilabial	160 Bilabial	401 Examples:
177 Dental	162 Dental/alveolar	101 + 401 Bilabial
178 (Post)alveolar	164 Palatal	103 + 401 Dental/alveolar
179 Palatoalveolar	166 Velar	109 + 401 Velar
180 Alveolar lateral	168 Uvular	132 + 401 Alveolar fricative

OTHER SYMBOLS

169 Voiceless labial-velar fricative	182 183 Alveolo-palatal fricatives
170 Voiced labial-velar approximant	181 Alveolar lateral flap
171 Voiced labial-palatal approximant	175 Simultaneous ∫ and X
172 Voiceless epiglottal fricative	Affricates and double articulations
174 Voiced epiglottal fricative	can be represented by two symbols 433 (509)
173 Epiglottal plosive	joined by a tie bar if necessary.

VOWELS

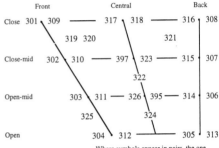

Where symbols appear in pairs, the one to the right represents a rounded vowel.

SUPRASEGMENTALS

501	Primary stress
502	Secondary stress
	ˌfoʊnəˈtɪʃən
503	Long eː
504	Half-long eˑ
505	Extra-short ĕ
507	Minor (foot) group
508	Major (intonation) group
506	Syllable break ɹi.ækt
509	Linking (absence of a break)

DIACRITICS   Diacritics may be placed above a symbol with a descender, e.g. 119 + 402B

402A	Voiceless	n̥ d̥	405	Breathy voiced	b̤ a̤	408	Dental t̪ d̪
403	Voiced	s̬ t̬	406	Creaky voiced	b̰ a̰	409	Apical t̺ d̺
404	Aspirated	tʰ dʰ	407	Linguolabial	t̼ d̼	410	Laminal t̻ d̻
411	More rounded	ɔ̹	420	Labialized	tʷ dʷ	424	Nasalized ẽ
412	Less rounded	ɔ̜	421	Palatalized	tʲ dʲ	425	Nasal release dⁿ
413	Advanced	u̟	422	Velarized	tˠ dˠ	426	Lateral release dˡ
414	Retracted	e̠	423	Pharyngealized	tˤ dˤ	427	No audible release d̚
415	Centralized	ë	428	Velarized or pharyngealized 209		
416	Mid-centralized	e̽	429	Raised	e̝	(ɹ̝ = voiced alveolar fricative)
431	Syllabic	n̩	430	Lowered	e̞	(β̞ = voiced bilabial approximant)
432	Non-syllabic	e̯	417	Advanced Tongue Root	e̘		
419	Rhoticity	327 ɚ	418	Retracted Tongue Root	e̙		

TONES AND WORD ACCENTS

LEVEL			CONTOUR		
512	519	Extra high	524	529	Rising
513	520	High	525	530	Falling
514	521	Mid	526	531	High rising
515	522	Low	527	532	Low rising
516	523	Extra low	528	533	Rising-falling
517	Downstep		510	Global rise	
518	Upstep		511	Global fall	

Table 1 The IPA Number Chart

02CE if it follows the symbol. When this character set is in wide use, it will be the normal way to encode IPA symbols.

In cooperation with ISO, the Association for Font Information Interchange (AFII) maintains a registry of glyphs. The IPA symbols have been registered with AFII, and their registered glyph numbers are indicated with a hexadecimal number in the AFII Code column of tables 3, 4, 5 and 6. The AFII glyph registry may be used for font standardization in the future.

A TEI writing system declaration (wsd) has been drawn up for the IPA symbols. This document gives information about the symbol and its IPA function, as well as its encoding in the accompanying SGML document and in Unicode/UCS and in AFII. The writing system declaration can be read as a text document or processed by machines in an SMGL process.

Table 2 illustrates that the 26 roman characters within the IPA symbol set have retained their original or 'ASCII' numbers as their UCS codes. They belong to the 00 or 'base' table of Unicode/UCS. More specialized phonetic symbols have been assigned to subsequent tables.

Table 2

UCS codes retain original ASCII coding for roman characters in the IPA set.

Symbol	Symbol Name	Phonetic Description / *Status*	IPA Number	UCS Code	AFII Code
a	Lower-case A	Open front unrounded vowel	304	0061	E25B
b	Lower-case B	Voiced bilabial plosive	102	0062	E2A3
c	Lower-case C	Voiceless palatal plosive	107	0063	E2D9
d	Lower-case D	Voiced dental or alveolar plosive	104	0064	E2B1
e	Lower-case E	Close-mid front unrounded vowel	302	0065	E256
f	Lower-case F	Voiceless labiodental fricative	128	0066	E2AC
g	Looptail G	Voiced velar plosive *Equivalent to 110*	210	0067	E2E3
h	Lower-case H	Voiceless glottal fricative	146	0068	E2EE
i	Lower-case I	Close front unrounded vowel	301	0069	E251
j	Lower-case J	Voiced palatal approximant	153	006A	E2DB
k	Lower-case K	Voiceless velar plosive	109	006B	E2DE
l	Lower-case L	Voiced dental or alveolar lateral approximant	155	006C	E2BD
m	Lower-case M	Voiced bilabial nasal	114	006D	E2A1
n	Lower-case N	Voiced dental or alveolar nasal	116	006E	E2AF

o	Lower-case O	Close-mid back rounded vowel	307	006F	E269
p	Lower-case P	Voiceless bilabial plosive	101	0070	E2A2
q	Lower-case Q	Voiceless uvular plosive	111	0071	E2E6
r	Lower-case R	Voiced dental or alveolar trill	122	0072	E2C0
s	Lower-case S	Voiceless alveolar fricative	132	0073	E2B6
t	Lower-case T	Voiceless dental or alveolar plosive	103	0074	E2B0
u	Lower-case U	Close back rounded vowel	308	0075	E265
v	Lower-case V	Voiced labiodental fricative	129	0076	E2AD
w	Lower-case W	Voiced labial-velar approximant	170	0077	E2A8
x	Lower-case X	Voiceless velar fricative	140	0078	E2E0
y	Lower-case Y	Close front rounded vowel	309	0079	E252
z	Lower-case Z	Voiced alveolar fricative	133	007A	E2B7

The Kiel Convention Workgroup on Pathological Speech and Voice Quality has developed specialized symbols and diacritics with IPA Numbers from 600 to 699. They are described in Duckworth, Allen, Hardcastle and Ball (1990), and listed together with their Number assignments in Ball (1991). They are not included in the present tables because they were not considered among the original submissions made to ISO for universal coding. At the moment, therefore, there are no UCS codes or AFII codes that can be easily associated with the 'Extended IPA' characters for disordered speech and voice quality of the 600 series.

Table 3 lists all phonetic consonant and vowel symbols that have been given a code in the universal coded character set, cross-referencing symbol shape, symbol name, articulatory description, IPA Number, UCS code, and AFII code. The symbols are arranged in pseudo-alphabetical order. Table 4 lists all phonetic diacritic and suprasegmental symbols that have been given a code in the universal coded character set, arranged in the order of the original 1993 IPA Chart. Symbols in the declaration which are not IPA symbols and those which are no longer in IPA usage are specified, with an indication of the date when they were removed from IPA usage or superseded by other symbols. Supplementary tables 5 and 6 offer a cross-referenced listing of all phonetic consonant and vowel, diacritic and suprasegmental symbols in numerical order by IPA Number. An earlier version of these tables appeared in the *Handbook of Standards and Resources for Spoken Language Systems* (Gibbon, Moore and Winski 1997). The publication of these lists of coding assignments should not be construed as an endorsement by the IPA of every character in the list, but as a convenient reference to the location of any potential phonetic character in the coding tables as currently constituted.

Table 3

IPA symbols: Phonetic consonant/vowel symbol codes
(in pseudo-alphabetical order by symbol shape)

Symbol	Symbol Name	Phonetic Description / *Status*	IPA Number	UCS Code	AFII Code
a	Lower-case A	Open front unrounded vowel	304	0061	E25B
ɐ	Turned A	Near-open central vowel	324	0250	E263
ɑ	Script A	Open back unrounded vowel	305	0251	E26C
ɒ	Turned script A	Open back rounded vowel	313	0252	E26D
æ	Ash; Lower-case A-E ligature	Near-open front unrounded vowel	325	00E6	E25A
b	Lower-case B	Voiced bilabial plosive	102	0062	E2A3
ɓ	Hooktop B	Voiced bilabial implosive	160	0253	E2A9
ʙ	Small capital B	Voiced bilabial trill	121	0299	E2F0
β	Beta	Voiced bilabial fricative	127	03B2	E2A5
c	Lower-case C	Voiceless palatal plosive	107	0063	E2D8
ƈ	Hooktop C	Voiceless palatal implosive *Withdrawn (1993)*	163	0188	2376
č	C wedge	Voiceless postalveolar affricate *Not IPA usage*	299	010D	F1AE
ç	C cedilla	Voiceless palatal fricative	138	00E7	E2DA
ɕ	Curly-tail C	Voiceless alveolo-palatal fricative	182	0255	E2CE
ʗ	Stretched C	Postalveolar click *Superseded by 178 (1989)*	202	0297	E2C4
d	Lower-case D	Voiced dental or alveolar plosive	104	0064	E2B1
ɗ	Hooktop D	Voiced dental or alveolar implosive	162	0257	E2C2
ɖ	Right-tail D	Voiced retroflex plosive	106	0256	E2C8
ᶑ	Hooktop right-tail D	Voiced retroflex implosive *Not explicitly IPA approved*	219	------	E219
ʣ	D-Z ligature	Voiced alveolar affricate *Superseded by 104+133*	212	02A3	E2F9
ʤ	D-Ezh ligature	Voiced postalveolar affricate *Superseded by 104+135*	214	02A4	E2FA
ʥ	D-Curly-tail-Z ligature	Voiced alveolo-palatal affricate *Superseded by 104+183*	216	02A5	E2FB
ð	Eth	Voiced dental fricative	131	00F0	E2B3
e	Lower-case E	Close-mid front unrounded vowel	302	0065	E256

ə	Schwa	Mid central vowel	322	0259	E25F
ᵊ	Superscript schwa	Mid central vowel release	218	------	E21A
ɚ	Right-hook schwa	R-coloured mid central vowel *Equivalent to 322+419*	327	025A	E260
ɘ	Reversed E	Close-mid central unrounded vowel	397	0258	E26E
ɛ	Epsilon	Open-mid front unrounded vowel	303	025B	E258
ʚ	Closed epsilon	*Superseded by 395 (1996)*	396	029A	E273
ɜ	Reversed epsilon	Open-mid central unrounded vowel	326	025C	E262
ɞ	Closed reversed epsilon	Open-mid central rounded vowel	395	025E	E270
f	Lower-case F	Voiceless labiodental fricative	128	0066	E2AC
ɡ	Opentail G	Voiced velar plosive *Equivalent to 210*	110	0261	E2DF
ɠ	Hooktop G	Voiced velar implosive	166	0260	E27E
g	Looptail G	Voiced velar plosive *Equivalent to 110*	210	0067	E2E3
ɢ	Small capital G	Voiced uvular plosive	112	0262	E2E7
ʛ	Hooktop small capital G	Voiced uvular implosive	168	029B	E2F1
ɣ	Gamma	Voiced velar fricative	141	0263	E2E1
ˠ	Superscript gamma	Velarized	422	02E0	E28B
ɤ	Ram's horns	Close-mid back unrounded vowel	315	0264	E268
h	Lower-case H	Voiceless glottal fricative	146	0068	E2EE
ʰ	Superscript H	Aspirated	404	02B0	D565
ħ	Barred H	Voiceless pharyngeal fricative	144	0127	E2EB
ɦ	Hooktop H	Voiced glottal fricative	147	0266	E2EF
ɧ	Hooktop heng	Simultaneous voiceless postalveolar and velar fricative	175	0267	E2D6
ɥ	Turned H	Voiced labial-palatal approximant	171	0265	E2A6
ʜ	Small capital H	Voiceless epiglottal fricative	172	029C	E2F2
i	Lower-case I	Close front unrounded vowel	301	0069	E251
ı	Undotted I	*Not IPA usage*	394	0131	00F5
ɨ	Barred I	Close central unrounded vowel	317	0268	E25D
ɪ	Iota	Near-close near-front unrounded vowel *Superseded by 319 (1989)*	399	0269	E253

ɪ	Small capital I	Near-close near-front unrounded vowel	319	026A	E254
j	Lower-case J	Voiced palatal approximant	153	006A	E2DB
ʲ	Superscript J	Palatalized	421	02B2	D567
ʝ	Curly-tail J	Voiced palatal fricative	139	029D	E2F3
ǰ	J wedge	Voiced postalveolar affricate *Not IPA usage*	298	01F0	E290
ɟ	Barred dotless J	Voiced palatal plosive	108	025F	E2D9
ʄ	Hooktop barred dotless J	Voiced palatal implosive	164	0284	E27C
k	Lower-case K	Voiceless velar plosive	109	006B	E2DE
ƙ	Hooktop K	Voiceless velar implosive *Withdrawn (1993)*	165	0199	2363
ʞ	Turned K	*Withdrawn (1979)*	291	029E	E2F4
l	Lower-case L	Voiced dental or alveolar lateral approximant	155	006C	E2BD
ˡ	Superscript L	Lateral release	426	02E1	FDA3
ɫ	L with tilde	Velarized voiced dental or alveolar lateral approximant	209	026B	E27D
ɬ	Belted L	Voiceless dental or alveolar lateral fricative	148	026C	E2BB
ɭ	Right-tail L	Voiced retroflex lateral approximant	156	026D	E2CC
ʟ	Small capital L	Voiced velar lateral approximant	158	029F	E2F5
ɮ	L-Ezh ligature	Voiced dental or alveolar lateral fricative	149	026E	E2BC
λ	Lambda	Voiceless dental or alveolar lateral fricative *Not IPA usage*	295	03BB	266E
ƛ	Barred lambda	Voiceless dental or alveolar lateral affricate *Not IPA usage*	294	019B	FD7B
m	Lower-case M	Voiced bilabial nasal	114	006D	E2A1
ɱ	Left-tail M (at right)	Voiced labiodental nasal	115	0271	E2AB
ɯ	Turned M	Close back unrounded vowel	316	026F	E264

ɰ	Turned M, right leg	Voiced velar approximant	154	0270	E2E2
n	Lower-case N	Voiced dental or alveolar nasal	116	006E	E2AF
ⁿ	Superscript N	Nasal release	425	207F	FDA8
ŋ	N, right leg	Syllabic nasal *Withdrawn (1976)*	293	019E	E2E5
ɲ	Left-tail N (at left)	Voiced palatal nasal	118	0272	E2D7
ŋ	Eng	Voiced velar nasal	119	014B	E2DD
ɳ	Right-tail N	Voiced retroflex nasal	117	0273	E2C6
ɴ	Small capital N	Voiced uvular nasal	120	0274	E2E4
o	Lower-case O	Close-mid back rounded vowel	307	006F	E269
☉	Bull's eye	Bilabial click	176	0298	E2AA
ɵ	Barred O	Close-mid central rounded vowel	323	0275	E261
ø	Slashed O	Close-mid front rounded vowel	310	00F8	E257
œ	Lower-case O-E ligature	Open-mid front rounded vowel	311	0153	E259
Œ	Small capital O-E ligature	Open front rounded vowel	312	0276	E25C
ɔ	Open O	Open-mid back rounded vowel	306	0254	E26B
ω	Closed omega	Near-close near-back rounded vowel *Superseded by 321 (1989)*	398	0277	E266
p	Lower-case P	Voiceless bilabial plosive	101	0070	E2A2
ɓ	Hooktop P	Voiceless bilabial implosive *Withdrawn (1993)*	159	01A5	2378
ɸ	Phi	Voiceless bilabial fricative	126	0278	E2A4
q	Lower-case Q	Voiceless uvular plosive	111	0071	E2E6
ɋ	Hooktop Q	Voiceless uvular implosive *Withdrawn (1993)*	167	02A0	E2F6
r	Lower-case R	Voiced dental or alveolar trill	122	0072	E2C0
ɾ	Fish-hook R	Voiced dental or alveolar tap	124	027E	E2C1
ɼ	Long-leg R	*Withdrawn (1989)*	206	027C	E2BE
ɺ	Turned long-leg R	Voiced alveolar lateral flap	181	027A	E2BF
ɽ	Right-tail R	Voiced retroflex flap	125	027D	E2CD
ɹ	Turned R	Voiced dental or alveolar approximant	151	0279	E2BA

ɹ	Turned R, right tail	Voiced retroflex approximant	152	027B	E2CB
ʀ	Small capital R	Voiced uvular trill	123	0280	E2EA
ʁ	Inverted small capital R	Voiced uvular fricative	143	0281	E2E9
s	Lower-case S	Voiceless alveolar fricative	132	0073	E2B6
ˢ	Superscript S	*Withdrawn (1989)*	207	02E2	FDA7
š	S wedge	Voiceless postalveolar fricative *Not IPA usage*	297	0161	F1DC
ʂ	Right-tail S (at left)	Voiceless retroflex fricative	136	0282	E2C9
ʃ	Esh	Voiceless postalveolar fricative	134	0283	E2D0
ʆ	Curly-tail esh	*Withdrawn (1989)*	204	0286	E2D2
t	Lower-case T	Voiceless dental or alveolar plosive	103	0074	E2B0
ƭ	Hooktop T	Voiceless dental or alveolar implosive *Withdrawn (1993)*	161	01AD	2379
ƫ	Left-hook T	Palatalized voiceless dental or alveolar plosive *Withdrawn (1989)*	208	01AB	E2A0
ʈ	Right-tail T	Voiceless retroflex plosive	105	0288	E2C7
ts	T-S ligature	Voiceless dental or alveolar affricate *Superseded by 103+132*	211	02A6	E2FC
ʧ	T-Esh ligature	Voiceless postalveolar affricate *Superseded by 103+134*	213	02A7	E2FD
ʨ	T-Curly-tail-C ligature	Voiceless alveolo-palatal affricate *Superseded by 103+182*	215	02A8	E2FE
ʇ	Turned T	Dental click *Superseded by 177 (1989)*	201	0287	E2C3
θ	Theta	Voiceless dental fricative	130	03B8	E2B2
ᶿ	Superscript theta	Voiceless dental fricative release	217	------	E21B
u	Lower-case U	Close back rounded vowel	308	0075	E265
ʉ	Barred U	Close central rounded vowel	318	0289	E25E
ʊ	Upsilon	Near-close near-back rounded vowel	321	028A	E267
v	Lower-case V	Voiced labiodental fricative	129	0076	E2AD
ʋ	Cursive V	Voiced labiodental approximant	150	028B	E2AE
ʌ	Turned V	Open-mid back unrounded vowel	314	028C	E26A

w	Lower-case W	Voiced labial-velar approximant	170	0077	E2A8
ʷ	Superscript W	Labialized	420	02B7	D56E
ʍ	Turned W	Voiceless labial-velar fricative	169	028D	E2A7
x	Lower-case X	Voiceless velar fricative	140	0078	E2E0
ˣ	Superscript X	Voiceless velar fricative release	292	02E3	D56F
χ	Chi	Voiceless uvular fricative	142	03C7	E2E8
y	Lower-case Y	Close front rounded vowel	309	0079	E252
ʎ	Turned Y	Voiced palatal lateral approximant	157	028E	E2DC
ʏ	Small capital Y	Near-close near-front rounded vowel	320	028F	E255
z	Lower-case Z	Voiced alveolar fricative	133	007A	E2B7
ž	Z wedge	Voiced postalveolar fricative *Not IPA usage*	296	017E	F1F0
ʑ	Curly-tail Z	Voiced alveolo-palatal fricative	183	0291	E2CF
ʐ	Right-tail Z	Voiced retroflex fricative	137	0290	E2CA
ʒ	Ezh; Tailed Z	Voiced postalveolar fricative	135	0292	E2D1
ʓ	Curly-tail ezh	*Withdrawn (1989)*	205	0293	E2D3
ƻ	Barred two	*Withdrawn (1976)*	290	01BB	E2B5
ʔ	Glottal stop	Glottal plosive	113	0294	E2ED
ʡ	Barred glottal stop	Epiglottal plosive	173	02A1	E2F7
ʖ	Inverted glottal stop	Alveolar lateral click *Superseded by 180 (1989)*	203	0296	E2C5
ʕ	Reversed glottal stop	Voiced pharyngeal fricative or approximant	145	0295	E2EC
ˤ	Superscript reversed glottal stop	Pharyngealized	423	02E4	E28C
ʢ	Barred reversed glottal stop	Voiced epiglottal fricative or approximant	174	02A2	E2F8
ǀ	Pipe	Dental click	177	01C0	23A6
ǂ	Double-barred pipe	Palatoalveolar click	179	01C2	23A4
ǁ	Double pipe	Alveolar lateral click	180	01C1	23A7
ǃ	Exclamation point	(Post)alveolar click	178	01C3	23A5

Table 4
Phonetic diacritic and suprasegmental symbol codes
(in 1993 IPA Chart order)

Symbol	Symbol Name	Phonetic Description	Placement/ *Status*	IPA Number	UCS Code	AFII Code
ʼ	Apostrophe	Ejective	pʼ kʼ tsʼ ʧʼ	401	02BC	E249
̥	Under-ring	Voiceless	n̥ d̥	402A	0325	E229
̊	Over-ring	Voiceless	ŋ̊ g̊	402B	030A	00CA
̬	Subscript wedge	Voiced	s̬ k̬	403	032C	E22A
ʰ	Superscript H	Aspirated	pʰ tʰ	404	02B0	D565
̹	Subscript right half-ring	More rounded	e̹ ɔ̹	411	0339	E23C
̜	Subscript left half-ring	Less rounded	ɔ̜	412	031C	E232
̟	Subscript plus	Advanced	u̟	413	031F	E233
̠	Under-bar	Retracted	e̠	414	0320	E234
̈	Umlaut	Centralized	ë	415	0308	E221
̽	Over-cross	Mid-centralized	ẽ	416	033D	2311
̩	Syllabicity mark	Syllabic	ɹ̩ n̩ l̩	431	0329	E22E
̯	Subscript arch	Non-syllabic	e̯	432	032F	23FA
˞	Right hook	Rhoticity	e˞ ɚ o˞ a˞	419	02DE	E28A
̤	Subscript umlaut	Breathy voiced	b̤ a̤	405	0324	E22B
̰	Subscript tilde	Creaky voiced	b̰ a̰	406	0330	23D8
̼	Subscript seagull	Linguolabial	t̼ d̼	407	033C	22E8
ʷ	Superscript W	Labialized	tʷ dʷ	420	02B7	D56E
ʲ	Superscript J	Palatalized	tʲ dʲ	421	02B2	D567
ˠ	Superscript gamma	Velarized	tˠ dˠ	422	02E0	E28B
ˤ	Superscript reversed glottal stop	Pharyngealized	tˤ dˤ	423	02E4	E28C
̪	Subscript bridge	Dental	n̪ d̪	408	032A	E22C
̺	Inverted subscript bridge	Apical	n̺ d̺	409	033A	23FD
̻	Subscript square	Laminal	n̻ d̻	410	033B	23FE
̃	Superscript tilde	Nasalized	ẽ ã	424	0303	E222

ⁿ	Superscript N	Nasal release	dⁿ	425	207F	FDA8
ˡ	Superscript L	Lateral release	dˡ	426	02E1	FDA3
˺	Corner	No audible release	p˺ d˺	427	031A	23F9
~	Superimposed tilde	Velarized or pharyngealized	ᵽ đ	428	0334	E226
˔	Raising sign	Raised	ẹ̝ ɹ̝ (e̝ o̝)	429	031D/ 02D4	E22F
˕	Lowering sign	Lowered	ẹ̞ β̞ (e̞ o̞)	430	031E/ 02D5	E231
˴	Advancing sign	Advanced tongue root	u̘	417	0318	23F7
˵	Retracting sign	Retracted tongue root	e̙	418	0319	23F8
⌒	Top tie bar	Affricate or double articulation	k͡p g͡b t͡s d͡ʒ	433	0361	E225
˞	Subscript right hook	Rhoticity	e˞ ʞ˞ a˞ ʔ˞ *Superseded by 419 (1989)*	489	0322	E228
˹	Open corner	Release/ burst	*Not IPA usage*	490	------	E218
,	Comma	Pause (comma)	*Not IPA usage*	491	002C	002C
'	Reversed apostrophe	Weak aspiration	*Withdrawn (1979)*	492	02BB	00A9
˙	Over-dot	Palatalization/ centralization	*Withdrawn (1979)*	493	0307	E224
˗	Minus sign	Retracted variety (backed)	*Use 414 or 418 (1989)*	494	02D7	E239
+	Plus sign	Advanced variety (fronted)	*Use 413 or 417 (1989)*	495	02D6	E238
ʸ	Superscript Y	High-front rounding/ palatalized	*Not IPA usage*	496	02B8	D570
̣	Under-dot	Closer variety/ fricative	*Use 429 (1989)*	497	0323	E230
ˎ	Subscript left hook	Palatalized	*Superseded by 421 (1989)*	498	0321	E227
ᵂ	Subscript W	Labialized	*Superseded by 420 (1989)*	499	032B	E22D

Suprasegmentals

'	Vertical stroke (Superior)	Primary stress	ˌfoʊnəˈtɪʃən	501	02C8	E23E
ˌ	Vertical stroke (Inferior)	Secondary stress	ˌfoʊnəˈtɪʃən	502	02CC	E23F
ː	Length mark	Long	eː	503	02D0	E23A
ˑ	Half-length mark	Half-long	eˑ	504	02D1	E23B
˘	Breve	Extra-short	ĕ	505	0306	E223
.	Period	Syllable break	ɹi.ækt	506	002E	002E
	Vertical line (thick)	Minor (foot) group		507	007C	007C
‖	Double vertical line (thick)	Major (intonation) group		508	2016	2142
‿	Bottom tie bar	Linking (absence of a break)	ˌfɑːɹ‿əˈweɪ	509	203F	230F

Tones and word accents

˝	Double acute accent (over)	Extra high level	a̋	512	030B	00CD
´	Acute accent (over)	High level	á	513	0301	00C2
‾	Macron	Mid level	ā	514	0304	00C5
`	Grave accent (over)	Low level	à	515	0300	00C1
˵	Double grave accent (over)	Extra low level	ȁ	516	030F	23E2
˥	Extra-high tone letter	Extra high level	ma˥	519	02E5	E28D
˦	High tone letter	High level	ma˦	520	02E6	E28E
˧	Mid tone letter	Mid level	ma˧	521	02E7	E28F
˨	Low tone letter	Low level	ma˨	522	02E8	E29F
˩	Extra-low tone letter	Extra low level	ma˩	523	02E9	E29E
ˇ	Wedge; háček	Rising contour	ǎ	524	030C	00CF
ˆ	Circumflex	Falling contour	â	525	0302	00C3
᷄	Macron plus acute accent	High rising contour	a᷄	526	------	E296
᷅	Grave accent plus macron	Low rising contour	a᷅	527	------	E297

‿	Grave plus acute plus grave accent	Rising-falling contour	ã	528	------	E298
⟋	Rising tone letter	Rising contour	ma⟋	529	------	E299
⟍	Falling tone letter	Falling contour	ma⟍	530	------	E29A
⌐	High-rising tone letter	High rising contour	ma⌐	531	------	E29B
⟋	Low-rising tone letter	Low rising contour	ma⟋	532	------	E29C
⊣	Rising-falling tone letter	Rising-falling contour	ma ⊣	533	------	E29D
↓	Down arrow	Downstep		517	2193	EEAF
↑	Up arrow	Upstep		518	2191	EEAD
↗	Upward diagonal arrow	Global rise		510	2197	EF3E
↘	Downward diagonal arrow	Global fall		511	2198	EF3D
⌢	Superscript arch	Long falling tone/ advanced/ palatal	*Not IPA usage*	595	0311	23F2
ˇ	Wedge; háček	Falling-rising tone	*Usage re-defined (1989) See 524*	596	02C7	E247
ˆ	Circumflex	Rising-falling tone	*Usage re-defined (1989) See 525*	597	02C6	E246
ˎ	Subscript grave accent	Low falling tone	*Superseded (1989)*	598	0316/ 02CE	E245
ˏ	Subscript acute accent	Low rising tone	*Superseded (1989)*	599	0317/ 02CF	E243

Transcription delimitation characters

Symbol	Symbol Name	Phonetic Description / *Status*	IPA Number	UCS Code	AFII Code
[	Left square bracket	Begin phonetic transcription	901	005B	005B
]	Right square bracket	End phonetic transcription	902	005D	005D
/	Slash	Begin/end phonemic transcription	903	002F	002F
(	Left parenthesis	Indistinguishable utterance (begin)	906	0028	0028
)	Right parenthesis	Indistinguishable utterance (end)	907	0029	0029

((	Left double parenthesis	Sound obscured (begin)	908	0028+ 0028	2127
))	Right double parenthesis	Sound obscured (end)	909	0029+ 0029	2128
{	Left brace	Begin prosodic notation	910	007B	007B
}	Right brace	End prosodic notation	911	007D	007D

Table 5
IPA symbols: Phonetic consonant/vowel symbol codes
(in numerical order by IPA Number)

Symbol	Symbol Name	Phonetic Description / *Status*	IPA Number	UCS Code	AFII Code
p	Lower-case P	Voiceless bilabial plosive	101	0070	E2A2
b	Lower-case B	Voiced bilabial plosive	102	0062	E2A3
t	Lower-case T	Voiceless dental or alveolar plosive	103	0074	E2B0
d	Lower-case D	Voiced dental or alveolar plosive	104	0064	E2B1
ʈ	Right-tail T	Voiceless retroflex plosive	105	0288	E2C7
ɖ	Right-tail D	Voiced retroflex plosive	106	0256	E2C8
c	Lower-case C	Voiceless palatal plosive	107	0063	E2D8
ɟ	Barred dotless J	Voiced palatal plosive	108	025F	E2D9
k	Lower-case K	Voiceless velar plosive	109	006B	E2DE
g	Opentail G	Voiced velar plosive *Equivalent to 210*	110	0261	E2DF
q	Lower-case Q	Voiceless uvular plosive	111	0071	E2E6
ɢ	Small capital G	Voiced uvular plosive	112	0262	E2E7
ʔ	Glottal stop	Glottal plosive	113	0294	E2ED
m	Lower-case M	Voiced bilabial nasal	114	006D	E2A1
ɱ	Left-tail M (at right)	Voiced labiodental nasal	115	0271	E2AB
n	Lower-case N	Voiced dental or alveolar nasal	116	006E	E2AF
ɳ	Right-tail N	Voiced retroflex nasal	117	0273	E2C6
ɲ	Left-tail N (at left)	Voiced palatal nasal	118	0272	E2D7
ŋ	Eng	Voiced velar nasal	119	014B	E2DD
ɴ	Small capital N	Voiced uvular nasal	120	0274	E2E4
ʙ	Small capital B	Voiced bilabial trill	121	0299	E2F0
r	Lower-case R	Voiced dental or alveolar trill	122	0072	E2C0
ʀ	Small capital R	Voiced uvular trill	123	0280	E2EA
ɾ	Fish-hook R	Voiced dental or alveolar tap	124	027E	E2C1
ɽ	Right-tail R	Voiced retroflex flap	125	027D	E2CD

ɸ	Phi	Voiceless bilabial fricative	126	0278	E2A4
β	Beta	Voiced bilabial fricative	127	03B2	E2A5
f	Lower-case F	Voiceless labiodental fricative	128	0066	E2AC
v	Lower-case V	Voiced labiodental fricative	129	0076	E2AD
θ	Theta	Voiceless dental fricative	130	03B8	E2B2
ð	Eth	Voiced dental fricative	131	00F0	E2B3
s	Lower-case S	Voiceless alveolar fricative	132	0073	E2B6
z	Lower-case Z	Voiced alveolar fricative	133	007A	E2B7
ʃ	Esh	Voiceless postalveolar fricative	134	0283	E2D0
ʒ	Ezh; Tailed Z	Voiced postalveolar fricative	135	0292	E2D1
ʂ	Right-tail S (at left)	Voiceless retroflex fricative	136	0282	E2C9
ʐ	Right-tail Z	Voiced retroflex fricative	137	0290	E2CA
ç	C cedilla	Voiceless palatal fricative	138	00E7	E2DA
ʝ	Curly-tail J	Voiced palatal fricative	139	029D	E2F3
x	Lower-case X	Voiceless velar fricative	140	0078	E2E0
ɣ	Gamma	Voiced velar fricative	141	0263	E2E1
χ	Chi	Voiceless uvular fricative	142	03C7	E2E8
ʁ	Inverted small capital R	Voiced uvular fricative	143	0281	E2E9
ħ	Barred H	Voiceless pharyngeal fricative	144	0127	E2EB
ʕ	Reversed glottal stop	Voiced pharyngeal fricative or approximant	145	0295	E2EC
h	Lower-case H	Voiceless glottal fricative	146	0068	E2EE
ɦ	Hooktop H	Voiced glottal fricative	147	0266	E2EF
ɬ	Belted L	Voiceless dental or alveolar lateral fricative	148	026C	E2BB
ɮ	L-Ezh ligature	Voiced dental or alveolar lateral fricative	149	026E	E2BC
ʋ	Cursive V	Voiced labiodental approximant	150	028B	E2AE
ɹ	Turned R	Voiced dental or alveolar approximant	151	0279	E2BA
ɻ	Turned R, right tail	Voiced retroflex approximant	152	027B	E2CB
j	Lower-case J	Voiced palatal approximant	153	006A	E2DB
ɰ	Turned M, right leg	Voiced velar approximant	154	0270	E2E2
l	Lower-case L	Voiced dental or alveolar lateral approximant	155	006C	E2BD
ɭ	Right-tail L	Voiced retroflex lateral approximant	156	026D	E2CC
ʎ	Turned Y	Voiced palatal lateral approximant	157	028E	E2DC

L	Small capital L	Voiced velar lateral approximant	158	029F	E2F5
ƥ	Hooktop P	Voiceless bilabial implosive *Withdrawn (1993)*	159	01A5	2378
ɓ	Hooktop B	Voiced bilabial implosive	160	0253	E2A9
ƭ	Hooktop T	Voiceless dental or alveolar implosive *Withdrawn (1993)*	161	01AD	2379
ɗ	Hooktop D	Voiced dental or alveolar implosive	162	0257	E2C2
ƈ	Hooktop C	Voiceless palatal implosive *Withdrawn (1993)*	163	0188	2376
ʄ	Hooktop barred dotless J	Voiced palatal implosive	164	0284	E27C
ƙ	Hooktop K	Voiceless velar implosive *Withdrawn (1993)*	165	0199	2363
ɠ	Hooktop G	Voiced velar implosive	166	0260	E27E
ʠ	Hooktop Q	Voiceless uvular implosive *Withdrawn (1993)*	167	02A0	E2F6
ʛ	Hooktop small capital G	Voiced uvular implosive	168	029B	E2F1
ʍ	Turned W	Voiceless labial-velar fricative	169	028D	E2A7
w	Lower-case W	Voiced labial-velar approximant	170	0077	E2A8
ɥ	Turned H	Voiced labial-palatal approximant	171	0265	E2A6
ʜ	Small capital H	Voiceless epiglottal fricative	172	029C	E2F2
ʡ	Barred glottal stop	Epiglottal plosive	173	02A1	E2F7
ʢ	Barred reversed glottal stop	Voiced epiglottal fricative or approximant	174	02A2	E2F8
ɧ	Hooktop heng	Simultaneous voiceless postalveolar and velar fricative	175	0267	E2D6
ʘ	Bull's eye	Bilabial click	176	0298	E2AA
ǀ	Pipe	Dental click	177	01C0	23A6
ǃ	Exclamation point	(Post)alveolar click	178	01C3	23A5
ǂ	Double-barred pipe	Palatoalveolar click	179	01C2	23A4
ǁ	Double pipe	Alveolar lateral click	180	01C1	23A7
ɺ	Turned long-leg R	Voiced alveolar lateral flap	181	027A	E2BF
ɕ	Curly-tail C	Voiceless alveolo-palatal fricative	182	0255	E2CE
ʑ	Curly-tail Z	Voiced alveolo-palatal fricative	183	0291	E2CF
ʇ	Turned T	Dental click *Superseded by 177 (1989)*	201	0287	E2C3

ɕ	Stretched C	Postalveolar click *Superseded by 178 (1989)*	202	0297	E2C4
ʖ	Inverted glottal stop	Alveolar lateral click *Superseded by 180 (1989)*	203	0296	E2C5
ʆ	Curly-tail esh	*Withdrawn (1989)*	204	0286	E2D2
ʓ	Curly-tail ezh	*Withdrawn (1989)*	205	0293	E2D3
ɼ	Long-leg R	*Withdrawn (1989)*	206	027C	E2BE
ˢ	Superscript S	*Withdrawn (1989)*	207	02E2	FDA7
ţ	Left-hook T	Palatalized voiceless dental or alveolar plosive *Withdrawn (1989)*	208	01AB	E2A0
ɫ	L with tilde	Velarized voiced dental or alveolar lateral approximant	209	026B	E27D
g	Looptail G	Voiced velar plosive *Equivalent to 110*	210	0067	E2E3
ts	T-S ligature	Voiceless dental or alveolar affricate *Superseded by 103+132*	211	02A6	E2FC
ʣ	D-Z ligature	Voiced alveolar affricate *Superseded by 104+133*	212	02A3	E2F9
ʧ	T-Esh ligature	Voiceless postalveolar affricate *Superseded by 103+134*	213	02A7	E2FD
ʤ	D-Ezh ligature	Voiced postalveolar affricate *Superseded by 104+135*	214	02A4	E2FA
ʨ	T-Curly-tail-C ligature	Voiceless alveolo-palatal affricate *Superseded by 103+182*	215	02A8	E2FE
ʥ	D-Curly-tail-Z ligature	Voiced alveolo-palatal affricate *Superseded by 104+183*	216	02A5	E2FB
θ	Superscript theta	Voiceless dental fricative release	217	------	E21B
ə	Superscript schwa	Mid central vowel release	218	------	E21A
ɗ	Hooktop right-tail D	Voiced retroflex implosive *Not explicitly IPA approved*	219	------	E219
ƻ	Barred two	*Withdrawn (1976)*	290	01BB	E2B5
ʞ	Turned K	*Withdrawn (1979)*	291	029E	E2F4
ˣ	Superscript X	Voiceless velar fricative release	292	02E3	D56F
ƞ	N, right leg	Syllabic nasal *Withdrawn (1976)*	293	019E	E2E5
ƛ	Barred lambda	Voiceless dental or alveolar lateral affricate *Not IPA usage*	294	019B	FD7B
λ	Lambda	Voiceless dental or alveolar lateral fricative *Not IPA usage*	295	03BB	266E

ž	Z wedge	Voiced postalveolar fricative	296	017E	F1F0
		Not IPA usage			
š	S wedge	Voiceless postalveolar fricative	297	0161	F1DC
		Not IPA usage			
ǰ	J wedge	Voiced postalveolar affricate	298	01F0	E290
		Not IPA usage			
č	C wedge	Voiceless postalveolar affricate	299	010D	F1AE
		Not IPA usage			
i	Lower-case I	Close front unrounded vowel	301	0069	E251
e	Lower-case E	Close-mid front unrounded vowel	302	0065	E256
ɛ	Epsilon	Open-mid front unrounded vowel	303	025B	E258
a	Lower-case A	Open front unrounded vowel	304	0061	E25B
ɑ	Script A	Open back unrounded vowel	305	0251	E26C
ɔ	Open O	Open-mid back rounded vowel	306	0254	E26B
o	Lower-case O	Close-mid back rounded vowel	307	006F	E269
u	Lower-case U	Close back rounded vowel	308	0075	E265
y	Lower-case Y	Close front rounded vowel	309	0079	E252
ø	Slashed O	Close-mid front rounded vowel	310	00F8	E257
œ	Lower-case O-E ligature	Open-mid front rounded vowel	311	0153	E259
Œ	Small capital O-E ligature	Open front rounded vowel	312	0276	E25C
ɒ	Turned script A	Open back rounded vowel	313	0252	E26D
ʌ	Turned V	Open-mid back unrounded vowel	314	028C	E26A
ɤ	Ram's horns	Close-mid back unrounded vowel	315	0264	E268
ɯ	Turned M	Close back unrounded vowel	316	026F	E264
ɨ	Barred I	Close central unrounded vowel	317	0268	E25D
ʉ	Barred U	Close central rounded vowel	318	0289	E25E
ɪ	Small capital I	Near-close near-front unrounded vowel	319	026A	E254
ʏ	Small capital Y	Near-close near-front rounded vowel	320	028F	E255
ʊ	Upsilon	Near-close near-back rounded vowel	321	028A	E267
ə	Schwa	Mid central vowel	322	0259	E25F
ɵ	Barred O	Close-mid central rounded vowel	323	0275	E261
ɐ	Turned A	Near-open central vowel	324	0250	E263
æ	Ash; Lower-case A-E ligature	Near-open front unrounded vowel	325	00E6	E25A
ɜ	Reversed epsilon	Open-mid central unrounded vowel	326	025C	E262

Symbol	Name	Description	IPA Number	UCS Code	AFII Code
ɚ	Right-hook schwa	R-coloured mid central vowel *Equivalent to 322+419*	327	025A	E260
ı	Undotted I	*Not IPA usage*	394	0131	00F5
ɞ	Closed reversed epsilon	Open-mid central rounded vowel	395	025E	E270
ʚ	Closed epsilon	*Superseded by 395 (1996)*	396	029A	E273
ɘ	Reversed E	Close-mid central unrounded vowel	397	0258	E26E
ω	Closed omega	Near-close near-back rounded vowel *Superseded by 321 (1989)*	398	0277	E266
ι	Iota	Near-close near-front unrounded vowel *Superseded by 319 (1989)*	399	0269	E253

Table 6
Phonetic diacritic and suprasegmental symbol codes
(in numerical order by IPA Number)

Symbol	Symbol Name	Phonetic Description	Placement/ *Status*	IPA Number	UCS Code	AFII Code
’	Apostrophe	Ejective	pʼ kʼ tsʼ tʃʼ	401	02BC	E249
̥	Under-ring	Voiceless	n̥ d̥	402A	0325	E229
̊	Over-ring	Voiceless	ŋ̊ g̊	402B	030A	00CA
̬	Subscript wedge	Voiced	s̬ t̬	403	032C	E22A
ʰ	Superscript H	Aspirated	pʰ tʰ	404	02B0	D565
̈	Subscript umlaut	Breathy voiced	b̤ a̤	405	0324	E22B
̰	Subscript tilde	Creaky voiced	b̰ a̰	406	0330	23D8
̼	Subscript seagull	Linguolabial	t̼ d̼	407	033C	22E8
̪	Subscript bridge	Dental	n̪ d̪	408	032A	E22C
̺	Inverted subscript bridge	Apical	n̺ d̺	409	033A	23FD
̻	Subscript square	Laminal	n̻ d̻	410	033B	23FE
̹	Subscript right half-ring	More rounded	e̹ ɔ̹	411	0339	E23C
̜	Subscript left half-ring	Less rounded	ɔ̜	412	031C	E232
̟	Subscript plus	Advanced	u̟	413	031F	E233
̠	Under-bar	Retracted	e̠	414	0320	E234

	Name	Meaning	Example	No.		
¨	Umlaut	Centralized	ë	415	0308	E221
˟	Over-cross	Mid-centralized	ë̽	416	033D	2311
ˌ	Advancing sign	Advanced tongue root	u̟	417	0318	23F7
ˌ	Retracting sign	Retracted tongue root	e̠	418	0319	23F8
˞	Right hook	Rhoticity	e˞ ɚ o˞ ɑ˞	419	02DE	E28A
ʷ	Superscript W	Labialized	tʷ dʷ	420	02B7	D56E
ʲ	Superscript J	Palatalized	tʲ dʲ	421	02B2	D567
ˠ	Superscript gamma	Velarized	tˠ dˠ	422	02E0	E28B
ˤ	Superscript reversed glottal stop	Pharyngealized	tˤ dˤ	423	02E4	E28C
˜	Superscript tilde	Nasalized	ẽ ɑ̃	424	0303	E222
ⁿ	Superscript N	Nasal release	dⁿ	425	207F	FDA8
ˡ	Superscript L	Lateral release	dˡ	426	02E1	FDA3
˺	Corner	No audible release	p̚ d̚	427	031A	23F9
˷	Superimposed tilde	Velarized or pharyngealized	ħ ɫ	428	0334	E226
˔	Raising sign	Raised	e̝ ɹ̝ (e̞ o̞)	429	031D/ 02D4	E22F
˕	Lowering sign	Lowered	e̞ β̞ (e̞ o̞)	430	031E/ 02D5	E231
̩	Syllabicity mark	Syllabic	ɹ̩ n̩ l̩	431	0329	E22E
̯	Subscript arch	Non-syllabic	e̯	432	032F	23FA
‿	Top tie bar	Affricate or double articulation	k͡p g͡b t͡s d͡ʒ	433	0361	E225
ˌ	Subscript right hook	Rhoticity	e̜ ɹ̜ a̜ ʔ̜ *Superseded by 419 (1989)*	489	0322	E228
⌐	Open corner	Release/ burst	*Not IPA usage*	490	------	E218
,	Comma	Pause (comma)	*Not IPA usage*	491	002C	002C
ʻ	Reversed apostrophe	Weak aspiration	*Withdrawn (1979)*	492	02BB	00A9

·	Over-dot	Palatalization/ centralization	*Withdrawn (1979)*	493	0307	E224
-	Minus sign	Retracted variety (backed)	*Use 414 or 418 (1989)*	494	02D7	E239
+	Plus sign	Advanced variety (fronted)	*Use 413 or 417 (1989)*	495	02D6	E238
ʸ	Superscript Y	High-front rounding/ palatalized	*Not IPA usage*	496	02B8	D570
.	Under-dot	Closer variety/ fricative	*Use 429 (1989)*	497	0323	E230
ˌ	Subscript left hook	Palatalized	*Superseded by 421 (1989)*	498	0321	E227
ω	Subscript W	Labialized	*Superseded by 420 (1989)*	499	032B	E22D
'	Vertical stroke (Superior)	Primary stress	ˌfoʊnə'tɪʃən	501	02C8	E23E
ˌ	Vertical stroke (Inferior)	Secondary stress	ˌfoʊnə'tɪʃən	502	02CC	E23F
ː	Length mark	Long	eː	503	02D0	E23A
'	Half-length mark	Half-long	e'	504	02D1	E23B
˘	Breve	Extra-short	ĕ	505	0306	E223
.	Period	Syllable break	ɹi.ækt	506	002E	002E
|	Vertical line (thick)	Minor (foot) group		507	007C	007C
‖	Double vertical line (thick)	Major (intonation) group		508	2016	2142
‿	Bottom tie bar	Linking (absence of a break)	ˌfɑːɹ‿ə'weɪ	509	203F	230F
↗	Upward diagonal arrow	Global rise		510	2197	EF3E
↘	Downward diagonal arrow	Global fall		511	2198	EF3D
˝	Double acute accent (over)	Extra high level	a̋	512	030B	00CD
´	Acute accent (over)	High level	á	513	0301	00C2
¯	Macron	Mid level	ā	514	0304	00C5

`	Grave accent (over)	Low level	à	515	0300	00C1
˶	Double grave accent (over)	Extra low level	ȁ	516	030F	23E2
↓	Down arrow	Downstep		517	2193	EEAF
↑	Up arrow	Upstep		518	2191	EEAD
˥	Extra-high tone letter	Extra high level	ma˥	519	02E5	E28D
˦	High tone letter	High level	ma˦	520	02E6	E28E
˧	Mid tone letter	Mid level	ma˧	521	02E7	E28F
˨	Low tone letter	Low level	ma˨	522	02E8	E29F
˩	Extra-low tone letter	Extra low level	ma˩	523	02E9	E29E
ˇ	Wedge; háček	Rising contour	ǎ	524	030C	00CF
^	Circumflex	Falling contour	â	525	0302	00C3
ˉ	Macron plus acute accent	High rising contour	a̍	526	------	E296
ˎ	Grave accent plus macron	Low rising contour	a̋	527	------	E297
˷	Grave plus acute plus grave accent	Rising-falling contour	a̎	528	------	E298
∧	Rising tone letter	Rising contour	ma∧	529	------	E299
∨	Falling tone letter	Falling contour	ma∨	530	------	E29A
˄	High-rising tone letter	High rising contour	ma˄	531	------	E29B
ˏ	Low-rising tone letter	Low rising contour	ma˓	532	------	E29C
˒	Rising-falling tone letter	Rising-falling contour	ma ˧	533	------	E29D
⌢	Superscript arch	Long falling tone/ advanced/ palatal	*Not IPA usage*	595	0311	23F2
˅	Wedge; háček	Falling-rising tone	*Usage re-defined (1989) See 524*	596	02C7	E247
˄	Circumflex	Rising-falling tone	*Usage re-defined (1989) See 525*	597	02C6	E246
ˎ	Subscript grave accent	Low falling tone	*Superseded (1989)*	598	0316/ 02CE	E245
ˏ	Subscript acute accent	Low rising tone	*Superseded (1989)*	599	0317/ 02CF	E243

Acknowledgements

We would like to thank Alexandra (Smith) Gaylord for initiating discussion in 1989 between the phonetics community and the Text Encoding Initiative, and for interpreting phonetic symbols in the context of coding standardization. We are also indebted to Hans G. Tillmann, William J. Barry, and H. Joachim Neuhaus for their contribution to the Workgroup on Computer Coding of IPA Symbols and Computer Representation of Individual Languages, and for their advice on developing principles for the computerized documentation of phonetic databases. Suggestions on the technical presentation of these tables and on details of symbol coding from Christoph Draxler and from Michael Everson are gratefully acknowledged.

References

BALL, M. J. (1991). Computer coding of the IPA: Extensions to the IPA. *Journal of the International Phonetic Association* 21, 36–41.

DUCKWORTH, M., ALLEN, G., HARDCASTLE, W. AND BALL, M. J. (1990). Extensions to the International Phonetic Alphabet for the transcription of atypical speech. *Clinical Linguistics and Phonetics* 4, 273–80.

ESLING, J. H. (1988). Computer coding of IPA symbols and Detailed phonetic representation of computer databases (1989 Kiel Convention coordinator's report). *Journal of the International Phonetic Association* 18, 99–106.

ESLING, J. H. (1990). Computer coding of the IPA: Supplementary report. *Journal of the International Phonetic Association* 20, 22–6.

GIBBON, D., MOORE, R. AND WINSKI, R. (editors) (1997). *Handbook of Standards and Resources for Spoken Language Systems*. Berlin: Mouton de Gruyter.

IPA (1989a). The International Phonetic Alphabet (revised to 1989). *Journal of the International Phonetic Association* 19(2), centre pages.

IPA (1989b). The IPA Kiel Convention Workgroup 9 report: Computer coding of IPA symbols and computer representation of individual languages. *Journal of the International Phonetic Association* 19, 81–2.

IPA (1993). The International Phonetic Alphabet (revised to 1993). *Journal of the International Phonetic Association* 23(1), centre pages.

PULLUM, G. K. AND LADUSAW, W. A. (1986). *Phonetic Symbol Guide*. University of Chicago Press.

PULLUM, G. K. AND LADUSAW, W. A. (1996). *Phonetic Symbol Guide*, 2nd edition. University of Chicago Press.

UNICODE CONSORTIUM (1996). *The Unicode Standard, Version 2.0*. Reading, MA: Addison-Wesley Developers Press.

Appendix 3

Extensions to the IPA: The ExtIPA Chart

This section on extended IPA symbols was prepared by the Executive Committee of the International Clinical Phonetics and Linguistics Association (ICPLA), which can be contacted through the Secretary of the ICPLA, Wolfram Ziegler, Städt. Krankenhaus München-Bogenhausen, EKN, Dachauer Str. 164, D-80992 München, Germany. The original text and chart first appeared as an article in the *Journal of the International Phonetic Association* 24, 95–8 (1994), entitled 'The ExtIPA Chart', by the ICPLA Executive Committee. The list of IPA Numbers for ExtIPA symbols which has been added here appeared originally in an article by Martin J. Ball entitled 'Computer coding of the IPA: Extensions to the IPA' in the *Journal of the International Phonetic Association* 21, 36–41 (1991).

1 Introduction

At the 1989 Kiel Convention of the IPA, a sub-group was established to draw up recommendations for the transcription of disordered speech. The report produced at the Convention appeared in print in Duckworth, Allen, Hardcastle, and Ball (1990), being mainly a list of symbols, termed 'Extensions to the IPA', or 'ExtIPA' for short. Examples of the use of the ExtIPA symbols are given in Ball (1991), Howard (1993) and Ball, Code, Rahilly and Hazlett (1994) among others, and Ball (1993) includes them at textbook level. Various changes and additions to the original set of symbols are reported in Bernhardt and Ball (1993). The changes meant, however, that there was a need for a listing of the current set of symbols, preferably in as concise a form as possible. There was also felt to be a need for the symbol set to receive overt recognition from a relevant society, therefore the 1994 publication in *JIPA* marked the official adoption of the ExtIPA symbols by the International Clinical Phonetics and Linguistics Association (ICPLA).

2 The Chart

The chart included here is clearly based on the current format of the IPA Chart to make it directly comparable and equally user-friendly. There are, however, a few comments that will aid in the use of the chart. First, shaded squares on the main chart represent – as in the IPA Chart – articulations that are deemed impossible to make. Blank squares stand for sounds for which the IPA already provides symbols, or for sounds that are possible to make but for which no symbols are available. Clearly, this difference is straightforward to resolve with access to both charts.

The place of articulation labels used on the chart are mostly straightforward: dentolabial is the reverse of labiodental (upper lip to lower teeth), labioalveolar is needed for speakers with gross overbite such that bilabial and labiodental target articulations are realized with the lower lip articulating against the alveolar ridge. The linguolabial place of articulation does appear (as a diacritic) on the IPA Chart, but it is also included here as it does occur reasonably frequently in disordered speech. The velopharyngeal place of articulation occurs only as a fricative: the friction originates at the velopharyngeal port (and can also accompany other articulations as noted below).

The manner of articulation labels are similar to those used on the IPA Chart with three exceptions: the lateral plus central (median) fricative manner involves a simultaneous central and lateral release of friction, such as is found with some misarticulations of target alveolar fricatives. The percussive manner involves the striking together of two rigid or semi-rigid articulators. While the most common example of a percussive is found with a bidental place of articulation, bilabial percussives are occasionally found also. Finally, there is the nareal fricative category. This sound type involves audible nasal release during the production of a nasal segment. As noted below, a diacritic is available to mark audible nasal release with other sound types, and is used on the chart with nasal symbols as they are probably the most common sounds to occur of this variety. These symbols replace previously proposed composite symbols of the type [h̃m], the change being approved at the 1994 ICPLA Symposium.

At the 1989 IPA meeting at Kiel, the sub-group on disordered speech, following on from the recommendations of the PRDS Group (1983), recommended that as an alternative to [ɱ], clinical phoneticians might wish to employ [m̪], to pattern with the symbols for labiodental plosives. This might be especially useful in a patient presenting with labiodental as a favourite articulation, in that the use of the dental diacritic added to a range of different symbols would clearly stand out in a transcription. This usage was, however, controversial as it was the only symbol directly competing with an official IPA symbol, and recognition was withdrawn from it at the 1994 ICPLA Symposium.

The sets of diacritics beneath the main chart are mainly self-explanatory. The back-slash for reiterated articulation can be used between individual segments or between syllables, but presupposes rapid reiteration; reiteration with pauses between the segments should be shown with the pause markings listed in the 'Connected Speech' section. Sliding articulation is described more fully in Bernhardt and Ball (1993), but we can note here that it is to be used to mark a rapid movement from one place of articulation to a neighbouring place within the time normally allotted to a single segment. The nasal escape diacritic is used to mark audible nareal friction accompanying another sound and, similarly, velopharyngeal friction accompanying another sound is marked with the double tilde.

The voicing diacritics allow fine discrimination of amounts of voicing with particular sounds. There is also a diacritic for unaspirated plosives. It might be argued that it is unnecessary to mark the absence of something (i.e. aspiration). However, speech pathologists have found such a diacritic useful due to the ambiguous nature of a plain fortis plosive symbol, standing in narrow transcription for an unaspirated plosive, but in broad transcription for a plosive unspecified for aspiration, and the need some transcribers might have to note overtly a non-normal lack of aspiration.

Finally, the symbolizations in the 'other' category can be commented on. The 'indeterminate' system utilizes the 'balloon' to mark sounds about which the transcriber is uncertain. The amount of information the transcriber *is* sure about is entered within the balloon in terms of categories (e.g. consonant), or features (e.g. bilabial, plosive, etc.). The transcriber can also enter a specific phonetic symbol, in which case this is read as meaning 'probably [f]' etc. 'Silent articulation' or 'mouthing' is relatively common in some disordered speakers. Here there is a visible articulatory gesture, but no sound is made. Naturally, labial gestures may be the only ones easily spotted here, but the use of this marking convention does allow the analyst to distinguish between speakers who omit a sound and those who attempt it.

3 Conclusion

As with the IPA Chart, we expect this chart to be subject to regular revision by ICPLA members, especially in the light of clinical experience. The chart may be copied by those interested in clinical phonetic transcription, as long as acknowledgement is made to the ICPLA. ExtIPA symbols are listed in the following table, with an indication of the IPA Number that has been assigned to each symbol. Any symbol which also appears in the tables in appendix 2 is cross-referenced here.

Extended IPA character set: Symbol names and IPA Numbers

Symbol Name	Phonetic Symbol	Phonetic Description	IPA Number
Consonant/vowel symbols			
Double bridge	[ꞎ]	Bidental percussive	601
F-Eng ligature	[ꬵ]	Velopharyngeal fricative	602
L-S ligature	[ꞎ]	Lateralized [s]	603
L-Z ligature	[ꞎ]	Lateralized [z]	604
Indeterminacy symbols			
Balloon	◯	Unidentified segment(s)	611
Asterisk	*	Placeholder symbol	612
Voice symbols			
Upper-case V	V	Voice	621 (= 722)
Upper-case F	F	Falsetto	622 (= 706)
Upper-case W	W	Whisper	623 (= 723)
Upper-case C	C	Creak	624 (= 703)
Upper-case L	L	Larynx	625 (= 712)
Upper-case J	J	Jaw	626 (= 710)
Upper-case O-E ligature	Œ	Oesophageal speech	627
Upper-case Greek Theta	Θ	Protruded-tongue voice	628

Connected speech

Bracketed single period	(.)	Short pause	631 (use 506)
Bracketed double period	(..)	Medium-length pause	632 (use 506)
Bracketed triple period	(...)	Long pause	633 (use 506)
Forte	*f*	Loud speech	634
Fortissimo	*ff*	Louder speech	635
Piano	*p*	Quiet speech	636
Pianissimo	*pp*	Quieter speech	637
Allegro	*allegro*	Fast speech	638
Lento	*lento*	Slow speech	639
Numeral one	1	Slight degree	640
Numeral two	2	Moderate degree	641
Numeral three	3	Extreme degree	642

Diacritics

Superscript bridge	[͆]	Dentolabial	651
Subscript double arrow	[͍]	Labial spreading	652
Superscript+subscript bridge	[̪͆]	Bidental articulation	653
Superscript slashed tilde	[͊]	Denasal	654
Superscript dotted tilde	[͋]	Nasal escape	655
Superscript double tilde	[͌]	Velopharyngeal friction	656
Subscript double syllabicity mark	[͈]	Stronger articulation	657
Subscript corner	[͉]	Weaker articulation	658
Backslash	[\]	Reiterated articulation	659
Subscript upward arrow-head	[͎]	Whistled articulation	660
Down full arrow	[↓]	Ingressive air flow	661
Up full arrow	[↑]	Egressive air flow	662
Left-sited subscript wedge	[ˬ]	Pre-voicing	663 (use 403)
Right-sited subscript wedge	[ˬ]	Post-voicing	664 (= 403)
Bracketed subscript wedge	[(ˬ)]	Partial voicing	665
Left-bracketed subscript wedge	[(ˬ]	Initial partial voicing	666
Right-bracketed subscript wedge	[ˬ)]	Final partial voicing	667
Bracketed under-ring	[(˳)]	Partial devoicing	668
Left-bracketed under-ring	[(˳]	Initial partial devoicing	669
Right-bracketed under-ring	[˳)]	Final partial devoicing	670

Left-sited superscript H	[ʰ]	Pre-aspiration	671 (use 404)
Right-sited double exclamation point	[‼]	Ventricular	672
Superscript cursive V	[ᶹ]	Labiodentalized	673
Subscript right arrow	[⃗]	Slurred articulation	674
Subscript equals sign	[₌]	Alveolarized	675
Superscript inverted small capital R	[ʶ]	Uvularized	676
Superscript double-barred H	[ᶣ]	Faucalized	677
Superscript O-E ligature	[ꟹ]	Labialized: Open-rounded	678
Right-sited exclamation point	[!]	Harsh	679
Superscript equals sign	[⁼]	Unaspirated	680
Subscript left pointer	[˂]	Laterally offset to the right	681
Subscript right pointer	[˃]	Laterally offset to the left	682
Right-sited subscript tilde	[̰]	Creaky	683 (= 406)

Existing IPA diacritic symbols

Under-ring	[̥]	Voiceless	402
Subscript wedge	[̬]	Voiced/ Diplophonia (VQ)	403 (= 663, 664)
Superscript H	[ʰ]	Aspirated	404 (= 671)
Subscript umlaut	[̈]	Breathy	405
Subscript tilde	[̰]	Creaky	406
Subscript seagull	[̼]	Linguolabial	407
Subscript bridge	[̪]	Dental	408
Inverted subscript bridge	[̺]	Apical	409
Subscript square	[̻]	Laminal	410
Subscript plus	[̟]	Advanced	413
Retracting sign	[̠]	Retracted	418
Right hook	[˞]	Rhoticity (Retroflex)	419
Superscript W	[ʷ]	Labialized: Close-rounded	420
Superscript J	[ʲ]	Palatalized	421
Superscript gamma	[ˠ]	Velarized	422
Superscript reversed glottal stop	[ˤ]	Pharyngealized	423
Superscript tilde	[̃]	Nasalized	424
Raising sign	[̝]	Raised	429
Lowering sign	[̞]	Lowered	430
Comma	,	Comma	491

Under-dot	[.]	Whispery	497
Period	.	Pause	506
			(631,632,633)
Bottom tie bar	[‿]	Linking	509

Upper-case letters

Upper-case A	A	A	701
Upper-case B	B	B	702
Upper-case C	C	C (Creak)	703 (use 624)
Upper-case D	D	D	704
Upper-case E	E	E	705
Upper-case F	F	F (Falsetto)	706 (use 622)
Upper-case G	G	G	707
Upper-case H	H	H	708
Upper-case I	I	I	709
Upper-case J	J	J (Jaw)	710 (use 626)
Upper-case K	K	K	711
Upper-case L	L	L (Larynx)	712 (use 625)
Upper-case M	M	M	713
Upper-case N	N	N	714
Upper-case O	O	O	715
Upper-case P	P	P	716
Upper-case Q	Q	Q	717
Upper-case R	R	R	718
Upper-case S	S	S	719
Upper-case T	T	T	720
Upper-case U	U	U	721
Upper-case V	V	V (Voice)	722 (use 621)
Upper-case W	W	W (Whisper)	723 (use 623)
Upper-case X	X	X	724
Upper-case Y	Y	Y	725
Upper-case Z	Z	Z	726

Transcription delimitation characters

Left square bracket	[	Begin phonetic transcription	901
Right square bracket	]	End phonetic transcription	902
Slash	/	Begin/ end phonemic transcription	903
Left parenthesis	(	Silent articulation (Mouthing)	906
Right parenthesis	)	Silent articulation (Mouthing)	907

Left double parenthesis	((	Sound obscured	908
Right double parenthesis	))	Sound obscured	909
Left brace	{	Begin prosodic notation	910
Right brace	}	End prosodic notation	911

References

BALL, M. J. (1991). Recent developments in the transcription of non-normal speech. *Journal of Communication Disorders* 24, 59–78.

BALL, M. J. (1993). *Phonetics for Speech Pathology,* 2nd edition. London: Whurr Publishers.

BALL, M. J., CODE, C., RAHILLY, J. AND HAZLETT, D. (1994). Non-segmental aspects of disordered speech: Developments in transcription. *Clinical Linguistics and Phonetics* 8, 67–83.

BERNHARDT, B. AND BALL, M. J. (1993). Characteristics of atypical speech currently not included in the Extensions to the IPA. *Journal of the International Phonetic Association* 23, 35–8.

DUCKWORTH, M., ALLEN, G., HARDCASTLE, W. AND BALL, M. J. (1990). Extensions to the International Phonetic Alphabet for the transcription of atypical speech. *Clinical Linguistics and Phonetics* 4, 273–80.

HOWARD, S. (1993). Articulatory constraints on a phonological system: A case study of cleft palate speech. *Clinical Linguistics and Phonetics* 7, 299–317.

PRDS GROUP (1983). *The Phonetic Representation of Disordered Speech: Final Report.* London: The King's Fund.

ExtIPA SYMBOLS FOR DISORDERED SPEECH

(Revised to 1997)

CONSONANTS (other than those on the IPA Chart)

	bilabial	labiodental	dentolabial	labioalv.	linguolabial	interdental	bidental	alveolar	velar	velophar.
Plosive		p̪ b̪	p͆ b͆	p͇ b͇	t̼ d̼	t̪͆ d̪͆				
Nasal			m͆	m͇	n̼	n̪͆				
Trill					r̼	r̪͆				
Fricative: central			f͆ v͆	f͇ v͇	θ̼ ð̼	θ̪͆ ð̪͆	h̪͆ h̪͆			ʩ
Fricative: lateral+ central								ʪ ʫ		
Fricative: nareal	m͋							n͋	ŋ͋	
Percussive	ʬ						ʭ			
Approximant: lateral					l̼	l̪͆				

DIACRITICS

↔ labial spreading s͍	͈ strong articulation f͈	͊ denasal m͊
͆ dentolabial v͆	͉ weak articulation v͉	͋ nasal escape v͋
̪͆ interdental/bidental n̪͆	\ reiterated articulation p\p\p	͌ velopharyngeal friction s͌
͇ alveolar t͇	͎ whistled articulation s͎	↓ ingressive airflow p↓
̼ linguolabial d̼	→ sliding articulation θ͢s	↑ egressive airflow !↑

CONNECTED SPEECH

(.)	short pause
(..)	medium pause
(...)	long pause
f	loud speech [{*f* laʊd *f*}]
ff	louder speech [{*ff* laʊdɚ *ff*}]
p	quiet speech [{*p* kwaɪət *p*}]
pp	quieter speech [{*pp* kwaɪətɚ *pp*}]
allegro	fast speech [{*allegro* fɑːst *allegro*}]
lento	slow speech [{*lento* sloʊ *lento*}]
crescendo, rallentando, etc. may also be used	

VOICING

ˬ	pre-voicing	ˬz
ˬ	post-voicing	zˬ
₍ ̥₎	partial devoicing	₍z̥₎
₍ ̥	initial partial devoicing	₍z̥
̥₎	final partial devoicing	z̥₎
₍ ̬₎	partial voicing	₍s̬₎
₍ ̬	initial partial voicing	₍s̬
̬₎	final partial voicing	s̬₎
⁼	unaspirated	p⁼
ʰ	pre-aspiration	ʰp

OTHERS

(_) indeterminate sound	(( )) extraneous noise ((2 sylls))
(V̲), (P̲l̲) indeterminate vowel, plosive, etc.	¡ sublaminal lower alveolar percussive click
(P̲l̲.̲v̲l̲s̲) indeterminate voiceless plosive, etc.	!¡ alveolar & sublaminal click ('cluck-click')
( ) silent articulation (ʃ), (m)	* sound with no available symbol

Appendix 4

About the International Phonetic Association

The History of the International Phonetic Association

1 The Association

The Association was founded in Paris early in 1886 under the name of *Dhi Fonètik Tîcerz' Asóciécon* (the *FTA*), which was itself a development of *L'Association Phonétique des Professeurs d'Anglais*. A small group of language-teachers came together, under the leadership of Paul Passy, to press the case for phonetic notation to be used in schools as a method of helping children to acquire a realistic pronunciation of foreign languages. A further use of phonetic notation was seen to be in the teaching of reading to young children. In these aims, particularly the former, the Association was supported by the examples and encouragement of language-teachers and phoneticians in other countries such as Johan Storm in Norway, Henry Sweet and Henry Widgery in Britain, and Hermann Klinghardt and Wilhelm Viëtor in Germany.

In less than a year, the membership had grown from an initial eleven members in France to 58 in twelve countries, mainly in Western Europe. By the summer of 1914, which was the high point of the Association's existence in terms of membership and influence in education circles, there were 1751 members in 40 countries. In January 1889, the name of the Association was changed to *L'Association Phonétique des Professeurs de Langues Vivantes (AP)*, and, in 1897, to *L'Association Phonétique Internationale (API)* – in English, the *International Phonetic Association (IPA)*. The Association's activities were severely disrupted by the First World War and its aftermath. No journal appeared between October 1914 and December 1922, although circumstances did allow the occasional publication of a handful of Supplements on particular aspects of phonetics.

It was the Danish phonetician Otto Jespersen who first suggested, in 1886, that there should be what he called an 'International Phonetic Association', which would devise an international alphabet rather than a set of different alphabets specific to particular languages (see 4 below on the development of the Alphabet). Passy himself favoured the compromise of an 'International Society' made up of a confederation of national bodies, whose aim would be 'the advancement of the science of phonetics and its application to practical teaching'. Jespersen's proposal, however, failed to get the support of a majority of the FTA's membership, and the Association continued as a forum for language-teachers dedicated to the cause of phonetic script rather than as an organization of academic phoneticians. Within a few years, the gradual increase in the number of items in the journal dealing with matters unconnected with the concerns of mainstream language-teachers (for example, specimens of Mandarin Chinese and Armenian) heralded the shift towards phonetic rather than applied phonetic concerns. Items dealing with language-teaching matters have, nevertheless, always continued to be published in the journal.

2 The journal

During the first few months of 1886, the Association's members kept each other informed of developments in the application of phonetic techniques in schools with the help of an 'ever-circulator', but in May of that year a journal was published, *Dhi Fonètik Tîcer* ('The Phonetic Teacher') – *FT* for short. It quickly established itself as the focus of the Association's activities. (Another journal of the same name, emanating from the United States, dealt solely with questions of spelling reform and was unconnected with the *FT*.) In January 1889, the name of the journal was changed to *Le Maître Phonétique* (**mf**), at the same time as French became the Association's official language. In 1971 the **mf** became the *Journal of the International Phonetic Association* (*JIPA*), and the official language reverted to English.

The journal was, from the very start, published as far as possible in phonetic script. (In many issues, a variety of phonetic scripts illustrating the range of symbolizations possible within the Association's conventions was the norm.) It was only with the publication of *JIPA* from 1971 onwards that phonetic script gave way to traditional orthography. The format of each issue of the journal has tended to be one of articles on aspects of the descriptive phonetics of languages or language-varieties, comments on phonetic notation and examples in phonetic script (**spesimen**, as they were known in French in the **mf**) of the pronunciation of languages. The reading passage used to illustrate the pronunciation was, normally, from 1911 onwards, the fable of 'The North Wind and the Sun'. In addition, smaller items were published describing the academic and social activities of members of the so-called *famille phonétique*. Although the character of the articles has always tended to reflect the descriptivist articulatory phonetic leanings of the Association, experimental work of various kinds is increasingly represented in the journal.

3 Supplements to the journal

A series of Supplements and loose inserts to the journal has been published at irregular intervals since 1888. One of the most important of these has been the *Principles of the International Phonetic Association*, which first appeared in French in 1900, in English in 1904, in German in 1928, in Italian in 1933 and in Spanish in 1944. The *Principles* (of which this *IPA Handbook* is the successor) included an introductory section explaining phonetic notation, which was followed by transcriptions of 'The North Wind and the Sun' in about 50 languages from around the world. Further **spesimen** covering about another 100 languages can be found in the journal itself. In addition, three issues of *Miscellanea Phonetica*, collections of articles on phonetic topics, have been published (1914 (issued 1925), 1954, 1958).

4 The development of the Association's Alphabet

Phonetic notation has been one of the Association's central concerns from the very beginning. The first alphabet that was employed and promulgated was a modification of the '1847 Alphabet' of Isaac Pitman and Alexander J. Ellis. Originally, the aim was to make available a set of phonetic symbols which would be given *different* articulatory values, if necessary, in different languages. The choice of symbols was dictated by the need to keep them as simple as possible, for the benefit of both teachers and school-children. Since a large proportion of the membership was from Western Europe (or was linked in cultural and linguistic terms with Western Europe), it was inevitable that a roman base should be used for the Alphabet. Thus, to begin with, 'c' stood for the [ʃ] in the English word *sheep,* but the [ʃ] of French *chat* was represented by an 'x'. Then, as now, the policy for the development of the Alphabet involved members making proposals for changes, which were published in the journal and voted on by the Association's Council. During the first half of 1887 there were some small alterations to the list of symbols. Twelve months later, in August/September 1888, further revisions were proposed in the light of a set of policy statements. The latter were to exert a profound effect and determine the content of most later versions of the Alphabet:

> In choosing between the various proposals that have been made for revising our alphabet, we've been guided by the following principles, which I think are admitted by *most* of our readers as essential to a *practical* system of phonetic spelling:
>
> 1   There should be a separate sign for each distinctive sound; that is, for each sound which, being used instead of another, in the same language, can change the meaning of a word.
> 2   When any sound is found in several languages, the same sign should be used in all. This applies also to very similar shades of sound.
> 3   The alphabet should consist as much as possible of the ordinary letters of the roman alphabet; as few new letters as possible being used.
> 4   In assigning values to the roman letters, international usage should decide.
> 5   The new letters should be suggestive of the sounds they represent, by their resemblance to the old ones.
> 6   Diacritic marks should be avoided, being trying for the eyes and troublesome to write.

Other remarks emphasized the need for the transcription to be, in the terminology of twentieth century phonological theories, 'phonemic', for stress to be predicted as occurring on particular syllables within a word depending on the language in question, and for contributors to the journal to notate their own pronunciation of their language.

During the 1890s further changes were made to the Alphabet, mainly to provide a series of diacritics for transcriptions that were 'allophonic' (*pace* the 1888 proposal that phonetic notation should be 'phonemic'), for prosodic features, and for widening the compass of the Alphabet to accommodate languages well removed from the original cluster of English, French, and German – for example, Arabic. The relatively rapid development of the Alphabet can be judged from the fact that the one that was issued in August 1899 is in many respects similar to today's, despite certain divergences in the choice of symbols and their allocation to sound categories.

Clearly, at that time the Alphabet was already developing into a tool for general phonetic work rather than being merely a set of notational conventions for the phonemic transcription of certain major languages taught in schools. Even so, the 'phonemic' emphasis in defining the range of sounds to be symbolized has continued up to the present, as can be seen in successive elaborations of the Principles of the IPA. The most recent formulation can be found in appendix 1.

The development of the Alphabet has not been without controversy. Particularly during the 1920s, changes suggested by a specially convened Conference on Phonetic Transcription and Transliteration would have affected many of the conventions; few of them, however, were incorporated into the Alphabet. In addition, other Alphabets have existed alongside the IPA, especially during the early period of the Association's existence, for example Alexander Melville Bell's *Visible Speech* alphabet, later modified and renamed the *Organic Alphabet* by Henry Sweet; Johan Lundell's *Swedish Dialect Alphabet*; and Otto Jespersen's *Danish Dialect Alphabet*. None of them has, in the longer term, offered serious competition to the pre-eminence of the Alphabet of the International Phonetic Association as a widely, even if not universally, accepted standard. The Alphabet has always been subject to critical review, and consequent change, and this healthy cycle of renewal is certain to continue as new knowledge is brought to bear on it. It will be of considerable interest to see how it develops in the future, under the influence of developments in phonological theory, the needs of new practical applications, and the knowledge about speech production and perception which experimental methods will continue to provide.

5 Examinations in Phonetics

A further aspect of the Association's activities since 1908 has been the organization of examinations in phonetics, leading to the award of a Certificate of Proficiency in the phonetics of English, French, or German. Examinations are still held for English, and further details and entry forms are available from the following address: IPA Examination, Department of Phonetics and Linguistics, University College London, Gower Street, London WC1E 6BT, UK, or via the IPA World Wide Web page (see 'How to find out more...' below).

Statutes and By-laws of the Association

Statutes of the International Phonetic Association (1995)

1   The name of the Association is 'International Phonetic Association'.

2   The aim of the Association is to promote the scientific study of phonetics and the various practical applications of that science. In furtherance of this aim the Association publishes a journal entitled the *Journal of the International Phonetic Association*. The Association considers that in pursuing its aim it makes a contribution to friendly relations between peoples of different countries.

3   To become a member of the Association it is necessary to pay dues as fixed in the by-laws, and to be elected by vote of the Secretary acting on behalf of the Council.

4   The Association is administered by a Council of 30 members, 20 of whom will be elected by direct vote of the members. The elected Council has the power to co-opt up to 10 further members, so as to ensure a suitable representation of phoneticians throughout the world.

5   Elections for the Council will be held every four years, in a manner as prescribed in the by-laws.

6   The Council elects from its members a President, a Vice-President, a Secretary, a Treasurer, and an Editor; these officers form an Executive Committee, reporting to the Council, and running the current affairs of the Association.

7   The President and Vice-President are each elected for a single term of four years only. The Secretary, the Treasurer, and the Editor are each elected for a four-year term in the first place, and are eligible for re-election for not more than one further term of four years.

8   The Association holds a general business meeting at least once every four years, normally in conjunction with the four-yearly International Congress of Phonetic Sciences. At the request of any member present, any decisions taken at such a meeting are subject to ratification by mail ballot of the Association.

9   Modification of these statutes requires a mail ballot of the membership, with a two-thirds majority of those responding to the ballot.

By-laws of the International Phonetic Association (1997)

1   The annual dues are £13 or US $25 payable to the Treasurer on the first of January each year.

2   There are the following types of members:

Members, who pay annual dues.
Life members, who pay no annual dues. Any member who has paid full annual dues for 30 years will automatically become a life member. Alternatively, life membership may be obtained by paying a one-time sum of 15 times the annual dues.
Student members, who pay half the annual dues. Student members must include with their dues a letter from their Head of Department or supervisor, certifying that they are currently full-time students.
All of the above types of members are entitled to all the privileges of membership, including receipt of the Journal.
Institutional members, who pay twice the current annual dues, and who receive the Journal, but are not otherwise entitled to the privileges of membership.

3   Elections to the Council will be by mail ballot. The time schedule for the election of the Council of the IPA will be as follows: (a) 12 months before an International Congress of Phonetic Sciences – the Secretary to request nominations for membership of the Council; (b) 10 months before – closing date for receipt of nominations, and for members nominated to have notified the Secretary if they are willing for their names to appear on a ballot; (c) 9 months before – ballot paper to be mailed to members; (d) 8 months before – completed ballot paper to be received by the Secretary; (e) 7 months before – the Secretary to request the new Council to make nominations for 10 co-opted members; (f) 6 months before – closing date for the receipt of nominations for co-opted members; (g) 5 months before – ballot paper for co-opted members to be mailed to Council; (h) 4 months before – completed ballot paper to be received by the Secretary; (i) 3 months before – the Secretary to request the new Council to make nominations for the posts of President, Vice-President, Secretary, Treasurer, and Editor; (j) 2 months before – closing date for the receipt of nominations for executive posts; (k) 2 months before – ballot paper for executive posts to be mailed to Council; (l) 1 month before – completed ballot paper to be received by the Secretary.

4   Modifications of these by-laws require a two-thirds majority of the Council voting in a mail ballot.

How to find out more about the Association
Members of the Association receive the twice-yearly *Journal of the International Phonetic Association*, which is also available in many libraries in academic institutions. This contains research articles, discussions, and news of the Association's activities.

A monthly electronic newsletter for the phonetic sciences, *foNETiks*, carries regular announcements of IPA news and activities. This can be joined by sending an e-mail message to: mailbase@mailbase.ac.uk. The message should consist of one line as follows: Join fonetiks firstname(s) lastname. There is also an IPA page on the World Wide Web; this gives up-to-date information about the IPA, including useful addresses and current subscription rates. The URL is: **http://www.arts.gla.ac.uk/IPA/ipa.html**

How to join the Association
An application form is included in each number of the *Journal of the International Phonetic Association* and on the IPA Web Site. Completed application forms should be returned to the Treasurer.

Appendix 5

Reference charts

This appendix contains larger-scale versions of the IPA Chart together with the corresponding IPA Number Chart, divided into sections for ease of reference. The charts may be copied and used while consulting parts 1 and 2 of the *Handbook*, or enlarged for teaching purposes.

CONSONANTS (PULMONIC)

	Bilabial	Labiodental	Dental	Alveolar	Postalveolar	Retroflex	Palatal	Velar	Uvular	Pharyngeal	Glottal
Plosive	p b			t d		ʈ ɖ	c ɟ	k ɡ	q ɢ		ʔ
Nasal	m	ɱ		n		ɳ	ɲ	ŋ	ɴ		
Trill	ʙ			r					ʀ		
Tap or Flap				ɾ		ɽ					
Fricative	ɸ β	f v	θ ð	s z	ʃ ʒ	ʂ ʐ	ç ʝ	x ɣ	χ ʁ	ħ ʕ	h ɦ
Lateral fricative				ɬ ɮ							
Approximant		ʋ		ɹ		ɻ	j	ɰ			
Lateral approximant				l		ɭ	ʎ	ʟ			

Where symbols appear in pairs, the one to the right represents a voiced consonant. Shaded areas denote articulations judged impossible.

NUMBER CHART

CONSONANTS (PULMONIC)

	Bilabial	Labiodental	Dental	Alveolar	Postalveolar	Retroflex	Palatal	Velar	Uvular	Pharyngeal	Glottal
Plosive	101 102			103 104		105 106	107 108	109 110	111 112		113
Nasal	114	115		116		117	118	119	120		
Trill	121			122					123		
Tap or Flap				124		125					
Fricative	126 127	128 129	130 131	132 133	134 135	136 137	138 139	140 141	142 143	144 145	146 147
Lateral fricative				148 149							
Approximant		150		151		152	153	154			
Lateral approximant				155		156	157	158			

Where symbols appear in pairs, the one to the right represents a voiced consonant. Shaded areas denote articulations judged impossible.

VOWELS

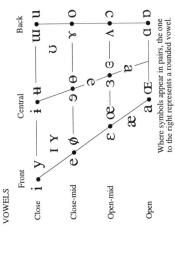

Where symbols appear in pairs, the one to the right represents a rounded vowel.

VOWELS

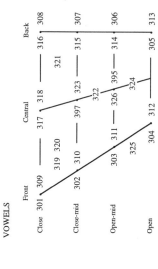

Where symbols appear in pairs, the one to the right represents a rounded vowel.

CONSONANTS (NON-PULMONIC)

Clicks		Voiced implosives		Ejectives	
⊙	Bilabial	ɓ	Bilabial	ʼ	Examples:
ǀ	Dental	ɗ	Dental/alveolar	pʼ	Bilabial
ǃ	(Post)alveolar	ʄ	Palatal	tʼ	Dental/alveolar
ǂ	Palatoalveolar	ɠ	Velar	kʼ	Velar
ǁ	Alveolar lateral	ʛ	Uvular	sʼ	Alveolar fricative

CONSONANTS (NON-PULMONIC)

Clicks		Voiced implosives		Ejectives		
176	Bilabial	160	Bilabial	401		Examples:
177	Dental	162	Dental/alveolar	101 +401		Bilabial
178	(Post)alveolar	164	Palatal	103 +401		Dental/alveolar
179	Palatoalveolar	166	Velar	109 +401		Velar
180	Alveolar lateral	168	Uvular	132 +401		Alveolar fricative

OTHER SYMBOLS

ʍ Voiceless labial-velar fricative

w Voiced labial-velar approximant

ɥ Voiced labial-palatal approximant

ʜ Voiceless epiglottal fricative

ʢ Voiced epiglottal fricative

ʡ Epiglottal plosive

ɕ ʑ Alveolo-palatal fricatives

ɺ Alveolar lateral flap

ɧ Simultaneous ʃ and x

Affricates and double articulations can be represented by two symbols joined by a tie bar if necessary.

k͡p t͡s

OTHER SYMBOLS

169 Voiceless labial-velar fricative

170 Voiced labial-velar approximant

171 Voiced labial-palatal approximant

172 Voiceless epiglottal fricative

174 Voiced epiglottal fricative

173 Epiglottal plosive

182 183 Alveolo-palatal fricatives

181 Alveolar lateral flap

175 Simultaneous ʃ and x

Affricates and double articulations can be represented by two symbols joined by a tie bar if necessary. 433 (509)

SUPRASEGMENTALS

ˈ Primary stress

ˌ Secondary stress

ˌfoʊnəˈtɪʃən

ː Long eː

ˑ Half-long eˑ

˘ Extra-short ĕ

| Minor (foot) group

‖ Major (intonation) group

. Syllable break ɹi.ækt

‿ Linking (absence of a break)

SUPRASEGMENTALS

501 Primary stress

502 Secondary stress

ˌfoʊnəˈtɪʃən

503 Long eː

504 Half-long eˑ

505 Extra-short ĕ

507 Minor (foot) group

508 Major (intonation) group

506 Syllable break ɹi.ækt

509 Linking (absence of a break)

TONES AND WORD ACCENTS

LEVEL			CONTOUR		
e̋ or ˥	Extra high	ě or ʌ	Rising		
é ˦	High	ê ˅	Falling		
ē ˧	Mid	e᷄ ˧˦	High rising		
è ˨	Low	e᷅ ˦˧	Low rising		
ȅ ˩	Extra low	e᷈ ˧	Rising-falling		
↓	Downstep	↗	Global rise		
↑	Upstep	↘	Global fall		

TONES AND WORD ACCENTS

LEVEL		CONTOUR	
512	519 Extra high	524	529 Rising
513	520 High	525	530 Falling
514	521 Mid	526	531 High rising
515	522 Low	527	532 Low rising
516	523 Extra low	528	533 Rising-falling
517	Downstep	510	Global rise
518	Upstep	511	Global fall

DIACRITICS   Diacritics may be placed above a symbol with a descender, e.g. ŋ̊

̥	Voiceless	n̥ d̥	̈	Breathy voiced	b̤ a̤	̪	Dental	t̪ d̪
̬	Voiced	s̬ t̬	̰	Creaky voiced	b̰ a̰	̺	Apical	t̺ d̺
ʰ	Aspirated	tʰ dʰ	̼	Linguolabial	t̼ d̼	̻	Laminal	t̻ d̻
̹	More rounded	ɔ̹	ʷ	Labialized	tʷ dʷ	̃	Nasalized	ẽ
̜	Less rounded	ɔ̜	ʲ	Palatalized	tʲ dʲ	ⁿ	Nasal release	dⁿ
̟	Advanced	u̟	ˠ	Velarized	tˠ dˠ	ˡ	Lateral release	dˡ
̠	Retracted	e̠	ˤ	Pharyngealized	tˤ dˤ	̚	No audible release	d̚
̈	Centralized	ë	̴	Velarized or pharyngealized	ɫ			
̽	Mid-centralized	e̽	̝	Raised	e̝	(ɹ̝ = voiced alveolar fricative)		
̩	Syllabic	n̩	̞	Lowered	e̞	(β̞ = voiced bilabial approximant)		
̯	Non-syllabic	e̯	̘	Advanced Tongue Root	e̘			
˞	Rhoticity	ɚ a˞	̙	Retracted Tongue Root	e̙			

DIACRITICS   Diacritics may be placed above a symbol with a descender, e.g. 119 + 402B

402A	Voiceless	n̥ d̥	405	Breathy voiced	b̤ a̤	408	Dental	t̪ d̪
403	Voiced	s̬ t̬	406	Creaky voiced	b̰ a̰	409	Apical	t̺ d̺
404	Aspirated	tʰ dʰ	407	Linguolabial	t̼ d̼	410	Laminal	t̻ d̻
411	More rounded	ɔ̹	420	Labialized	tʷ dʷ	424	Nasalized	ẽ
412	Less rounded	ɔ̜	421	Palatalized	tʲ dʲ	425	Nasal release	dⁿ
413	Advanced	u̟	422	Velarized	tˠ dˠ	426	Lateral release	dˡ
414	Retracted	e̠	423	Pharyngealized	tˤ dˤ	427	No audible release	d̚
415	Centralized	ë	428	Velarized or pharyngealized	209			
416	Mid-centralized	e̽	429	Raised	e̝	(ɹ̝ = voiced alveolar fricative)		
431	Syllabic	n̩	430	Lowered	e̞	(β̞ = voiced bilabial approximant)		
432	Non-syllabic	e̯	417	Advanced Tongue Root	e̘			
419	Rhoticity	327 a˞	418	Retracted Tongue Root	e̙